THE YARD

THE YARD
HOW A HORSE HEALED MY HEART

GRACE OLSON

BROWN
DOG
BOOKS

Published under licence by Brown Dog Books and
The Self-Publishing Partnership Ltd, 10b Greenway Farm, Bath Rd,
Wick, nr. Bath BS30 5RL

www.selfpublishingpartnership.co.uk

ISBN printed book: 978-1-83952-511-7
ISBN e-book: 978-1-83952-512-4

Cover design by Andrew Prescott
Cover image: 'Our Hearts' watercolour on langton board © Ruth Buchanan
2017
Internal design by Andrew Easton

Printed and bound in the UK

This book is printed on FSC certified paper

Dedication

This book is dedicated to the memory of my wonderful mum. She laughed her head off typing up the first chapters of the original version. I am gutted she didn't get to read the whole thing.

Most importantly, this book is dedicated to my amazing, talented, hilarious daughter.

Chapter 1

My love of horses was reignited on a rather nondescript sort of a day. The kind of day you could easily forget about if nothing in particular happened to change it into a more noteworthy experience. I was cleaning the sink in my therapy room, preparing for the next client, when my phone pinged.

"Hiya! Not going to be able to come today. Got to wait in for the gardener!" messaged the irksome client.

My heart dropped and I instantly felt panic about not earning enough money that day. She often cancelled appointments at the last moment and it stressed me out a lot. I phoned her immediately because I felt I'd be able to get her booked in more easily via a call rather than a text.

"Hi! I got your message!" I said in a cheery voice, pretending I was unperturbed. "Would you like to rearrange? I can do next Monday at the same time."

"Yes, great! See you then. Got to dash now, bye!" She hung up.

"Bloody hell," I sighed to myself. "She didn't even apologise or offer to pay for wasting my time again! I suppose I should have mentioned a cancellation policy earlier. So I can't really expect her to offer."

I felt utterly crap. I had an hour and a half to fill but as I worked from home, filling the time was not a problem. Why is it that washing always needs doing along with cooking and cleaning and other dismal, monotonous chores? And why is it always left to me? I swore out loud as I dashed downstairs, almost tripping over the cat, to hurl a mountain of endless laundry into the machine and then flew back upstairs to chop a load of vegetables for a curry. Our house was on four levels, so doing anything always involved lots of stairs, which seemed to add to the irritation of getting things done.

"Crikey! Is that the time already?" I grabbed the dog, dashed to the car and opened the boot.

"Quickly! In you get!" I commanded.

The dog looked at me blankly.

"Come on! Get in!" I gestured to the boot space.

No response at all from the dog.

"For God's sake! Hurry up!"

I rummaged around in my pocket for a biscuit. There was no biscuit so I had to admit defeat, scoop him up and put him in the car feeling very annoyed. I had foolishly believed life would become easier once our daughter, Florence, had started school. But it wasn't. It was actually harder and God only knows how that was even possible.

I had really looked forward to being a mum. We had bought a ridiculously large house to accommodate a family because I had been absolutely certain I wanted at least three children. I was so enthusiastic, I even went on a hypno-birthing course so that I could experience a natural delivery. Unfortunately, the total opposite happened. I had to be induced, which involved a shocking amount of pain. I had all the drugs on the trolley and even that wasn't enough, so an epidural was fitted. The baby was stuck so I was eventually rushed in for an emergency caesarean, during which the anaesthetic wore off. I could feel the searing pain of being sewn up, which was horrifying beyond description. Bizarrely, none of the medical staff said anything when I cried out. They all ignored me. It was like being in a horror film.

Unsurprisingly, I didn't want any more children after that experience. I had terrible postnatal depression. I was beyond exhausted and I was stunned at how difficult it was to have a baby to look after. It was so hard! And it wasn't just the lack of sleep, it was the total destruction of my former self that blew my mind to bits.

Before becoming a mum, I had been the very confident lead singer in an indie band and life was full of fun. I also thoroughly enjoyed my work as a self-employed massage therapist, and I was physically very fit and healthy. Motherhood was like a wrecking ball. Not only did it destroy my body – I gained so much weight – but it also destroyed my self-confidence. I became as quiet as a mouse and as enormous as an elephant. Luckily, I managed to lose the worst of the excess weight but I was still big and I felt uncomfortable, unhealthy and extremely depressed. I also stopped singing because I felt too fat to go on stage. I weighed ten stone but I was only five foot four, with a very light skeleton, and all the weight was round my tummy so I still looked heavily pregnant. When the window cleaner asked me when I was due it took all my inner strength to resist pushing him off his ladder.

Every day was a struggle and I coped with it by creating strict routines that did help to make Florence a very contented baby but caused a lot of pressure for me. We had to be up at 7am for the first feed; nap at 9am; up and out to a group by 10am and then lunch and nap at 12. Another outing in the afternoon, followed by a 4pm nap, followed by bath, book and bed by 7pm. I was terribly regimented and if something random happened to threaten the routine my heart would begin to palpitate and I would lose my temper. As you can imagine this put a lot of strain on my relationships with everyone, especially my husband.

Fortunately, I had watched *Mary Poppins* several times during my childhood so I was able to fake being a 'fun mum'. I would sing and dance and do mad things that made Florence laugh her head off but it was all just an act. Inside I was extremely miserable and grieving for a life I felt I had lost, while battling with guilt for not feeling full of joy. I hated self-pity and I was cross with myself for feeling so down but I knew it was genuine depression. Not that being aware of that fact helped very much. The doctor was kind and prescribed homeopathy, which was very open-minded, but I needed something else. I needed a therapy that would help me find happiness but I never felt I had the time to invest in such a thing. Nor did I feel I could justify spending that sort of money on myself.

Now Florence was five and had started school. I honestly thought this would be a fantastic opportunity to have some time to myself. The reality was that by the time I'd dropped her at school and walked the dog, there was only time to treat one or two clients and do some housework before the mad dash back to school to collect her.

I hated the school run. Firstly, there was never anywhere to park due to the fleet of weird parents who seemed to regularly arrive more than fifteen minutes early. Why would anyone want to sit and wait for that long? Do they not have other things to do? Secondly, there were so many bitchy mums at my daughter's school and they all looked at me as if I was a piece of chewing gum stuck on their expensive designer shoes. They all appeared to be very wealthy and didn't need to work. I assumed they probably spent their days at cafes and spas because they turned up to school looking glamorous and relaxed. In contrast, I was always in a rush and felt like a rather sweaty mess. So I lingered in the background, avoiding any eye contact, praying the dog wouldn't embarrass me further by doing a poo in the playground.

The bitchy mums were like a coven of witches, gossiping and cackling. One of them looked over at me and then turned to her friend and said something I couldn't hear. Both of them laughed, which made me feel hot and very self-conscious. Luckily the dog saw another dog in the distance and pulled me away to investigate, which was a huge relief.

After what felt like an eternity, Florence skipped out of school and chattered about her day. None of it made any sense but I listened and smiled. In the car on the way home she insisted we listened to ghastly songs from musicals and as usual, I forced myself to sing along so that the journey home was fun for her. It was a Monday, which meant my mum would be coming over to babysit so that I could continue working. Mum was a very jolly woman who was genuinely like Mary Poppins and I often marvelled at how easy-going and positive she was. When Mum played mad games with Florence she really did enjoy herself, which always amazed me.

I sighed and got ready for my next, new client while my mum got dinner ready for Florence. I felt so heavy in my heart and desperately wished I could be the happy person I had been several years ago but I had forgotten who that 'me' was. However, I didn't have much time to think more about it because the doorbell rang and in swept Lady Alexa Heptonstall.

"Sorry about the smell! I've come straight from the stables

and the haylage is particularly pongy!" she greeted as she walked through the door.

"That's fine, don't worry!" I laughed, taken aback by such a funny introduction. She really did smell.

"I must say I do hope you can sort me out. I don't have the time for this backache nonsense anymore!" exclaimed Alexa, marching up the stairs to my therapy room as if she had been there before.

I followed her up, fascinated that she knew which room to go in. She flung herself on the sofa as if she was an old friend and reeled off a frighteningly long list of horse-related accidents she had sustained. Alexa had a wonderful plummy accent that sounded almost identical to Princess Anne but she was surprisingly down to earth despite her lofty upbringing. I was amazed that she was actually still alive, let alone still riding horses, after all her terrible injuries. She had broken or sprained almost every bone and joint in her body over the years and yet she simply laughed about it and put it down to experience.

"It's all part and parcel of the joy of horses!" laughed Alexa at my shocked expression.

"Wow! You are hardcore!" I laughed. "Let's get you on the couch and I'll have a look at your back."

Alexa undressed and jumped on to the massage couch. Her back was as solid as a rock.

"Do you ride?" she asked.

"I haven't for years but I used to love riding when I was younger," I replied as I began the process of softening her tense shoulders.

"Oh, marvellous! Did you have a pony?" she asked.

"Sadly no!" I laughed. "I just had a riding lesson every Saturday. It was the highlight of my life!"

"Ah, lovely!" replied Alexa. "I was so fortunate. Ma insisted that I should always have at least one pony. Usually there were two or three on the go at once as Ma was so keen on competitions. I think that's why I have two horses now."

"Wow! You have two horses?"

I was absolutely fascinated. I didn't know anyone who had a horse and suddenly, here was somebody who had two of them.

"Yes, I'll show you a photo when you've finished, if you like."

"Ooh yes!" I replied with great enthusiasm.

I couldn't wait for the massage to be finished so I could have a look at Alexa's horses. It turned out she had a beautiful dapple-grey Irish Sport Horse and a huge Cleveland bay. Both were for showjumping as that was her passion. The two gorgeous horses were kept at a posh livery yard in Harrogate. This surprised me, considering she had mentioned her family had a very impressive, sprawling mansion.

"Pa collects vintage hot-air balloons so the stables are full of them," explained Alexa.

"Wow, that sounds fun! Do you go up in them?" I asked.

"Oh no, Pa just collects them. He never actually goes up in the air in them. They're just his weird hobby!" laughed Alexa. "Also, he's very allergic to horses so they're not allowed anywhere near the house unfortunately. It's such a shame as I can't stand the bitchiness of livery yards."

"Bitchiness?" I asked.

"Oh yes. Livery yards seem to attract the worst sort of females!" She chuckled.

"Really? I thought they'd be lovely places full of women all enjoying horse riding!" I said, surprised.

Alexa laughed her head off at that comment.

"If only! They are full of stupid idiots who have all the gear but no idea."

She proceeded to tell me about how, in general, livery yards consist mainly of "unfriendly women full of their own self-importance with warm blood horses that they can't control. They only ride round the block, because they daren't go any further, wearing the latest equestrian clothing and do a bit of dressage not particularly well."

"How depressing!" I exclaimed. "I couldn't stand being with people like that."

"I can't either!" said Alexa. "This place is not too bad so far."

Later that evening, I sat down with a cup of tea in the living room and the cat jumped on to my knee and curled in to a ball. I stroked her soft black fur absentmindedly as I thought about the conversation I'd had with Lady Alexa. My mind was alight with memories I hadn't thought about for many years. I had loved ponies when I was little and regularly asked my parents to buy me one but they couldn't afford it. Even as an adult, whenever I saw a horse I felt a pang of sadness and wished that I could have one. Unfortunately, life was full of expensive responsibilities and I truly believed that horses would always remain a dream that could never happen for me.

The rest of the week passed by in a blur of chores, work and general gloom but I cheered up when I realised that Lady Alexa was coming for another treatment.

"Bloody hell! Those horrible women at the yard were the last straw today!" exclaimed Alexa as she came through the door, marched upstairs, flung her clothes off and leaped on to the couch.

"Oh dear! What happened?" I asked.

"Well, I arrived at the livery yard much earlier than usual and found one of the grooms punching my dapple-grey horse in the face!"

"Oh my God! Why?" I asked.

"Apparently he'd nipped her! I told her I'd do more than nip her if I found her anywhere near my horse again! I was furious, let me tell you!"

"What did you do about it?" I was so absorbed in the drama I almost forgot to continue massaging.

"I complained to the yard owner and the groom was sacked on the spot. And then I packed up all my things and left immediately!"

"Oh blimey! Where are your horses now?"

"Luckily I have a friend called Tony who owns his own breeding yard at an old farm in Ilkley. It used to be a fabulous yard but unfortunately the glory days have well and truly gone! It's an absolute dump now but I don't care. So long as I don't have to deal with any more bitchy women, I'm happy!"

I was so fascinated by the conversation about horses I had to keep reminding myself to focus on work. I must have given her such a rubbish massage and I was amazed she bothered to book in again. I found it interesting that I hardly knew Alexa, yet I felt as if we had been friends for years. Being in her company perked me up a lot and I looked forward to hearing more of her horsey dramas. Luckily, I didn't have to wait too long.

"Ahoy there! Fancy coming to see my new foal? I just bought one from Tony!" Alexa texted a few days later.

I was surprised to receive her message and felt quite emotional to have been asked.

"Yes, I'd love to!" I replied instantly. How could I resist such an invitation?

We made a date for the following day as I had no work booked in. I was excited to go but felt very apprehensive when it was time to set off and it really hit home how much confidence I had lost since having a child. Before being a mum, I would have thought nothing of leaping into the car and heading off to do gigs with the band in other cities. Ilkley was only twenty minutes away but it felt like an expedition to me. I looked through the route very thoroughly, several times, and then had to dash back into the house to go to the toilet.

"I think I should call and say I can't come," I said out loud to myself.

No! You can do this! It's horses! said my inner voice.

"But I feel too self-conscious. I look like I'm pregnant! I can't go out looking like this!"

Don't be so ridiculous. Nobody cares what you look like!

"What if I get lost on the way? Farms never have signs outside!"

Then just phone Alexa!

I really did want to go but I felt such crippling anxiety. After another toilet trip I took a deep breath.

Now get the hell in the car, woman, and get going! You will regret it if you don't! my inner voice commanded.

I marched myself to the car and made myself set off. I put some calming music on and ignored all my negative thoughts about getting lost. After a while, the beautiful scenery soothed my nerves and I loved looking out at the rolling fields of the farms I passed. There's something very relaxing about watching sheep grazing lazily on the hillsides and I thoroughly enjoyed seeing all the old stone cottages along the way. By the time I arrived I felt much better.

"Hello!" Alexa waved as I drove into the yard.

She was surrounded by a gaggle of Jack Russells who were very keen to say hello too, yapping and wagging their tails. I stepped out of the car and had a good look around. It was exactly as Alexa had described. You could tell it had once been a super-luxurious equestrian yard but now it was very shabby and decrepit. Every expense had been spared on the maintenance of the place and if something could be fixed by a bit of gaffer tape then that had been used to do the job. However, it was brimming with horses, which was very exciting indeed.

"Do come and meet Henrietta, she really is a pet!" enthused Alexa as she led me past a row of beautiful showjumpers looking out of their stables, to a small paddock in which there was the most adorable little bay foal I had ever seen.

"Oh wow, she's so cute!" I gasped.

"Isn't she just? But don't be fooled! She's already quite a little madam, aren't you, Henrietta?"

Alexa laughed but I could tell she was very proud of her really.

Henrietta had very long legs so it was clear she was born to jump. Her mother had won many prizes so Alexa had high hopes for the future.

"So long as she doesn't break her legs, of course! She's already tried to jump out of here, haven't you, little monkey?" Alexa chuckled.

Alexa's other horses were grazing in a nearby paddock so we went to see them and gave them apples, which they enjoyed very much.

"They're absolutely beautiful!" I said wistfully, looking around at the outdoor arena and wishing that I could have a ride.

"They are, aren't they? I know I'm very lucky."

A sudden crash of a door banging shut made us both jump.

"Oh, it's Tony!" exclaimed Alexa as a very dishevelled man almost seemed to fall out of a barn door, carrying several saddles.

"Bluddy 'ell!" he yelled, tripping over the reins of a bridle, slung over his arm.

The saddles flew in all directions and Alexa and I dashed over to help.

"You silly clot! What are you doing now?" laughed Alexa as she pulled Tony back on to his feet.

"I forgot we was goin' to that show tomorrow," mumbled Tony, looking very embarrassed in my direction. His thick Yorkshire accent was an interesting contrast to Alexa's cut-glass one.

"Tony, this is Grace, my magical masseuse!" said Alexa by way of an introduction. "And Grace, this is Tony."

We both said hello and Tony blushed. He appeared to be quite uncomfortable.

"All this tack wants a clean-up," Tony grunted. "An' that bloody wall has fallen o'er there. I dunno which to sort fust?"

Alexa looked over at the dry-stone wall that had tumbled down in the middle and was scattered across a footpath.

"You do the wall! I'll do the tack," she said and Tony nodded, muttered something incoherent and wandered off to look for tools.

"He's a bit shy!" laughed Alexa as we walked to the tack room to clean the saddlery.

The tack room was dusty and full of mouldering saddles from hundreds of years ago. Cobwebs decorated most of the ceiling, and the windowpanes were cracked but it filled me with great joy as youthful memories of my riding-school days flooded back.

As I was driving home all I could think about was how much I had loved riding ponies. The thrill of cantering along soft turf and flying over jumps like a bird. The lovely moments in the stable, grooming and tacking up, when the pony would blow softly on your face. The smell of the saddles and bridles hanging up in the tack room. Such happy, fun-filled days. Why did I ever stop?

Chapter 2

I had started riding as a child so I suppose you could actually blame my mother for my love of horses. She took my sister and I to a very rickety riding school in, of all places, Meanwood, which was and still is a very busy suburb. I use the word *rickety* because the whole place looked like it was being held together by a piece of bailer twine and could fall down at the slightest gust of wind. There was no school so all the lessons were done 'on the hoof' as it were – while we were out on a hack. We would ride through the local housing estate, with the instructor also riding a horse. Every so often we would stop and do various exercises like Round the World, which is a great test of balance.

In this exercise you begin by bringing your right leg over the neck of the horse so you're sitting sideways. Then you bring your left leg over its bottom so you're facing backwards. Then you bring your right leg over the bottom so you're sitting to the other side and finally you bring your left leg over its neck so you're sitting forward again. The aim is to be able to remain on the horse throughout and not slide off on to the ground with a painful thud. It must have been quite amusing for any onlookers watching us do this in the middle of the road.

Eventually that particular riding school closed down thanks to one of the local twats who set fire to the place. Luckily all the horses had been turned out that night as it had been a warmer day than usual, but had it been cold they would have died. I don't know what happened to the horses when it shut but we then went to another, slightly more upmarket riding school called Ringways.

Ringways belonged to the most eccentric woman I have ever met, called Mrs Falkingham-Brown. She was of a very solid build and always wore hunting tweeds. Her wispy grey hair seemed to have a life of its own, flying about madly around her leathery old face. She was either very brisk and jolly, shouting, "Come along, chaps! Up and at 'em!" or she would suddenly come rushing out of the tack room, shrieking, "I've had enough!" and promptly sack all of the staff. Everyone ignored her except for the senior instructor. She would say "Right!" and would march off towards her car, at which point Mrs Falkingham-Brown would burst into tears and fall on to her knees and beg her to come back. This pantomime was a regular feature of our lessons at Ringways and we all got so used to it that we would hardly bat an eyelid eventually.

The ponies were lovely and all had their own peculiar quirks that have been etched into my memory. The biggest character belonged to a little black Shetland. I remember taking him back to his stable, which was actually one of a row of old railway carriages. I put the Shetland in his carriage, untacked him and mooched back up the path, feeling very sad that the lesson was over and that I would have to wait a whole week before riding again. You can imagine my surprise, therefore, when I got to the door of the tack room and discovered that he was right behind me – and no doubt sniggering to himself. I was so shocked I almost dropped his saddle. I quickly hung his tack up and tried to catch him, which took a while as he was enjoying himself far too much. Mrs Falkingham-Brown screaming her head off probably didn't help matters either.

Eventually, the Shetland was caught and I took him back to his carriage. Right in front of my face, the clever little bugger got down on to his knees and crawled out under the ridiculously useless chain that was meant to keep him in. The chaos began again, only this time with more comedy value as he shot straight past me and into one of the top fields where a gate had been left open and a lesson was going on. The Shetland cantered round and round, egged on by the shrieks of laughter from the kids having a lesson.

"Whoa! Whoa!" shouted the instructor, flailing her arms about in a useless attempt at stopping him.

But he was not in the mood for stopping as he whizzed round and round, laughing his head off and probably swearing too and then laughing even more. I like to think that if he could talk he would have been yelling the most disgusting obscenities and insults to everyone. Eventually, someone had the presence of mind to bring a bucket of feed. He had run out of steam by this point so wasn't too bothered about giving up the game. The naughty Shetland was instantly moved into a proper stable with a door that was, unfortunately, too high for him to look out. Poor little man.

My worst memory of Ringways was when I arrived for my lesson to find that several of the ponies had been shot. Apparently, Mrs Falkingham-Brown had decided they were no longer fit enough to work in the riding school. She could not afford to allow them to simply retire so the vet had come out and euthanised them with a captive bolt gun. I was so shocked I cried and a particularly heartless girl just looked at me with disdain and said, "Well, that's what you've got to do with them when they can't work any more!" My mother was disgusted and promptly found me another riding school to go to.

Mount Heather Riding School was in Collingham (a frightfully posh village) and was a whole different class from the previous riding schools I'd been to. This one was actually clean, for a start, and it had a really nice indoor arena that made winter riding much more fun. All the tack was immaculate and the stables were light and airy.

I really learned how to ride properly at that place because the instructor was amazing. She taught us how to do dressage and often had the whole class riding in formation like a military parade. She also taught us how to jump correctly and we spent hours working on our positions in the saddle. I remember doing a bit of horse vaulting too, which was tremendous fun. We did things like Round the World while in canter, which I absolutely loved and was a real test of core strength. Sadly, that particular teacher suffered from depression and had a nervous breakdown, so she left. I stopped having lessons at that point too, at the age of sixteen.

I stopped riding all together at the age of eighteen. I had just been given free use of an ex-racehorse called Tommy, who lived on a dairy farm next door to my cousin's house where, as twelve-year-olds, we had helped with milking. Tommy belonged to the farmer's wife, Jane, who didn't have much time for horse riding any more. He was an excellent horse to ride because he was so laid-back and happy to hack out anywhere. We had some lovely times together and he was so pleased that someone was taking him out.

Although I really loved Tommy and enjoyed our rides together, I stopped going because I felt so intimidated by Jane. Looking back as an adult, I really don't know why because she was so lovely. However, when I was eighteen I was very self-conscious and massively lacking in confidence. Jane was a typical tough Yorkshire farmer with a very no-nonsense way about her that just highlighted my general lack of common sense and made me feel a bit idiotic.

I felt guilty for many years about leaving Tommy and I never forgot how much I loved riding. It never occurred to me to do anything about it, though, because I was too busy working and singing to find time for horses. But they were always a wistful dream in the back of my mind.

A few days after visiting Alexa at her new yard, I related the tale of my horsey childhood during her massage.

"So why did you stop riding Tommy?" she asked.

"I really don't know. I suppose it was because of feeling a bit weird around his owner and wanting to spend my spare time with my boyfriend."

"Golly! I wouldn't give up horses for any boyfriend!" exclaimed Alexa, clearly horrified by the mere thought.

"I really miss riding, especially when I hear all your horsey stories," I sighed.

"Well, what's stopping you from going back to it?"

That question struck me like a thunderbolt. What *was* stopping me from going back to it?

"I don't know. Nothing! Only me is stopping me!" I laughed.

"You do realise there's a riding school literally five minutes down the road from here?"

"Really?" I'd not noticed it.

"Yes, you silly clot! It's called Amber Rose. How on earth have you never noticed the giant sign by the turn-off? It's opposite Homebase!"

After Alexa had left I sat and pondered the conversation and wondered if I should phone and book a lesson. So many ifs and buts whirled through my mind. Mainly, I felt guilty about spending money on myself. Life had become all about Florence and although I did my best to be a good mum, I was still really struggling with it. I needed to find *me* again. The *me* that was not just a mum or a wife but the *me* that still loved horses.

I remembered my old bedroom as a child and how the walls were completely covered in posters of horses. My favourite book had been a Reader's Digest pocket book of horse breeds and I read it so often I knew all about each breed. I was very careful with that little book because I did not want to damage any of the pages. I still have it to this day and it's still in excellent condition. I also had several toy horses and would spend hours brushing their manes and tails, completely absorbed in my imagination in which they were all real.

My husband, James, walked into the room, disturbing my reverie.

"I'm thinking of maybe going and having some riding lessons," I said as he sat down on the sofa.

"Riding lessons?" asked James. "What for? I thought you knew how to ride."

"Yes, but I haven't ridden for years and I need to do something that will make me feel happy," I replied.

"How much will that cost?"

My heart sank.

"I don't know. I suppose about twenty pounds?"

"OK. That's not so bad and I hope it helps. Have you got dinner ready?"

I breathed a sigh of relief and went into the kitchen to dish up. I assumed he'd be much more negative about the whole thing and start worrying about money. Ever since we had bought the new house his personality had become a bit 'Victorian husband'. He was always asking what I had bought whenever I used the bank card, which was extremely irritating, but I never felt I had the energy to stick up for myself. I could see that our relationship was becoming very unhealthy in that I had begun to do all the housework as well as the lion's share of the childcare but I just never felt strong enough to demand a change. However, I was very pleased that the horse-riding discussion had resulted in a positive outcome so I didn't bother to say anything else.

The following day I plucked up the courage to call Amber Rose riding school and book a lesson. It's surprising how difficult it can be to do things like that when you are depressed. Booking a lesson sounds so simple but it was a big step for me at that time. I picked up my phone and dialled the number. It rang. I felt sick and hung up. All sorts of extremely negative thoughts spiralled through my mind like a terrible kaleidoscope of fear.

Won't they think it's a bit sad that an adult wants to have lessons?

Won't they think I'm totally crap?

I'll make such a fool of myself because I can't even remember how to tack up!

But I want to ride! I love horses! I've always missed it. It's the place where I am happiest, a little voice replied, somewhere in the back of my mind.

That little voice became louder and more urgent. There was no ignoring it so I picked up the phone and swallowed my fears.

"Hello! Amber Rose Equestrian Centre!" greeted a very jolly lady.

"Hi . . . erm, I . . . erm, ahem!" My throat felt horribly gravelly and I had to cough several times.

"Can I help you? Would you like to book a lesson?" she asked kindly.

I was relieved to hear that question because it was very easy to answer.

"Yes, please!" I almost squeaked. "I've not ridden for years, though!"

"That's all right. We have lots of adult returners!" she laughed.

"I'm a bit overweight too," I said, suddenly feeling self-conscious about my size.

"Ha! Me too! What do you weigh?"

"I'm about ten stone," I replied.

"Oh, that's nothing! And anyway, we've got lots of strong cobs so don't you worry."

I felt so much better for speaking to that lady and I was very glad I'd gathered up the courage to make the call.

Amber Rose riding school was literally a five-minute drive from my house, just off the main road. I'm ashamed to say that in all the years I had lived there I had not noticed the enormous sign saying, AMBER ROSE EQUESTRIAN CENTRE with an arrow pointing to the slip road that led on to the bumpy track that was the driveway up to the school.

In my defence, you couldn't actually see anything of the riding school from the road as it was all hidden behind an extremely tall hedge line. You can imagine my surprise when I drove up the track and discovered a very pretty lodge house surrounded by well-kept modern stables, pristine paddocks and a lovely outdoor arena. I stepped out of the car and looked around in amazement. Then I suddenly felt a bit weird because other than a black-and-white cat the whole place appeared to be deserted and there was a strange hushed atmosphere. It was a stark contrast to the noisy and busy riding schools of my youth.

Presently a very brisk woman appeared.

"Now then!" she greeted in a strong Yorkshire accent. "You must be Grace?"

"Yes!" I replied, relieved to see someone.

"I'm June the yard manager. Yer gonna have a lesson wi' Jim – he's waiting fer you up 'ere."

June took me through the stable yard to a winding path that led into a large sand school where she left me with Jim.

Jim was an alcoholic and the ex-head groom for the German Olympic team. How he had gone from such prestige to the bottom of the pile at Amber Rose Equestrian Centre, I never got to find out. But there he was and although he kept popping into the shed next to the arena for a swig of Special Brew, he was actually an excellent rider and lots of fun to have as an instructor. I instantly felt at ease with Jim as he was so laid-back and non-judgemental.

The horse for my first lesson was a giant grey cob. She was built like a tank and I had to use a mounting block to get on. This was all new to me. In my younger days, we just sprang up from the ground but there was no way I could do that with this horse, especially with my lack of fitness. Once I was on I almost cried with happiness. It felt like I'd come home.

I must have been in a bit of a daze because eventually Jim said, "Well, I've never seen such a big smile! Do you want to start walking?"

"Oh yes! Sorry. I just can't believe how amazing this feels!"

Jim laughed. He must have witnessed the same scene many times.

"When horses are in your blood, you can't stay away from them for too long." He winked and walked into the centre of the school to begin the lesson.

I could hardly remember how to sit properly or what to do but it didn't seem to matter. Jim took great care to remind me of all the basics of riding and gave lots of praise when I did things right. I went home feeling on top of the world and even though my legs were in agony, I looked forward to my next lesson. It was as if a little spark of a flame had been rekindled in my body and mind. I felt more awake and life seemed more hopeful. I even bought a horsey magazine to help remind me of all the things involved with riding and it was so nice to sit and read it in the evening, knowing that it was relevant to me.

After a few weeks, I began to improve a lot so Jim decided to change the routine.

"Let's have a bit of fun!" he announced.

He gave me a half-hour lesson and then he grabbed a horse for himself and we rode off into the nearby woods for a lovely hack. The woods were beautiful and peaceful with a wide stream bubbling through the remains of a derelict flax mill. Large old stones covered in moss and full of stories of lives long forgotten, almost seemed to whisper their secrets as we rode past. It was quite an ethereal place to be on a horse. We had some lovely rides where Jim would tell me amusing stories of his time in Germany and now and again he would mention his father, who had basically told him he was worthless, which was very sad. Maybe that was why he was an alcoholic and working at a riding school?

My riding lessons with Jim helped me to feel lighter and a bit less stressed at home. He was so easy-going, it was very soothing to be in his company. Even when I got silly things wrong he would make a joke out of it in a very avuncular way, and remind me what I should be doing instead. It was as if it was all right to be wrong – it really didn't matter. I had spent so much time worrying about getting motherhood right that it was almost like therapy sessions.

It was while I was paying for my riding lesson that I mentioned to June, the yard manager, that I would love to have my own horse. June was a very bulky and stocky woman with short black hair and a very weathered face. She looked at me with her beady black eyes and breathed deeply on her ever-present cigarette. A plume of smoke coiled out of her nostrils in a very dragon-like way.

"You don't wanna do that, luv," she rasped in her deep Yorkshire and very knackered voice. "It's bloody expensive. No, luv, what you wanna do is part-loan some other bugger's horse and let them have the expense."

"She's right, you know," agreed Jim. "When you own a horse you've got livery costs, feed costs, hay and straw, shoes and vet's bills – it's a fortune. But you could part-loan a horse for about twenty quid a week, which is actually less than what you pay us for a half-hour riding lesson."

I had never in my life heard of such a thing as 'part-loaning a horse' so I was stunned and really excited.

"D'you know who'd be good fer 'er?" growled June. (Her voice was absolutely destroyed from smoking so much. She was probably weaned on cigarettes.) "Mad Mel!" She nodded knowingly.

"Ah yes!" agreed Jim emphatically.

"Mad Mel is lookin' fer a small steady cob that 'ud be just right fer you. She's a very nervous rider and she always wants someone to loan 'er 'orses. But –" she gave me a hard stare and pointed at me – "you'll end up doin' all the work because she's a bugger fer that so watch out!"

"Oh!" I said, surprised by everything she'd said. "Who is Mad Mel and why is she mad?" I was a bit wary of someone with the word *Mad* as their title.

"Mad Mel," explained Jim, "is a woman who has had quite a few horses but always ends up selling them because she thinks they're too fast for her."

He went on to say she had a Connemara at the riding school that she had asked them to import for her. The first time she rode the horse, it ran off with her. She totally freaked out and still hadn't paid for it but wanted them to sell it and find her a nice quiet Gypsy cob.

"She can only ride at weekends so she'll be wanting someone to ride it during the week. I'll have a word with her and let you know when she's got it," said Jim.

I drove home, my head spinning with excitement. I couldn't believe I had never heard of this concept of loaning a horse before.

When James came in that night I told him all about it in a rather jumbled mess of excitement. Sadly, he did not share my enthusiasm.

"Mad Mel?" he said. "That sounds a bit dangerous to me and you don't have time to be riding every day for some mad woman who buys a horse but doesn't have time to ride it. You've got Florence to think of now and you should be building up your massage work."

He took the wind right out of my sails. Although he was glad my lessons were cheering me up, James didn't have any interest in horses and couldn't really understand my passion for them. Now that our daughter had just started school, James wanted me to do more work and earn more money. Of course, that's totally fair enough. We had a new house and a big mortgage and before I got pregnant my massage therapy business was bringing in a lot of money. James is an osteopath and also self-employed. So, yes, I could see his point about earning money. However, he had spent a huge chunk of his life travelling the world, busking and having fun, whereas I had spent years working. Massage – proper deep-tissue massage, not whimsy beauty therapy massage – is a very hard physical job that takes a lot of energy and knackers your thumbs, wrists and back (which is how I met my husband – he fixed my back).

Before we got married, I had my own house and bills to pay and although I had the fun of being in a band, life mainly revolved around my work. Now I was a mum with postnatal depression. I had a bigger house to clean, a child to look after and I was working part-time. I just wanted to fulfil my lifelong dream of having a horse. I cried as I explained all of that to James, and as I rarely expressed my emotions he relented.

"Why don't you google 'horses to loan' and see if there's one available with an owner that's not mad and just wants someone to ride it once or twice a week?"

That was an excellent idea so I rushed off to have a look. I was astounded. There were so many websites advertising horses available to loan with literally hundreds of people crying out for help with their horses. I had a great time reading all the ads. After a while my eye fell on one that looked just right for me.

"Quiet cob available for hacking on a part-loan, mid-week basis. Perfect for a novice rider. Good company available at a small friendly yard in Thorner."

I was so excited. Thorner is a chocolate-box village, only ten minutes' drive from our suburban house, with loads of beautiful Yorkshire countryside. It's where I used to ride Tommy when I was younger so I knew the area well. The owner of the horse was called Carmel and although I felt anxious and terribly self-conscious I took a deep breath and gave her a call. My nerves subsided as soon as she answered her phone with a very jolly "Hello!" and after a brief chat we arranged to meet at the yard the following evening.

Chapter 3

The yard was opposite the dairy farm I used to play at when I was younger and where Tommy had lived. Fond memories came flooding back as soon as I turned on to the road. My cousin, who lived next door to the farm, had been given a cow called Vanilla. Vanilla was very intelligent. You could call out her name and she would come trotting over to greet you and she gave lovely cuddles and kisses. I remembered their ginger, woolly bull called Uncle, who lived in the same field as the cows. He was as soft as butter and would stand peacefully while we brushed him and made a fuss of him. He was such a lovely, gentle soul.

It's a real shame that not many people know how affectionate cows can be. In fact, they really are very similar in nature to dogs. They are very family orientated, just like us, and love to play. I find it fascinating that when cows are allowed to birth naturally, their mums and aunties come to help.

I loved being with the cows at that farm. I'll never forget a particularly hilarious day when we were helping to milk. The cows were all in their places, with the machines on their udders, standing on a raised platform round the sides of the milking room. My cousin and I were standing in the middle of the dairy, luckily towards the back. The farmer was at the front of the room, standing behind Vanilla. Suddenly, without warning, Vanilla lifted her tail and let out an almighty power jet of stinking liquid shit that quite literally covered him from head to foot. To this day I have never laughed so much in my life. Ah yes, it was great to be back near some happy memories.

I pulled up outside the yard. It looked very posh and clean and very well maintained. I could see the impressive arena with its set of wonderful show jumps and the sunlight was glinting off the white stripes on the poles.

Wow! I thought. *This is great!*

I had visions of myself flying over those jumps on a fantastic glossy black horse— My phone rang and jolted me out of my daydream. It was Carmel.

"Hiya! Is that gold Honda yours?" she asked.

"Yes, where are you?" I replied.

"You're at the wrong yard! I'm just further down the road ahead."

I had a look and saw a car at the next bend in the road and set off.

Carmel was very glamorous and dressed in head-to-toe designer gear. She was tall and slender with a very glossy, jet-black bob and had sparkly ice-blue eyes. Her long nails were beautifully French-manicured, I noticed, as she greeted me with a warm handshake. She looked like the bitchy mums from school and I suddenly felt a bit nervous and embarrassed about myself.

"That was the posh yard!" said Carmel cheerily. "It's not like ours!"

She wasn't lying. This yard was most definitely *not* like that one. Whereas everything at the posh yard was perfect and new, like Barbie's Equestrian Centre, this was like Steptoe and Son. Everything had seen better days. A forlorn beige caravan, encrusted with filth, was parked almost centrally in front of the 'feed room', which was basically a large, ancient, mouldering shed.

The flagged stable yard was uneven and haphazard with weeds poking through all the cracks and the faded multicoloured stable doors were well worn and very shabby. They were all different shades of pastel colours, painted to look like beach huts when they were new. But now they looked like they'd been battered by too many high tides.

Carmel was very friendly, which was a relief, and she took me over to the field and called her horse. Well, I say *horse*, he was really a pony. A chubby little, 14.2hh black gypsy cob with a fat white stripe down his face, called Monty. Carmel looked very incongruous next to Monty. She looked like the sort of person who should have owned a sleek American Saddlebred Horse with a foaming mane.

"I only got him a couple of weeks ago," she chattered. "But he's great. Really easy to do and very laid-back. I used to own that one over there," she continued, pointing to a huge tricoloured cob with a really long, thick mane and tail. "She's called Vera. I really loved her – she was perfect."

"Oh, what happened? I asked.

"I was skint and I needed to buy a car, so Valerie bought her. Valerie owns this yard."

"Oh no, that's so sad!" I exclaimed.

"Yeah. I was so gutted but at least I know she's OK and now I've got Monty, so life moves on."

We took Monty into the yard, tied him to a rusty ring outside his stable and began brushing him. Suddenly there was a loud *moo* quite close by. Startled, I turned around and there, to my surprise, was a cow's head looking over the half-door of the stable next but one to us.

"Oh!" I said. "It's a cow!" I don't really know why I felt the need to state the obvious.

"Ha!" laughed Carmel. "That's Brunhilde. She's got something wrong with her foot so she's on box rest."

"Brunhilde? That's a strange name for a cow!"

"Yes, it's crazy, isn't it? Valerie is obsessed with Wagner so most of her animals are named after opera characters. She's nuts but you'll get used to her eccentric ways."

"Why is there a cow here?" I asked. It seemed so odd.

Carmel sighed and shrugged her shoulders. "Valerie rescued her from a dairy farm in the next village."

"Rescued her?"

"Yes. Apparently, she wasn't producing any milk so she was for the chop, so to speak. We don't really know how Valerie knew about it because she's not actually on speaking terms with the farmer but one day she just walked into the yard with the cow!"

"Wow! How bizarre!"

"Yes, that's one word for it! She's quite sweet really. The cow that is, not Valerie. Haha!"

I went over to say hello to Brunhilde and she was very sweet and licked my face. Her tongue was massive and very rough like sandpaper, which reminded me of the many face-scrubs I'd had from Vanilla.

We continued getting Monty ready. Carmel said she would walk with me down the road and back to see how I got on with him. I stepped on to the mounting block (which was two old milk-bottle crates gaffer-taped together), got on and off we went. Monty was a super little pony and he just plodded along without any bother.

"He's only five, so he'll need a lot of direction and schooling but he's laid-back, which is the main thing," said Carmel as we wandered along the quiet country lane,

I was a bit taken aback by that comment as the advert suggested the horse was suitable for a total novice. I wasn't expecting such a young animal.

"So have you done much riding?" she asked, as we continued along the road past a large field of sheep.

"I did loads of riding when I was younger," I replied. "Then I stopped for quite a long time but I've recently been having lessons again at Amber Rose riding school."

"Oh God, Amber Rose! I hate those people! They got me a really dangerous Connemara when they knew I was looking for a quiet plod. I refused to pay for it and they keep calling me and giving me loads of hassle!"

Bloody hell! It's Mad Mel! I thought.

I nearly fell off Monty with shock but managed to control myself. I couldn't believe what a coincidence that was. Out of all the hundreds of adverts for horses available in Leeds, I had managed unwittingly to find Mad Mel. It was obviously some kind of weird destiny so I said nothing of my conversation with the people at Amber Rose and just continued with the trial ride.

When I dismounted and gave Monty a pat, Mad Mel told me she was trying out another lady the following day. But she said she liked me and felt that she probably would choose me and she'd call to let me know.

I went home to tell my husband the crazy twist of fate. "Oh my God!" he said. "You couldn't make it up, could you? Well, it must be fate so you'll have to wait and see."

The following day I took Florence to a local fair with a friend but I couldn't enjoy myself as I was on tenterhooks about Monty. I was worried that Mel would prefer the other lady and I really, really wanted him. I had liked him instantly and loved that part of Leeds so I got myself all wound up about it.

"But if she says no –" my friend said, trying to calm me down – "then you will find another one. As you said yourself, there are loads available!"

Of course she made total sense but it just wound me up even more and by that point I was actually feeling a bit sick and just wanted to go home. Suddenly my phone rang and I jumped out of my skin. I had jelly hands and couldn't get it out of my bag, which really made me angry so my friend grabbed it and passed it to me.

"Hiya! It's Mel!"

"Hello!" I replied nervously.

"I didn't bother seeing that other woman cos I think Monty liked you. Do you want to come up tomorrow and meet the gang and we can sort out which days for you to ride?"

I was ecstatic and nearly whooped.

"Yes, brilliant!" I exclaimed. "Thank you, I'm so excited!"

"Thank God for that!" said my friend when I got off the phone and told her the news. We celebrated with ice creams and several chocolate muffins from a home-made cake stall.

Eventually we went home and I told James the news. He grumbled about how I would end up doing everything as June had warned and he also grumbled about the money. Twenty pounds a week, in comparison to owning a horse, is such a negligible amount and we weren't broke. Had I not begun to feel better thanks to my riding lessons, I think I would have crumbled and said, "OK, I won't bother then." However, I felt very strongly that I needed to do this and I knew we could afford it.

"I've been feeling shit for so long!" I shouted. "Can't you see I really need to do this? I don't drink! I don't smoke! I don't even sing anymore! I don't do anything except housework and mum stuff! When do I spend money on myself? Twenty pounds is bugger all!"

James was stunned by my outburst. "I'm sorry," he said. "You're right. You do need this and I'm just being a bit tight." He gave me a hug and I had to force myself to give him a hug back.

I sat down with a cup of chamomile tea and considered my current way of life. What had I become? A mum that was so uptight I found myself constantly tidying up, and almost every word that came out of my mouth was some kind of warning: "Be careful!" "Don't touch that – it's hot!" "Watch out – it's sharp!" And so on.

Going to work had become a break from the difficulties of 'mumming', which was the most surprising thing of all. My work was physically and mentally demanding because my role included being an ear for everyone's problems. If I found that to be a break, then there was something drastically wrong with my life balance. I was desperately in need of something joyful and that, to me, meant horses.

Chapter 4

The next day was Sunday and I had before me the excitement of going to the yard to meet *the gang*. I got up early to get ready because I was feeling nervous and didn't want to be late. If the girls hadn't got back from their ride, Mel had said that Valerie and Stan, the yard owners, would be there to meet me.

"How long will you be?" asked James as he rummaged around in a cupboard.

"I don't know. Not too long," I replied. I felt annoyance welling up in my chest. I also felt guilty that I was going to do something for myself that did not involve Florence.

"OK. What should I do with Florence while you're away? Will she need to eat?"

I had to bite my lip to avoid exploding.

"Why don't you take her to the park? That's the easiest thing to do and if she gets hungry, go to the café. I'm going now. Bye."

I dashed out of the house before James could utter another ridiculously annoying word. The last thing I needed was any sort of friction as I was suddenly feeling anxiety bubbling around in my stomach at the thought of meeting a load of new people.

I had no idea what to expect and by the time I arrived outside the yard, my mind started firing off terrible questions. My nerves had really got the better of me and I almost turned round to go home.

What happens if everyone thinks I'm a shit rider?

What if they're all really bitchy?

What if I make an absolute fool of myself in front of people I don't know?

Come on, Grace, you can do this! my inner voice commanded. *You used to get up and sing in front of hundreds of people, for God sake, woman! Get out of the car immediately!*

I swallowed my fears and stepped out of the car.

It was a fascinating experience to meet Valerie and Stan. As soon as I opened the gate I was greeted by the sound of German opera blaring out from the caravan. Mel had not been kidding when she said that Valerie was a big fan of Wagner. Stan, who was pottering around the yard, came to say hello to me first. He seemed very laid-back and mellow and had a lovely Scottish lilt.

"Ach, Valerie, love! Will you switch that awful racket off? I cannae hear myself think!" he called out.

"You uncultured brute! How dare you insult the greatest composer there ever was?" shrieked Valerie from inside the caravan.

"Grace is here, for goodness' sake, woman!"

A very small, wiry chap, Stan had an aura of grey about him. Grey wavy hair (slightly greasy), grey skin and grey-blue eyes. His fingertips were yellowed from smoking and his lips had a pale blue tinge to them. He was seventy but he looked older due to being outside so much. All he really wanted was to be sitting in front of the TV, watching sport and eating biscuits. How he managed to end up spending his retirement picking up equine poo was probably a complete mystery to the poor fellow. He was not a horse lover by any stretch of the imagination but he had no choice because Valerie wore the trousers in that relationship, which was clear from the moment I met her.

The thing that struck me the most about Valerie was the stench of donkey. It hit me like a Force Ten gale. I could actually taste it, such was the power of the aroma. Valerie was a very stout woman and she towered over Stan. Bushy pink hair was pinned up and rolled in a very glamorous style that reminded me of Mrs Slocombe from *Are You Being Served?*. She also had the most enormous bosom, which looked very uncomfortable. Valerie was a bit older than Stan at seventy-three but she could easily have passed for fifteen years younger. She was strikingly beautiful. Her flawless skin was tanned and her cheekbones, chin and neck were perfectly defined. Her mouth was fascinating as it was rounded in such a way that it looked rather like a horse's muzzle. She was wearing a pair of large diamond earrings that probably cost a lot more than my house, and a turquoise Puffa jacket that would have been lovely had it not been smeared with brown. Was it mud or poo, I wondered? Probably both.

Valerie was very suspicious and asked many questions in her very sharp Scottish accent so it felt like I was at an interview. However, as soon as she discovered that I had worked in the same complementary therapy clinic as her niece, her manner changed radically. She was suddenly *a friend*. She became completely different and started chatting about various people that we both knew and it seemed that I was a welcome member of the gang.

A youngish girl appeared round the corner, leading a very American-looking horse. The horse was mainly brown with white legs and specks of white on his bum, which looked like someone had splattered paint on him. This was Siegfried – he belonged to Valerie and he was her favourite horse.

"I bought him for Jenny," said Valerie quite sourly, chewing on a piece of nicotine gum. "I should have known better but she begged me so I stupidly said OK. Anyway, she was meant to loan him from me and then I was going to give Siegfried to her when I retired; you know what I mean? Well, she went and had a baby so now she's saying she doesn't have time for him."

A faint line of saliva trickled down the side of her chin and glistened in the sun, which I found quite distracting.

"Oh dear!" I replied, trying not to stare at her chin. "I suppose it's hard for her to find time at the moment then?"

This comment just fanned the fire.

"I managed to find time for all my horses when I had a baby!" said Valerie, horrified by my comment, which resulted in even more saliva trickling down her chin. "And I was a drama teacher at the same time, for goodness' sake!"

"But Valerie, love," Stan interjected. "We adopted Susan, so it's not quite the same really, is it?"

"Don't be so ridiculous!" Valerie glared a death stare at poor Stan. "What's the difference? It's still a baby that I had to look after – and work and do the horses!"

"But you only worked two mornings a week and you had a lot of help from your mother," Stan continued. "Would you like a tissue, love?"

"A *what*?"

"I think you need to wipe your chin, dearest," said Stan, handing her a tissue.

"Shut up, Stan!" barked Valerie, snatching the tissue and wiping her chin.

Just at that moment the girl put Siegfried's saddle on and all hell broke loose. He snorted and reared. "I think his back's gone again!" she shouted and quickly took the saddle off and leaped out of the stable.

"And that's Jenny's fault too!" shouted Valerie as she huffed and puffed her way into Siegfried's stable.

It turned out that when Jenny 'selfishly went off to have her baby', Valerie, desperate for someone else to exercise Siegfried, allowed the niece of one of the women at the yard to come and ride her. Now this niece was a very big stocky, heavy girl.

"She was far too heavy! She should never have ridden him!" said Valerie.

So why let her? I wondered quietly to myself.

"But I felt obliged because she was Jan's niece, you know what I mean?"

Suffice to say, this big girl loaned Siegfried for a few months until one day, poor Siegfried could hardly walk and had to have a physio and all sorts. He was a lot better now that he had a lighter jockey but every now and again his back would go and the physio would have to be called.

"Get him some bute! STAN!" Valerie shrieked at poor Stan, who was right behind the door.

"Oh, you're there!" she exclaimed, red-faced with her eyes almost popping out of her head. "What are you doing skulking around behind me? Get some bute, man!"

Stan shuffled off to the caravan to get some bute (the equine equivalent of ibuprofen). He opened the door and out bounded the biggest, scruffiest, bounciest lunatic dog.

"Isolde!" shrieked Valerie. "Come here!"

Isolde completely ignored her and bounced her way over to where I was standing, tongue lolling out and back end swinging crazily from side to side. She leaped up with such force she sent me flying into the stable behind. She was friendly though, so I didn't really mind, although I did end up with giant brown paw prints all over my T-shirt.

Bute was administered to Siegfried and Valerie looked for her phone to call the vet. Then came the sound of horses clattering along the road, heralding the return of the girls.

"STAN!" shrieked Valerie. "STAN! For God's sake, Stan! Get the gate! The girls are back!"

Poor Stan, who by now was sitting down in the caravan with a well-earned cup of tea, dragged himself up and went over to open the gate. "You could have got the gate," he muttered under his breath.

"What was that you said?" Valerie glared at him.

"Nothing, love!" he replied.

The girls rode in on their muddy horses and all of them gave me a big grin and said hello as they dismounted in a very haphazard sort of way. I have to say they were the friendliest bunch of people I've ever met. There was a tangible air of fun and camaraderie about them. They were all in scruffy riding gear spattered with mud, except for Mel, who was dressed super smartly, and all very smiley and happy. It was so lovely to be instantly welcomed into the group and all my nerves and self-consciousness dissolved.

When I saw Mel on Monty I was very surprised. It looked so wrong. She was far too tall for him and too elegant for a little black cob. She also looked very, very nervous. She dismounted and untacked him in a very brisk, heavy handed way. He appeared to be very unsettled around her and I felt a bit sorry for him. However, she was very friendly and introduced me to everyone.

The first to come over to say hello was a lady named Jan. She owned a black pony named Lucy, who looked almost identical to Monty.

"Welcome to the madhouse!" Jan looked around to check who was near. "Everyone's nice except Valerie," she whispered conspiratorially, "but you'll find that out for yourself!"

The next person to introduce herself was Jacqueline (or Jack as she preferred to be called). "Hello!" she greeted, removing her hat and shaking out her dreadlocks. "Mel said you might want to meet up for rides during the week."

"Yes, please! If that's OK with you?" I felt so relieved to have been asked.

"Of course!" Jack smiled warmly. "I'll help you to get settled with him and show you all the good places to ride." She winked and walked off with her horse, taking him back to the field.

After lovely cuddles with Monty, we all squashed into the caravan (which stank of smelly dog) and chatted for ages about horses and the ride that they'd just been on. Valerie had a deckchair at the head of the table that we were all sitting round. She was like the Queen on a throne except it was covered in mud and dog hair, as was Valerie.

I drove home feeling wonderful. I had been horribly worried that everyone would be a total bitch, after what Lady Alexa had said about livery yards, but nothing could have been further from the truth. All the girls had been so friendly and had given me such a welcome that I felt very buoyed up. For the rest of the day I did James's head in because all I could talk about was Monty and how nice everyone was at the yard.

The next morning I was like a whirlwind – everything was done at top speed.

"Don't forget I need you to wash my clinic coats!" shouted James as he left the house.

I dashed up the three flights of stairs to the bedroom and grabbed armfuls of clinic coats that were all in a heap in the washing basket. Then I flew all the way to the bottom of the house and stuffed them in the washing machine.

Florence was dropped at school, the dog was walked and I treated a new client. Lunch was speedily gobbled up while throwing a ball for the dog in the garden and then I excitedly changed into my riding clothes, leaped into the car and zoomed off to the yard. It felt thrilling to have something fun to do and I was really looking forward to getting to know Jack, as she had been so friendly. I must admit, though, I was also feeling guilty that I wasn't doing a million and one house chores.

You can do those later! You need to do this! said my inner voice firmly.

The yard was only a ten-minute drive from my house but then it could have been a different county. The dreary semi-detached houses gave way to moss-covered drystone walls, quaint cottages and the occasional grand Edwardian country manor. So many beautiful trees and wonderful rolling, green fields all dotted with cows and sheep and, of course, horses. I looked wistfully at the perfect posh yard as I drove past and pulled into the dishevelled and well-worn yard that was Valerie's.

Valerie seemed to be in a good mood when I arrived. She was sitting in a blue and white striped deckchair in front of the caravan, singing along to a section of Wagner's Ring Cycle while nursing a very bedraggled chicken. (I say *singing* but she was actually squawking and sounded quite similar to a chicken.) The chicken on Valerie's lap was wearing a knitted tabard in a Fair-Isle pattern of green, red and blue. A gaggle of similarly attired scruffy chickens were pottering around the yard, scratching here and there and making funny little chuckling noises.

"I rescued these from a battery farm," announced Valerie proudly. "Look at them all now! Don't they look happy? And I knitted all their wee jackets myself because of course they've got no feathers yet, you know what I mean?"

"You didn't knit all of them, Valerie, love. My sister did most of them, didn't she?" came Stan's voice from somewhere inside the caravan.

"Well, I made all of this one!" snapped Valerie, waving the chicken she was holding in the air, which suddenly looked terrified. She stood up to give me a tour of her yard, putting the chicken down, which ran off, relieved.

"I've had this place for twenty years!" she declared, bursting with pride. "This is Brunhilde," she continued, bustling over to the stable where the cow was on box rest. "She was going to be murdered because she had run out of milk. Isn't that disgusting? I wasn't going to stand for that, so I bought her. And now she is my little princess, aren't you, darling?" Valerie leaned over to give her a kiss.

Just at that moment Brunhilde produced some cud that oozed out of her mouth and *shlopped* on to Valerie's chin. It made me feel slightly nauseous but Valerie wasn't the least bit bothered – she just wiped it off.

"How did you know Brunhilde was going to be killed?" I asked. I was dying to know.

"I know everything that goes on around here!" replied Valerie very haughtily. "It was all just fields when I bought this place," she continued, "and I had the stables built and the barn…"

The wooden barn was a health-and-safety nightmare. Apart from the fact that it was falling apart and contained several dog poos (courtesy of Isolde), it was right behind the stables – that were also made of wood. It would only take one idiot with a cigarette and the entire place would be up in smoke. Behind the bales of hay there were piles of mucky horse rugs and right at the end was Monty's saddle, upside down and covered in straw.

Valerie tutted. "Ach, that's Mel for you. She just slings stuff anywhere!"

I pulled it out and brushed it off and felt a surge of excitement at the prospect of seeing Monty.

"Now over here," Valerie continued as she led me down a path strewn with weeds, "is where the donkeys live."

I stopped dead. I couldn't believe my eyes. I'd never seen such a sight in all my life. In stark contrast to the rest of the yard, Valerie had spared no expense on the donkey enclosure. It was like the set from the Teletubbies. Firstly, it was dotted with trees for natural shelter and secondly, the ground had been professionally landscaped to include large, raised grassy mounds and cobbled pathways. There was a plethora of toys to keep the donkeys entertained, such as giant, multicoloured beach balls, ropes dangling from branches with treat balls and, bizarrely, a set of funny mirrors.

"I found them in Scarborough," said Valerie proudly. "They were chucking them out at the fairground so I bought them. The donkeys absolutely love them!"

It did seem that they enjoyed them because one of the donkeys was indeed walking up and down in front of the mirrors looking at his reflection with an expression I can only describe as a combination of *What the hell?* and *Ha ha ha!*

There was a giant wooden shelter with fairy lights powered by solar panels on the roof, and inside were three extra large, custom-made settees, very low to the ground. Two donkeys were sprawled out enjoying the luxurious comfort. I was speechless.

The poor donkeys had been rescued from some grotty auction. There were eight altogether. Most of them had scars round their ankles from where they had been shackled, and at least two of them had had their vocal chords cut so they couldn't bray. They made a sound that is impossible to describe and truly horrible to hear. These donkeys were a rickety bunch and all but two were elderly and arthritic. They had certainly landed on their feet with Valerie, though. She absolutely doted on them. In fact, as she was telling me about one particularly abused donkey that had died (and was buried with a headstone by the donkey field), she started to cry. I didn't know what to do. Valerie wasn't a woman you could put your arm round, so I gave her a tissue.

She cheered up when she showed me her new outdoor school, which was opposite the donkey area. I say *outdoor school* in the loosest sense of the word. It was extremely small and would have been better used as a diet paddock. It was just large enough for a pony but you couldn't take a big horse in there. I don't know what the surface was made of but it sat in sad piles, waiting to be spread out.

Valerie's other hobby was Shetlands. She had four of them and they were all little gits and massively fat, even though they were kept on meagre rations. Valerie used to drive them in competitions and they had won lots of prizes in their prime. One of them was a particularly pretty dapple grey called Parsifal that she had bought for her grandchildren, in the hope that one of them would love riding. Unfortunately, none of them were interested. Poor Valerie. She had dreamed of having a daughter to share her horsey passion with but, sadly, her daughter Susan was not interested in horses at all. Then Susan produced six grandchildren and none of them were interested either.

What a waste! I thought to myself, remembering how as a child I had wished that my parents had horses.

I have to say, I found it most peculiar that Valerie should give her daughter the ordinary name of Susan when all of her pets had such exotic, Wagnerian names. Perhaps Stan had put his foot down? Although that was hard to imagine.

And so, on to the horses' field. Valerie gave me a head collar and lead rope and, full of excitement, I dashed off to get Monty. I stopped dead at the gate and suddenly felt a bit sick. Monty and Lucy were standing together and they looked exactly the same. It didn't occur to me to have a look for the one with a willy, so instead I called out his name in a vain hope of him coming to me. It worked. He lifted his head up and pootled towards me as if he had been my pony forever. I was very relieved.

I brought Monty into the yard and tied him up. Mel said she'd left a grooming kit in his stable so I went in to find it. I was surprised to discover it strewn all over the floor and covered in filth. However, I cleaned it up as best as I could and then Jack arrived.

"Hellooo!" she called out, grinning.

"Hello!" I replied. I was bending over at the tap, scrubbing the brushes.

"Is that Mel's grooming kit? She's a dirty cow, isn't she?" Jack laughed and went off to get her horse, Buddy.

It felt great to groom Monty and get him tacked up. It was like a dream come true. He was so docile and stood quietly, thoroughly relaxed and enjoying the attention. When it came to picking out his feet, though, his back leg was really jerky and it worried me because I thought he might accidentally kick me.

"Give him a crack!" yelled Valerie, sticking her head out of the caravan door. "He's being naughty!"

But I didn't want to give him *a crack* because that's not really in my nature. I could tell he wasn't being naughty – he was probably just young and unbalanced.

In a flash, Valerie strode over and walloped his bum. "Stand up!" she barked at him.

Monty looked at me in shock and stood quietly.

"Sometimes a firm hand is needed, my girl, or they'll always take advantage!" She marched back to the caravan before I could reply.

I was stunned. I wasn't expecting her to do that and I don't think that being aggressive is the right way to treat any animal. Jack, who by now was back with Buddy, rolled her eyes and grinned.

Buddy was a very striking, middle-weight, skewbald cob. He was 15.2hh and had a fabulously long, thick mane and tail. He certainly had a very strong presence and excellent self-carriage. He walked with a very proud and dominant demeanour that said, *Look at me – I'm a God!* Unfortunately, the effect was slightly ruined by a hand-sized grass stain on his right bum cheek, which stubbornly refused to be removed, but other than that, he was really stunning. We tacked up, climbed on to the wobbly milk-bottle crates and got on. It felt very exciting.

"We'll just do Bluebell Woods to see how you get on," said Jack.

Monty plodded along nicely and although I'd only been riding him for five minutes, I felt an instant connection with him, which was so lovely.

Jack was a very down-to-earth Yorkshire lass with a strong male energy about her. She was mixed race and lived on a council estate and, because of this, Valerie treated her as if she was totally beneath her. Weirdly, she had invited Jack (and the others) to her seventieth birthday party... where she proceeded to introduce her as "Jack, who lives on a council estate. Hasn't she got a lovely tan?"

"A lovely tan?" I gasped. "Did she really say that? And why did she need to mention where you live?"

"I know! It was so rude!" Jack laughed. "She can be a right old cow sometimes! I'd have left the yard but the girls are so nice and Valerie is awful to everyone, not just me."

Jack had obviously felt very upset at the time but Valerie had a strange ability to be as obnoxious as she wanted and no one dared to challenge her. Except for one particular lady. Jack related the tale as we clattered along the quiet country lane.

This lady had kept a horse at the yard and, as usual, Valerie was bossing her about, telling her that everything she was doing was completely wrong. Apparently, this had gone on for months, when suddenly the woman's patience snapped. She grabbed Valerie by the throat and literally pinned her up against the caravan, shrieking into her face. All her pent-up anger poured out. Poor Stan dived on to her to try to save Valerie but the enraged woman sent him flying across the yard. Hardly surprising, as Stan is matchstick-thin and probably only weighs three stone wet through. Luckily, Jan was there so she grabbed hold of the woman and pulled her off Valerie. Jan used to be in the military police so she didn't turn a hair at any of the drama.

"Get off my yard!" shouted Valerie once freed, "GET OFF MY YARD!" Apparently, she shouted that over and over until the woman had in fact got off her yard.

That would have been the end of the story because the woman was leaving that week to move to Birmingham. However, through absolute spite she bought the field immediately next to Valerie's yard – a field that Valerie had always wanted to buy but could not afford. The field joined on to a bridle path and would have completed Valerie's yard perfectly. But it wasn't meant to be and it was a subject that wound Valerie up pretty much on a daily basis. To this day the field has been empty and left to grow wild like a jungle. This drives Valerie mad because, "All her bloody weeds blow into my fields and ruin my grass!"

Jack and I laughed our heads off. The way she told the story was so visual I could see it all happening. Eventually we stopped laughing and I breathed deeply, completely immersed in the moment. It felt so good to be out riding such a lovely little horse. He felt like he belonged to me because there was an instant connection and he also reminded me of my favourite childhood books that featured a girl and her black pony. I had longed to be that girl when I was younger.

Jack was very thoughtful and kept turning round to make sure I was all right, which made me feel safe. I felt very relaxed in her company so I was able to thoroughly enjoy the whole experience.

Wandering along the beautiful, peaceful country lanes on a black pony was my dream come true. It was absolutely wonderful and it wasn't long before we were on a nice soft bridle path in the middle of some very pretty woods.

"How do you feel?" asked Jack.

"Great!" I replied, grinning.

"Do you want to try a short canter?" she asked.

"Is the Pope Catholic?" I replied.

"Ha! Good answer!" She laughed and Buddy began to trot.

"Are you ready?" called Jack.

"Yes!" I replied, with mild trepidation.

Buddy went into a canter, churning up large clods of mud that flew up into the air from his giant hooves. Poor Monty didn't seem to know what to do with his legs and he almost exploded into the canter. How I stayed on is a mystery. I lost both my stirrups and bumped around all over the place, probably very much like a sack of potatoes. Even so, it was huge amounts of fun and my face hurt from smiling so much.

"How was that?" asked Jack when we slowed back to a walk.

"It was brilliant!" I laughed. "But I've lost my stirrups!"

Jack laughed and halted Buddy so I could rearrange myself again.

"You'll get the hang of it eventually," said Jack kindly.

It was quiet at the yard when we arrived back after the ride. Valerie and Stan had gone home and Jack had to dash off to the dentist. I gave Monty a little massage that he enjoyed very much, then I let him wander around the yard as I cleaned his tack. I was transported back to treasured memories of my childhood and the simple enjoyment I had felt while cleaning saddles.

I drove away with a very wide smile on my face. I was so happy that I had met someone as lovely as Jack to ride out with and my cheeks were glowing from the blast of fresh air. I headed to school pick-up feeling energised and buoyant... but as soon as I arrived at the gates I could feel my chest tighten a bit. Looking around at the other mums always made me feel like an imposter. Everyone else seemed so much more competent than me, especially the mum of Florence's best friend who was already there waiting.

"Hello, Grace!" she greeted with a cheery smile. "Would you and Florence like to come to tea?"

She was such a lovely woman that I agreed to go but as usual I found the whole experience very difficult. Firstly, the conversation was all about children – what they were doing at school, who they liked to play with, what they did and didn't like to eat. Secondly, we couldn't just hang out in the kitchen and drink tea – oh no. This particular super mum was very hands-on, so we had to get involved with the games the girls were playing.

Watching this mum reminded me of my own mother and it made me feel so guilty that I had no enjoyment from playing these games. I wished that I could feel enthusiastic about playing hairdressers, but having my hair plaited and covered in glitter by two kids was the opposite of fun for me. However, I joined in with as much enthusiasm as I could muster because I wanted Florence to have good memories of her childhood. I didn't want her to look back as an adult and think her mother was a total misery guts.

By the time we left I was completely frazzled and, as usual, my brain launched a vicious attack. *Why am I such a shit mother? Why can't I enjoy playing hairdressers? What's wrong with me?*

We got home and I filled the bath. Florence loved bath time

and she splashed around, laughing her head off. My mind calmed down as I sat watching her play contentedly.

Thank God for Monty! I thought to myself guiltily as I tucked Florence into bed at 7pm. Even the simple thought of seeing him helped to lift my spirits, and the memory of the day's ride happily flooded back into my mind. Mel had said I could ride whenever I wanted midweek, so it was very thrilling to look through my diary to pencil in dates to see Monty.

Chapter 5

Monty was a baby and had spent most of his short life as nothing more than a field ornament. Mel had bought him from a breeder who had used him for driving once or twice. She then left him in a field for a year or so and then sold him to Mad Mel, who liked "young, untarnished" horses. For some reason, Mel thought that it was safer to get a youngster "because they haven't been ruined and you can put your own stamp on them". This is, of course, true and a perfectly sensible thing to do – if you are a knowledgeable, confident and experienced horse person with lots of time and patience. Mel, although experienced with having ridden many different horses, was by no means a confident rider and she certainly didn't have enough time to school a youngster.

It turned out that in the past two years alone, Mel had bought and sold eleven horses, which is an unbeatable record for a "Happy Hacker".

"Eleven horses?" I asked in horror when Valerie told me. I was dumbfounded.

"Aye! It's ridiculous!" she replied, her lips screwed up and her eyes narrowed.

"She's still got a Connemara at Amber Rose riding school!" Valerie exclaimed. "A Connemara! I said to her, 'You're mad – ye cannae cope with a horse like that!' They're very forward-going, not a novice ride, you know what I mean?"

Valerie, the expert on all things equine, was never more animated than when she was talking about how *wrong* other people were.

"But of course she dinnae listen to me," she continued, unaware that tiny bits of spit were flying out of her mouth with each word – which I had to politely dodge – "and so she got the Connemara and she rode it once and it moved so fast it scared the living daylights out of her!" Valerie pursed her lips further and breathed deeply through her nose, her nostrils flaring.

"And before that she bought a two-year-old off the internet without even going to see it! She just had it delivered here!"

"No! Really?" I couldn't believe my ears.

"Aye! I'm telling you she's absolutely potty!" exclaimed Valerie.

"Absolutely potty!" Stan agreed, nodding his head, sitting in a deckchair nearby.

"So, this horse arrives," continued Valerie, "and I kid ye not, it had the most revolting face!"

"Oh!" I said.

"It was disgusting!" she declared.

"Disgusting!" agreed Stan, still nodding.

"What did it look like?" I asked, very curious.

Valerie pulled a horrified face.

"It looked like it had a moustache which, on closer inspection, we discovered was made of warts!" She shuddered at the memory. "And not only that, but you couldn't catch the bugger. At least Mel couldn't catch it. I had to catch it, because they know I mean business. Horses don't mess around with me. They wouldn't bloody dare!" (This is true – most animals would not dare to mess around with Valerie.)

So the warty horse was swiftly despatched.

Valerie went through the list of Mel's horses – some good, some bad, but mostly terrible and it left my head whirling.

"*How long would she keep Monty?*" I wondered to myself anxiously.

"He won't be here long," said Valerie, as if reading my mind. "Three months maximum, I bet."

"Why?" I asked. "He's so lovely!"

"Aye, but he's young and he knows nothing. And she knows nothing and she doesn't have the time to train him to get him to be a nice safe hack." Valerie folded her arms. "He'll do something to scare her, mark my words, and he'll be sold quicker than you can say Christmas."

With that she walked off and I stood there with Monty, feeling extremely glum at the prospect. I choked back my tears. Crying in public was not something I was good at doing and I didn't want Valerie and Stan to know how depressed I was. I really liked Monty a lot and didn't want him to be sold on. He seemed such a lovely little chap with a very laid-back nature. I wished I could buy him but deep down I knew that would never be an option.

As warned, Mel turned out to be very slack where Monty was concerned. She was hardly ever there because of work, kids and a new boyfriend so I felt obliged to do as much with him as possible. This was not what I had in mind when I had originally looked for a horse to loan. I just wanted to have a pleasant, easy hack a couple of times a week that I could comfortably make time for. Instead, I ended up chasing my tail with parenting stuff, housework, massage work, dog training and now horse training.

I say *horse training* in the loosest sense because I didn't have a bloody clue what I was doing. However, Mel's slack behaviour had triggered my own innate pattern of doing too much for other people. Instead of walking away and finding an easier horse to loan, I felt duty-bound to help. I felt that if he was going to be sold on, then he would get a better home if he had more to offer someone. Also, I was really hoping that my husband would relent and let me buy him. Valerie, for all her cantankerous ways, understood where I was coming from, so she recommended a few lessons with Elise.

On the morning of my first lesson I had to sneak some cash out of my petty cash box so that James wouldn't know I was spending more money on horses. I didn't like how it felt to be doing such a thing.

"This is madness!" I thought to myself. *"But if he knows I'm paying for lessons to help somebody else's horse he'll go mad!"*

"You should just tell him to suck it up", said the bold part of me that didn't get out much.

"Ha yes! That would go down like a ton of bricks."

I managed to put the cash in my pocket unnoticed while James was making a cup of coffee. It made me feel guilty but I didn't want an argument. He went off to work and I dashed upstairs to change into my riding clothes and headed off to the yard. I felt quite apprehensive as I had no idea what Elise would be like or how Monty would react to being schooled.

"Well, well, well!" greeted Elise as she strode into the yard. She sounded like someone from the 1940s. "So this is Mel's recent mount, is it?" She stood back with her hands on her hips, scrutinising him. "He looks far too small for Mel but he's just right for you!"

I didn't really know what to say to that so I just smiled and gave Monty a bit of a scratch.

"Now first of all I want to check that the little fellow is comfortable in his tack or we'll get nowhere fast." Elise marched up to Monty and began checking every bit of tack thoroughly.

I stood to one side and had a look at Elise. She was a similar height to me and very stout with short dark hair and had a strong military air about her. She was wearing a very smart tweed jacket with navy breeches and sturdy brown walking boots.

"It'll do. At least it fits, even though the saddle is brown and the bridle is black, but never mind. Right, let's get going!" Elise walked briskly and I had to hurry to keep up.

Note to self – never book a riding lesson when Valerie is there. Even if she is busy she will drop everything to make sure the simple, short journey from the yard to the school is as stressful as possible.

"Don't open the gate like that! You'll damage the fence!" Valerie yelled.

Having appeared from nowhere she darted over and grabbed the gate, huffing and puffing. The fence was a total bodge job and the gate had to be opened in such a way so as not to knock half of the fence over. Valerie hopped from one foot to another, nervously shouting instructions. When the gate was finally opened and closed, without demolishing the fence, we then had to walk twenty-five metres through the wacky donkey paddock. Again, this was accompanied by a barrage of ridiculous instructions.

"Hold on tight to that lead rope! Don't let him go anywhere near the donkeys!"

This was impossible. A stranger entering their paddock was the absolute highlight of the day for the donkeys and they wanted in on the action.

"Watch out for Hermann! Don't let him kick Biterolf! Wait there until Reimar von Zweter has passed!"

By the time we got into the so-called school, I was a nervous wreck. Amazingly though, Elise was completely unruffled and calm.

"OK, Valerie! I'll take it from here!" called Elise and, thankfully, Valerie departed. "Right! I'd like you to walk him around the school before you get on," Elise commanded.

The school was a postage-stamp-sized square of sand that wasn't finished and there were still a few piles of *surface* waiting to be spread out. Luckily, as Monty was only a small chap, it was big enough for him and we walked around as instructed.

"OK! Now then, let's have you on board," called Elise, standing in the centre of the school with her hands on her hips.

I mounted with no trouble.

"Now ask him to walk on!"

I gave the aids to walk. Nothing happened. I tried again. Still nothing. "Come on, Monty!" I almost pleaded. "Walk on!"

Monty leaned down to nibble at his leg and then looked over towards the donkeys, who were beginning to wander quite close to the fence. He had clearly never been schooled and although I'd recently had a few lessons at Amber Rose, I had no experience of riding an untrained horse. Walking out on the roads following another horse was not difficult for Monty, but asking him to move correctly in the school seemed to be very much out of his comfort zone. I felt my face grow red as embarrassment welled up in me. I had no idea what to do and I felt like an absolute prat in front of Elise, who seemed very *sergeant major*. It didn't help to have an audience of donkeys... which fascinated Monty. He began pulling faces at them and snorting as if they were monsters about to eat him. At one point he even kicked out at one and hit the fence.

"*WATCH MY FENCE!*" screamed Valerie, once again appearing as if by magic just at that moment.

"Oh dear!" Elise chuckled. "It seems we have a problem! Don't worry, Valerie, I'll sort this out."

Valerie harrumphed and went away. With great calmness and kindness, Elise took hold of Monty's bridle and said "Walk on!" firmly. She then began walking and so did he. "Whoa!" said Elise, as she slowed to a stop and Monty stopped too.

After a few minutes of walking and halting with me, Elise wandered back into the middle of the school and Monty continued without her help. We managed to keep going for several circuits but I had to use voice commands to get halt and walk.

"You've done very well!" said Elise when she asked me to stop.

"I don't feel like I have!" I replied. "I feel like a crap rider, to be honest."

"Not at all! This is an unschooled horse. It's completely different from riding in a riding school. Those horses know their jobs and their job is to teach you how to ride. This young man needs someone to teach him everything by the looks of it and I doubt Mel will have the time to do it!"

"I can't do it either! I've never trained a horse! I have no idea how to do this!" I almost squeaked.

"Don't panic!" laughed Elise. "I'll help you! Just continue doing what we did today as often as you can – but only for short periods. Get him to walk and halt a few times in both directions. That's all you need to do until the next lesson."

"OK!" I replied, feeling a bit better about it all.

I drove home and mulled over the lesson. Monty was a challenge and I realised I had a lot to learn in order to help him to be his best. Elise had seemed very tough but I liked her a lot and could tell she was a very good horsewoman. I wondered how long I would get away with sneaking money for lessons and hoped that I wouldn't need too many.

A couple of weeks later, I was cleaning up before work when my phone pinged.

"Soz, can't make it today! Forgot I had dentist!"

I sat down with a heavy heart. It was bizarre how bad that woman made me feel about myself. However, as usual, I felt compelled to phone her instantly.

"Hi! Not to worry," I laughed falsely. "Would you like next Wednesday at ten?"

"Yeah, sure! See you then!" she trilled.

I wrote her appointment in my diary and then looked around the house at the umpteen jobs that needed doing.

Bugger it! said my inner voice. *Do it later. Go and ride!*

I felt guilty but rationalised it by deciding I would only spend half an hour, so I flew up to the yard to do a bit of schooling with Monty. However, it seemed fate had other plans and instead, I met Eva.

Eva was also a part-loaner at the yard. She rode a horse named Star, who was a very pretty dun Arab, around 14.3hh. Eva was immaculately dressed in Harry Hall breeches and a Caldene jacket. She was the only one there, other than Mel, who made an effort not to look like a total scruff. She was about ten years younger than me and appeared to be rather posh. She was very well spoken, which made me feel instantly self-conscious, and I assumed she would look down her nose at me.

"Hello! I'm going out for a hack. Would you like to come along?" she asked with a smile.

"OK, yes!" I replied, feeling ashamed that I had judged her unfairly.

Eva turned out to be a very lovely and friendly young woman. We pootled along at a leisurely pace, enjoying the glorious day and the fabulous countryside.

"I used to loan a horse from Mel," said Eva, as we wandered down the most beautiful bridle path that had stunning views of the surrounding rolling fields. "She was a lovely palomino Welsh D called Mitzi and I absolutely loved her."

"Oh, what happened?" I asked.

"Mel sold her," said Eva sadly. "She was a bit of a naughty horse but I love cheeky horses so I used to find it funny. But Mel didn't find it funny at all, especially when she bucked her over a hedge into a sheep field one day!"

"Oh no!" I exclaimed.

"It was terrible! Mel has a phobia of sheep so she was screaming her head off, running around the field trying to find the gate to get out. The sheep were following her, which made her scream even more! Jack had to go in and rescue her eventually!"

"Oh my God!" I was visualising the scene.

"Yes, it was so crazy! It was like something out of a Carry On film but that's why Mel decided to sell her. I was gutted because she got sold as soon as she was advertised. I didn't even have time to say goodbye and I really loved Mitzi"

It was such a sad story and it made me feel really worried that one day I would turn up to find Monty gone.

"Well, I wouldn't be surprised if she did end up selling him if he puts a foot wrong," said Eva when I voiced my concerns. "Could you buy him?"

"I don't think so," I said sadly. "We can't afford it."

That night, I told the sorry tale of Mitzi to my husband. He instantly became stressed and defensive.

"We are not buying a horse!" he said, before I'd even finished telling him.

"I didn't ask you to!" I replied.

"Well, that's what you're thinking, though, isn't it? And I'm just not paying for a horse – end of subject!"

I got really cross and went off to watch crap TV in a huff.

The following day I told Valerie about the conversation I'd had with James.

"I never told Stan when I bought a horse!" She was carrying a chicken under each arm, both of whom were wearing knitted tabards in Royal Stewart tartan. "It was none of his business!" she declared, drawing herself up to her full height.

The chickens began to look slightly nervous.

"I saw this horse, Venus. Skin and bone she was and I felt sorry for her, you know what I mean? So I bought her and took her up to the local livery yard."

Valerie put the chickens down. They instantly ran off, probably breathing a sigh of relief. Then she went into the caravan and scrabbled about through some drawers until she found some old photographs. Venus had indeed been a bag of skin and bones. Valerie had seen her advertised and had felt sorry for her. She bought her for next to nothing and restored her to surprisingly superb condition, which she showed me in the other photographs. Venus became a beautiful horse, an ethereal dappled cremello. There was a fabulous photo of Valerie sitting on her, wearing tweeds, at a show with a red rosette for coming first in the showing class. She then went on to regale me with tales of how she was a superb jumper and excellent at hunting, while Stan lingered in the background rolling his eyes and smirking.

Finally, Valerie's phone rang so I was able to escape to the field to get Monty.

"Monty!" I called as I arrived at the field gate.

Monty looked up from grazing and walked happily towards me. It was very gratifying. Slowly but surely Monty was embedding himself deeper into my heart, thanks to his lovely personality. He was so laid-back and cuddly. Being with him reminded me of the free spirit I had been as a child and the excitement I had felt during my riding lessons.

"I've got half an hour so let's just do some quick schooling because then I've got to go to the shops and get dinner ready before school pick-up!"

Schooling done, I hurriedly untacked, led Monty to his field and flew back to suburbia and the dullness of adult life.

"If only I had more time just to enjoy horsing!" I exclaimed to myself. "Lady Alexa is so lucky. She doesn't need to do any of this rubbish. She just rides horses!"

Although I was feeling quite uptight because of the overwhelming list of responsibilities, I was very happy with my progress with Monty. I could now get him to trot in the school, which was a great achievement, and I loved our hacks out with Jack and Buddy. I was also very much looking forward to my lesson the following day because I knew that Elise was going to teach me how to do lunging.

"Right, as you can see, this lunging head collar has three rings on the noseband," said Elise, holding up the strange contraption for me to inspect. "You can attach the lunge line to whichever ring you feel is best for the circumstances. Today we will use the inside rings, depending on which direction he's going in."

So far so good.

"OK. So attach the line to the one nearest to us and then we will stand in the middle of the school. Here's the whip. Use it to direct him, not to punish him! It's just an extension of your arm."

My hands felt so full of stuff and I had no idea what I was doing, so Elise gave me a demonstration. Of course, she made it look really easy. Then when I tried, it all went a bit wrong. The donkeys found it most entertaining to watch Monty hurtle round and round the school like a crazed lunatic with me running after him and Elise shouting her head off.

"Grace! Get back in the middle of the school! Stand still! He's meant to be the one moving, not you!" Elise had to duck her head to avoid being garrotted with the lunge line.

Eventually Monty calmed down and moved quite nicely but I think that was just luck.

Lunging is an art in itself – the aim being to get the horse to move round in a circle and exercise while you stand in the middle and watch. It's great when it works but when it doesn't, you find yourself doing more exercise than the horse as you run round all over the place, trying to keep up. When I first had a go on my own with Monty, I was definitely the one doing the most exercise. I huffed and puffed as I ran round after him. He didn't understand that he was meant to go in a circle and not zigzag around the school.

Then suddenly it clicked and he started going round me, so I could stop moving. He walked and trotted very nicely and changed direction very smoothly. I was pleased because it felt like such an accomplishment. It was so lovely to watch him learn to use his body more efficiently and carry his weight in a more balanced way. I never expected to have an opportunity to work with an unschooled horse and even though I felt completely out of my depth I also felt invigorated by the challenge.

My lunging session with Monty had perked me up so much that driving back home to work didn't feel as depressing as it usually did.

"Do tell me about Monty," said Lady Alexa during her massage. "I'm dying to hear how everything is going!"

"Well, he can now trot in the school and lunge," I replied.

"That's wonderful! Well done you!" she said enthusiastically.

"Hmmm! It's a bit pathetic in comparison to your standard," I laughed.

"Not at all! We all have to start somewhere and let's face it, this is the first time you've trained a horse, so I say jolly well done!" She was so kind and encouraging.

"Also," she continued, "it's much more difficult to train a horse of his age. Much easier to start basic training with a three-year-old, you know. Their brains are more amenable. Five-year-olds have their own minds and can be rather stubborn, so that's a double well done to you and I should give you a rosette!"

"Really? I didn't know that. I feel like I know nothing and everything I'm doing is just guesswork, to be honest. I'm just relieved it seems to be working!"

"Don't put yourself down! I think you are very capable of listening to him and giving him what he needs. That's the key, you know. Listening. Always observe his body language and you will know exactly how to respond! And let's face it, you are good at reading bodies because that's your job!" Lady Alexa laughed.

I loved talking about horses with Alexa. She had a wealth of experience and her kind, common-sense helped me to see that I was doing a good job. She made me feel so much more positive about myself and my abilities.

Chapter 6

One Tuesday morning, I received a text from Mel. She and Jan both had the day off work so Mel decided it would be nice for us all to ride out together. Valerie very kindly said that I could ride her horse, Siegfried, as Mel would be riding Monty. Jan would be riding Vera (the giant cob that used to belong to Mel but now belonged to Valerie) and Jack would be joining us too.

"Damn it!" I said out loud as I dashed back into the house to the toilet.

Maybe I should cancel? Once again, my mind began to unravel.

No! Don't be ridiculous! Commanded the sensible part of my brain.

But I don't really know Jan!

Stop being silly. She seems very nice!

Yes, but they will all be talking about things that I won't know about because they all know each other and I will just be really quiet and they'll think I'm really boring!

You are being mad! Get into the car and get going!

I took a swig of the Bach Flower Rescue Remedy and marched myself out of the house and into the car.

As soon as I arrived, I felt absolutely fine and my mind calmed down, thank goodness.

"Hiya!" greeted Mel as she waltzed in through the gate.

She was wearing a dazzling pair of bright pink tartan jodhpurs, studded with rhinestones, the likes of which I had never seen before and to be perfectly honest I didn't think such a garment would ever have existed. They were the sort of jodhpurs that Barbie would have worn but not a real live person.

"Wow! Very spectacular jodhpurs!" I said.

"Bloody hell!" exclaimed Jack. "They'll be able to see you from the moon in those!"

"What do you mean?" said Mel, looking down at herself. "They're fabulous!"

"Absolutely fabulous!" laughed Jan. She had just arrived too. "If you're riding with us wearing those, you're not allowed to get off when you get nervous."

"I won't be nervous. These are my new *confidence jodhpurs*!" grinned Mel and she shimmied off to the field to get Monty.

"I'll believe that when I see it," smirked Jack when Mel was out of earshot. "She always gets nervous about something and gets off. It's so annoying. I don't know why she bothers having a horse."

It felt very strange to collect Siegfried from the field and not Monty but he was easy to catch and seemed quite happy to be going out. Mel called out for Monty but he walked straight past her and came up to me.

"Not today, Monty!" I said, with false cheeriness.

"Come here, Monty," said Mel and she grabbed hold of his mane.

Jack gave me a wink as she walked past with Buddy, which eased my discomfort.

Siegfried was very relaxed when I tied him up outside his stable and he almost nodded off to sleep. All of his stuff was stored very tidily, which made a pleasant change, and his tack was impeccably clean too.

"Stand still!" commanded Mel.

I looked over. Monty was moving about a little.

"Stop moving, Monty!" Mel tied the lead rope tighter to the ring and began grooming him very briskly.

Monty snorted and shuffled around again.

"Stand still!" growled Mel.

Jack looked over at me and rolled her eyes.

"Have you had some Rescue Remedy?" asked Jan kindly.

"No! I'm fine," replied Mel as she tussled with Monty.

I felt quite awkward as I could sense she was already feeling nervous. Monty clearly could sense it too because he never moved around like that when I groomed him. However, Mel was his owner, and more experienced than me, so I felt unable to make any suggestions. I did my best to ignore her and focus on getting Siegfried groomed instead. Finally, we were all ready to go.

"STAN!" called Valerie through the caravan window. "STAN! Get the gate. The girls are going out!"

"Grace! Remember not to hold the reins too tight and don't use too much leg!" shrieked Valerie. "He doesn't like much contact! And don't let him eat any weeds while you're out!"

Poor Stan, who had been hiding in one of the Shetland's stables for a bit of peace and quiet, dragged himself out to open the gate for us.

Jack led the way on Buddy and I was next in line. Siegfried was very forward-going in comparison to laid-back Monty and he walked along purposefully with his ears pricked. Behind me was Mel on Monty and Jan took up the rear on Vera. Mel felt safer with someone in front and behind.

"Shall we do the duckpond ride?" called out Jack.

"Yes, good idea!" shouted Jan.

"What's the duckpond ride?" I asked. It sounded quite bizarre.

"It's great. You'll like it!" said Jack.

The duckpond ride involved going down the most beautiful country lanes that I had never seen before. We went past quaint, Christmas-card-style cottages with low roofs. They must have been very old buildings. Free-range, happy chickens wandered about on the grass verges, clucking and pecking at the ground. One cottage even had old-fashioned milk churns in the driveway and a white cat sitting nearby, licking her paws. I was like an owl, swivelling my head from side to side, wanting to look at everything. Eventually, the lane opened out to a very small village green that then led on to a dusty farm track.

"The wheels on the bus go round and round!" sang Mel suddenly, disturbing the peace.

I nearly jumped out of my skin with shock.

"We're not even there yet!" said Jack, turning to look at Mel with an expression of disbelief on her face.

"I know but I'm really nervous! I might get off!" squeaked Mel.

"You bloody will not!" commanded Jan in her sergeant-major voice. "Not in those jodhpurs. You are staying on! Keep singing!"

I looked all over to see what was making Mel so nervous but there was nothing. Monty was plodding along very calmly but Mel's face was white with fear. The more nervous she became the more it transferred to Monty, who pricked his ears up and began turning his head to see what it was that was making Mel so worried. The more Monty looked around, the more Mel got worried. It was a terrible vicious circle.

"The wheels on the bus go round and round!" sang Jan and Jack together. "Round and round – come on Mel, get singing!" called Jan.

"Round and round," sang Mel with a quivery voice.

Monty began walking faster as he soaked up Mel's irrational fear and almost walked into Siegfried's bottom.

"Whoa! Slow down!" said Mel, conjuring up a firm voice.

Siegfried sighed. He must have seen this before many times. I imagined that if he could have spoken, he would have said, "For God's sake, here we go again!"

It was a very peculiar, not to mention embarrassing, experience to be walking down a most beautiful Yorkshire farm track surrounded by fields bursting with barley, singing 'The Wheels on the Bus'. A couple of farm workers watched with amusement as we went by. God only knows what they were thinking.

Presently we arrived at the duckpond, which was at the end of a stony track and at the beginning of a lovely stretch of grass.

"I don't suppose we'll be having a canter then?" asked Jack doubtfully.

"Nooo!" squealed Mel.

"Are you serious?" said Jan.

"I feel sick!" said Mel.

"Why?" I asked.

"Because he might bolt!" said Mel, ashen-faced.

"He won't!" scoffed Jack. "He can't even be bothered to trot!"

This was true. Monty was generally rather lazy and preferred not to move any faster than was strictly necessary.

"I'm getting off!" said Mel.

"Oh my God! Mel don't be daft!" said Jan, annoyed.

Unfortunately, Mel's fearful mind was louder than anything anyone could have said and she leaped off with such gusto that she ended up stumbling sideways and fell, with a tremendous splash, into the duckpond.

The duckpond was full of muck and old rotten weeds. When Mel finally emerged, she was covered from head to foot in the stuff and looked exactly like a swamp monster. Algae oozed off her hat, and her beloved pink tartan jodhpurs were covered in a thick layer of stinking green sludge.

"Oh... my... God!" said Jan in utter disbelief, speaking for all of us.

I just sat with my mouth wide open in silent shock. Jack laughed her head off and Monty ignored the whole thing, taking the opportunity to stuff his face with the delights of the hedgerow. Poor Mel began to cry.

"Oh my God!" she blubbed.

I got off Siegfried to help her out of the pond, which really did stink to high heaven.

"Oh, Mel, you're such an idiot!" said Jan, also getting off her horse to help.

She had a few tissues in her pocket but obviously they didn't really do much good.

"I stink!" sobbed Mel.

"You're not wrong!" laughed Jack, which made Mel cry even more. Jack rolled her eyes skywards.

"I think you need to have some Rescue Remedy when you ride," suggested Jan kindly. "It works for me when I feel a bit nervous."

"I wouldn't bother riding if I was that nervous," said Jack, which wasn't particularly helpful but I suppose it was honest.

"I don't know why I get so nervous. It just comes over me," replied Mel sadly.

"It happens to a lot of riders," I said, hoping it would help her to feel better. "In fact it's funny Jan should mention Rescue Remedy because I use that too and it's really helpful."

Mel tried to scrape off the worst of the sludge but it didn't seem to make any difference.

The ride home seemed to take forever as Mel had to walk and lead Monty, squelching with every step and attracting all the flies in the neighbourhood. Luckily, Valerie and Stan had gone for lunch by the time we got back so we were able to hose Mel down without having to deal with any interference from them. It was quite satisfying to watch the green slimy contents of the pond trickle down Mel's body and reveal once again the bright pink tartan jodhpurs. It's a good job it was a warm day.

"Well, that was fun!" said Jack sarcastically. "Same time tomorrow, everyone?"

"You're not funny," sniffed Mel.

"Oh, come on. You've got to laugh or you'll just feel worse!" replied Jack. And surprisingly that actually helped to cheer Mel up.

"I don't think I'll wear these jodhpurs again – they didn't work!" laughed Mel.

We hurriedly turned the horses out into the field and dashed off before Valerie and Stan came back. It was the maddest ride I'd ever been on. I was stunned by Mel and her irrational fears but it made me feel better about my own state of mind. Although I wasn't a nervous rider, I did tend to doubt my abilities in general with most things in life. But this ride had helped me see that I did have a level of confidence that I hadn't been aware of for a number of years. I had ridden a strange horse without even thinking about it. For some people, that would have been very challenging and scary but not for me. That realisation made me feel stronger in myself and I faced the rest of the day feeling fantastic.

Chapter 7

It was around this time that Jan's horse, Lucy, began to show more of an interest in me. She started to come over to see me in the field, possibly because I was there so frequently. She also looked almost exactly like Monty so I often got them mixed up.

One day I went into the field and for once, Monty continued eating and didn't bother to look up. Lucy was standing near the gate next to me as I called out, "Monty, come on!"

Lucy kept tapping me with her nose until it dawned on me that it was actually Monty, not Lucy, standing next to me.

"Oh!" I exclaimed when I realised my mistake.

Are you bloody stupid or what? Monty most probably remarked, in his head. Luckily, nobody saw that or I would have been very embarrassed.

Lucy was the highest-ranking member of the herd because she was the oldest mare. Although knowing her, she would have been the highest-ranking at any age because she was so bossy. She was very much like an old lady pushing to the front of a bus queue and bashing people out of the way with her handbag. None of the other horses ever dared to challenge her. If she wanted to graze where another horse was grazing, that horse would move away without any arguments.

She had a small white scar on her neck from where she had been tethered too tightly by previous owners, who were total scumbags. Jan had bought Lucy on Valerie's advice. Note to self – never ever buy a horse on Valerie's advice.

The first horse Jan bought (before Lucy) was also on Valerie's advice. This surprised me because Jan was, in all other respects, a very sensible woman. She was around fifty and, as I said earlier, she was ex-military police and very no-nonsense.

Valerie had been at the York horse sales, she saw a horse and she called Jan. "There's a lovely young horse here that would be perfect for you!"

"Oh, really?" replied Jan. "I'm just in the middle of cooking dinner so I can't really talk. Also, I'd prefer to see a horse myself before I bought one."

"Never mind your dinner. You'd be mad not to get this horse!" Valerie blundered on, oblivious to Jan's sensible comment. "I'll buy it and you can pay me tomorrow." And with that she hung up.

Jan called her back in panic. Valerie didn't answer. Jan kept trying and after ten minutes, Valerie finally answered her phone.

"I'd really prefer not to buy a horse over the phone, Valerie!" said Jan.

"Well, it's too late! You should have told me that before! I've bought it now so you owe me two hundred pounds."

Jan was really annoyed but, like most people, she didn't dare to say so to Valerie's face.

The horse turned out to be a dark brown, middle-weight cob with a black mane and tail and lots of black feather, named Duncan. So far, so good. Unfortunately, Duncan was only fourteen months so he had to mature for a couple of years, which meant Jan was paying livery fees (to Valerie) without having the fun of even riding her own horse.

When it came to training Duncan, Valerie recommended a friend who was meant to be very knowledgeable but charged a fortune – £2000 per week. This man sent Duncan back after a few weeks, saying he had got so far with him but he could no longer cope with his bad behaviour. So, with the help of a friend, Jan decided to have a go herself. They took Duncan into the school, tacked him up and Jan got on board for the first time. All was going well until suddenly, for no apparent reason, Duncan went berserk. He started bouncing up and down like a rodeo horse, bucking and careering madly around the school. He zoomed towards the gate at top speed and smashed straight through it, at which point Jan flew off. It was remarkable that she'd lasted so long.

"My gate! My gate!" shrieked Valerie hysterically.

Suddenly, Duncan turned back and charged at Jan, who was lying on her back, unconscious, with a few broken ribs. Luckily, the friend managed to drag Jan to safety and Duncan galloped wildly off through the donkey paddocks.

"My donkeys!" shrieked Valerie. "Get him out of there! Get him out of there! Stan!!! Get that horse out of my donkey paddock!"

Never mind poor Jan lying unconscious.

Eventually, Duncan ended up in the yard next door where he calmed down and was duly returned. Stan dialled 999 and they said they'd send the air ambulance.

"Absolutely not!" said Valerie "It will scare the horses!"

So they sent a normal ambulance.

"No! You cannae park on my yard!" snapped Valerie, when they arrived. "My dog is running loose and you might run her over and no, she cannae go in the caravan because there is a chicken convalescing in there!"

No one dared argue with Valerie, or dare to suggest putting

Isolde in a stable. Poor Jan had to be bounced about on a stretcher as the paramedics stumbled over the uneven ground while trying to avoid donkey turds all the way to the ambulance.

It turned out that Duncan had a rare brain tumour that was causing him to be very aggressive. The kindest thing would have been to put him to sleep and release him from his mental torment, but Valerie wouldn't hear of such a thing.

"That's cruel!" she spluttered to the vet who suggested it.

So poor Duncan ended up in a sanctuary, alone, as he was too dangerous to be in with other horses. He lived a few lonely years and then got colic and died. At least that was the story. I bet they had him put to sleep because he was so dangerous but they daren't tell Valerie.

It amazed me that after that terrible experience, Jan would buy a horse on Valerie's suggestion, but she did. Lucy belonged to some friends of Valerie. They had rescued her from callous people and, coincidentally, she was living in a field a few streets away from our house. Before I'd got back into riding, I used to walk past that field, pushing Florence in her pram. We would talk to Lucy over the fence and give her carrots. (Obviously, I didn't know her name at that point.) She was so lovely, I wished that I could have a ride. If I'd known that eventually fate would grant this wish, I wouldn't have believed it.

Lucy was a laid-back, steady, black cob. In all senses, she was perfect for Jan, who was now a nervous rider after the experience with Duncan. Perfect, except in one vital department. Her height. She was a bit too small for Jan. But it was too late because Jan had already allowed Valerie to buy Lucy for her and they wouldn't take her back. Jan was a tall, stocky woman who needed to be on something around 15.2. Lucy was 14.2 and then only with shoes on. She was very strong, though, so she could easily carry Jan – it just looked odd.

Lucy restored Jan's confidence and then she realised she needed a bigger horse.

"I've bought Vera from Mel so you can keep Lucy and loan Vera from me," said Valerie, taking complete control of the situation as usual.

So Jan ended up with two horses to pay for. It surprised me that Valerie didn't change Vera's name to something more Wagnerian but it turned out that Vera was the name of her best friend, so Vera remained as Vera.

Lucy was pretty much retired, mainly because she had a bit of a dodgy back leg. Something had been wrong with a tendon, which led to an operation. Instead of the vet suggesting she walked around to stretch it all, he prescribed box rest, so she ended up with too much scar tissue, causing the leg to be tight and a bit limpy. She got ridden once a week by someone's eleven-year-old niece but it wasn't enough exercise for her, and poor Lucy was clearly very bored and depressed. I made a fuss of her each time I saw her and we would have a little chat, which seemed to lift her spirits.

I was also getting to know the girls a bit better, which was nice. Jack was not like anyone I had ever met before. Her hair was absolutely fascinating because it was very neat dreadlocks that never got ruined by her hat – unlike my own bird's nest, which always became very fuzzy after being in my hat.

"It's got a life of its own!" she said, when I remarked on its perfection.

Jack was very practical and her mind was very adept at

designing and problem-solving. She did a lot of fence-fixing and other odd jobs for Valerie because she was a joiner. She was very caring and happily went out of her way to help others and she was very funny without realising it. Unfortunately, she was also prone to doing mad things on the spur of the moment. Her first horse, Missy, was bought purely on impulse with no thought whatsoever. She literally woke up one day and decided to buy a horse so she went to some ghastly horse sale and found Missy. Not having anywhere to keep a horse, Missy was delivered to Jack's house and lived in the garden for several days until a friend found her a space at a livery yard – Valerie's livery yard.

Jack had not ridden a horse since she was twelve – so not only had she completely forgotten how to ride, she also had absolutely no idea how to care for a horse. Valerie was in her element. She thoroughly enjoyed instructing Jack on the *do's* and *don'ts* of horse ownership while the rest of the gang reminded her how to actually ride.

"That horse of yours is getting a bit fat," Valerie remarked on a daily basis. "There's something not right with her!"

Much to the horror of Jack, it transpired that Missy was in foal. To her credit, Valerie was amazing when the vet gave Jack the news. Most livery-yard owners would not allow a pregnant horse to stay but Valerie created a separate paddock for mum and baby and couldn't have been more helpful, if a bit bossy. Missy produced a beautiful piebald colt but sadly she never recovered fully from the pregnancy and had a bad back forever after, so couldn't be ridden again. The foal was sold to a friend of Valerie's after weaning, as Jack didn't know how to train a horse.

Jack then went back to the ghastly horse sales and luckily

found Buddy, who was an absolutely amazing horse. Valerie was hugely miffed by Jack buying a horse without her approval. "I found her a lovely horse that would have been perfect!" she said.

The reality was that Valerie had taken Jack to see a horse advertised in the *Yorkshire Post*. The horse turned out to be a pony and when Jack was mounted, her legs almost touched the floor. So Jack made the sensible decision to buy her own horse.

Jack loved 'going for a blast', as she called it, so all our rides were planned around places where the horses could let rip. I remember one particularly hairy moment where we zoomed pretty much uncontrollably down a long, winding bridle path with low branches overhanging. It was a popular dog-walking spot but probably not any more as we narrowly missed crushing a couple of elderly walkers to death. Luckily there was just enough time for them to flatten themselves against a tree as we careered past.

"Sorry!" yelled Jack.

I just had time to see the look of utter horror smeared across their faces. Thinking back, there is no way I would go that fast down that path ever again and I'm very glad we didn't kill anyone. However, Jack reignited the adventurer in me. She was so enthusiastic about finding new places to ride and was always upbeat and encouraging.

Chapter 8

It was the brink of autumn, when the leaves are just beginning to turn lightly golden and the air takes on a delicious aroma that's wonderful to smell but impossible to describe. Jack called to say that a group of them were heading out for a ride and asked if I was free to join in the fun. The way she described it made me envision a whole load of people that I didn't know. I was available because I had no clients booked in until late afternoon but I felt nervous about riding out with so many new people.

"I feel a bit self-conscious about riding with loads of people who I don't know. Is that silly?" I asked.

"I felt like that when I first came here," said Jack, "and I had to force myself to go out with them."

"Really? You seem so confident!" I replied, surprised.

"Yes, it was really difficult but I'm glad I made myself do it. Come on! There's only one person coming who you've not met yet and I'll look after you, so don't worry."

I instantly felt better knowing there was just one new person and it helped that Jack understood my state of mind, so I decided to go. I arrived just as Valerie was leaving for a day out to Scarborough. As usual she was shouting instructions to anyone who would listen, while Stan sat patiently in the car looking up towards the heavens, no doubt wondering what he'd done to deserve such a life.

"Brunhilde must stay in her stable until tomorrow, so for goodness' sake don't turn her out! She's got a terrible scratch all up her bottom!" Valerie yelled over to Jan, who was inside the feed room. "And remember to put some Sudocrem on it when you get back! Jan, did you hear me? And remember to put the chickens away later or the fox will have them!" continued Valerie at full volume. "Jack! JACK! Oh, for goodness' sake, where is that girl? Jack, remember to bring the donkeys in at four pm, no later! Satvinder! Satvinder, where are you? Remember that Siegmund will need his sheath cleaning today or the poor lad will be full of filthy lumps of muck! Satvinder! SATVINDER, did you hear me? Oh, for God's sake, where is everyone?"

Stan lost his patience at that point and tooted the horn loudly. "Valerie, will you get in the car? We're going to be late, woman!" he yelled.

It was the first time I'd ever heard Stan raise his voice. Valerie marched off to the car and was still shouting instructions out of the window as they drove away.

"Has she gone?" asked Jack, bobbing up from behind Buddy's stable door. "Bloody hell! It's enough to bring on a migraine," she grimaced.

"Yes, the coast is clear!" I laughed as Jan tiptoed out of the feed room and Satvinder appeared from the barn.

"I wish she'd call me Sukhi! Only my mum and dad call me Satvinder," she laughed.

Sukhi turned out to be a really lovely lady. Her confidence was a bit low due to her experiences with the horse she loaned from Valerie, named Siegmund.

Just to cause extreme confusion for everyone, Valerie had named one of her horses Siegfried and another Siegmund. Siegmund was a huge black tank of a cob. He had a particular loathing for rain, which is, unfortunately, a common weather phenomenon in the

UK. He was manageable when hacking with a group – he would just dance and snort and try to hide under trees. However, if it began to rain when out alone, he had a peculiar habit of spinning around and walking backwards. Sukhi had tried everything to stop him, turn him, encourage him to go forward, but nothing worked and she would often lose her balance and end up flying off. Valerie would be furious when this happened.

"Why didn't you keep hold of the reins and turn him? He could have got killed coming home on his own!" she would yell at poor Sukhi, not bothering to ask if she was OK.

After several incidents like this, Sukhi was ready to give up riding for life but the girls kept encouraging her to keep going and Sukhi did love Siegmund, despite his weird habit.

Just as Valerie and Stan drove away to Scarborough, Eva arrived, looking smart as usual. "Ah, did I miss Valerie? That's a shame!" she laughed.

"Right, let's get the horses and get out of here before she changes her mind and comes back!" laughed Sukhi, and we all dashed to the field to grab our respective mounts.

It was lots of fun grooming and tacking up and it wasn't long before we were all on board and ready to go. I was so glad I had been honest with Jack about my worries and been encouraged to come along.

"Oh, damn, we haven't got Stan to open the gate!" said Jan.

I was on the smallest horse so I got off to open it for everyone and then climbed up using it as a launch pad to get back on again.

"MY GATE!" shrieked Jan, impersonating Valerie perfectly and everyone laughed hysterically.

"Where shall we go?" asked Sukhi. "It's such a glorious day!

Let's go somewhere with excellent views!"

"How about doing the golf-course ride?" suggested Jack. "We've not been there for ages and Grace has never been."

"Good plan!" said Sukhi enthusiastically. "You'll love this ride, Grace!"

The golf course was a fifteen-minute hack down the lane. It had a lovely bridle path winding all the way round it, which eventually opened out on to an enormous field that was a great place for a canter. The views were spectacular and we could see for miles as the air was so clear and the sun was shining in that lovely, dappled autumnal way. It was just glorious.

I was at the back of the line, because Monty was the slowest. I was thoroughly enjoying myself when suddenly Star, at the front of the line, started bucking and snorting.

"There's something buzzing up her nose!" screeched Eva, hanging on for dear life. "Oh my God! What is it?!"

Star let out an almighty squeal and then bolted for all she was worth and, of course, all of our horses instinctively followed – for better or worse.

"Oh my fucking good God!" I heard Sukhi shriek from somewhere in front of me.

"Jesus Christ!" yelled Jan.

"Whoa there, Buddy! Whoa!" Jack engaged her deepest voice.

I was too busy trying to remember how to sit deeply and stay on to say anything. Fortunately, common-sense finally kicked in and I managed to slow Monty down to a canter and then to a trot. Jack managed to collect Buddy and that slowed Siegmund and Vera too, thank goodness. We all came to a raggedy halt, almost crashing into each other, and in the distance we could see Star still running at top speed. She was thundering down the bridle path that cut through the middle of a large stretch of the green. Golfers who had been crossing at that exact moment had to dive out of the way like skittles hurtling over.

"Oh my God! What shall we do?" asked Sukhi.

"We can't do anything because if we go after them it'll make Star run faster!" said sensible Jack.

All we could do was sit and watch the horror unfold before our eyes. Star was completely out of control and Eva was screaming her head off… and then it happened. Star took a sharp turn to the right and Eva flew off to the left. She did the most impressive commando roll straight into a sandy bunker.

"Well, at least she had a soft landing," said Jan.

We let the horses go and zoomed over to Eva as fast as we could. Jan leaped off and helped Eva up. Luckily, no major damage had been done but Star kept on running. Jack urged Buddy into a gallop and went after Star but then the unthinkable happened. Star swerved round and pelted towards us as fast as lightning. She shot past all of us and continued down the path we had come in on.

"Oh, for fuck's sake!" shouted Jack as she turned Buddy and galloped after Star. She was like a cowboy. Sukhi and I sped after her.

"Close the gate!" shouted Jack to the golfers near the car park.

They could see a riderless horse was belting towards them. Yet they stood motionless and allowed Star to fly through the gate into the car park and out on to the main road.

"You bloody idiots!" yelled Jack – and then one of Buddy's shoes pinged off and hit somebody's car.

"Oy! You'll bloody pay for that!" shouted one of the useless men who had not closed the gate.

Buddy almost screeched to a halt, puffing and blowing. He had had enough of running.

"And you'll pay for that horse if she gets hit by a car on the road, you moron! You should have closed the bloody gate!" shouted the enraged Jack.

The man backed down, completely squashed by Jack's anger.

By this time, Jan and Eva had managed to get to the car park, and a very helpful man offered Eva a lift in his Range Rover to go after Star. They caught up with her further down the busy road, covered in sweat and clearly stressed, with her reins trailing on the ground. Cars were driving past her very slowly but not one person had bothered to get out and catch her, which beggars belief. The helpful man turned out to be the owner of the golf course and he kindly accompanied Eva all the way back to the yard. He drove behind her slowly with his hazard lights flashing to make sure other people could see there was a problem.

Eventually, we all got back to the yard and, miraculously, there was no harm done to Star other than her nose being slightly swollen from where the wasp or bee had stung her. If I'd had that experience, it would have put me off riding for life – but not Eva. She was absolutely fine and even managed to see the funny side of the whole thing.

"I'm still in one piece!" she laughed as she hosed down the hot and sweaty Star, checking her body all over for any pain. Star was exhausted, so she was very happy to be led into her stable for the night with two giant hay nets and a sachet of bute to ward off any inflammation.

"Good job Valerie wasn't here. She would have gone berserk!" laughed Jan. "She'd never let anyone ride out again!"

We turned the horses into the field and collapsed in the smelly caravan for a very-much-needed cup of tea and several packets of biscuits.

"I am amazed by your sense of humour!" I exclaimed to Eva, who was grinning about the whole incident. "If that happened to me I'd die of shock."

"I was scared at the time but it's funny looking back on it now!" she laughed.

I thanked my lucky stars that Monty was so heavy and stocky he wouldn't be able to run as fast as Star, even if he wanted to.

"I think having kids makes you less likely to laugh at things like that," said Jan. "I wouldn't be laughing about it either."

I ruminated on Jan's words later that day while I was cleaning the kitchen. Being a mum had definitely reduced my bravery. When I was young I had no fear at all while riding. I loved to jump, and galloping was the best fun ever. I was much more cautious now and although I loved galloping with Monty, who was very slow, I did not ever want to ride a fast horse like Star. I suppose it is nature's way of ensuring you don't die while you have a young child to care for.

Chapter 9

A week after the terrible golf-course ride, Mel decided she would like to have a lesson at the same time as me to make sure we were both doing the same thing for Monty. I had been having weekly lessons and had improved so much that my first thought was, *Brilliant! I will be able to show off my new excellent riding skills.* This surprised me as I had been so down on myself for so long, I wasn't expecting a show of ego.

It was a Thursday, early evening and my wonderful mum was looking after Florence until James finished work, so I hopped in the car and sped off to the yard. Valerie had gone home, so there was just me, Jack, Mel and of course Elise, our instructor. The weather was lovely and warm and it was so peaceful, with just the odd bird call or moo drifting over from the dairy farm.

"Right, let's have Mel first!" said Elise in her brisk manner.

Mel was nervous and this instantly transferred to Monty, especially because he was young and didn't have the experience to judge for himself whether the situation was scary or not. An older, more worldly horse would be able to look around and think, *Is this scary? Yes or no?* Poor Monty, wondering, *What is out there that's scary?* began prancing around a little and it was enough to make Mel feel physically sick and leap off.

"Oh, Mel! What are you doing?" called Elise from her position in the middle of the school.

"I feel sick! Let Grace get on!" shouted Mel.

Jack was standing at the gate, grinning.

"Oh dear," she said. "Your turn!"

I mounted and managed to collect Monty and got him walking nicely. I felt rather smug, which was really out of character for me, and I did some circles and changes of rein.

"Let's try a trot!" called Elise and we went into a lovely sitting trot.

Elise had told me to stick to sitting trot as I had more control of him while he was young and still apt to try to bugger off elsewhere. I had worked hard at achieving a smooth trot and was very good at it by this point. Elise, who did not give compliments easily, was very pleased with it too.

"Well done, Grace! Just get him into the corners a bit more."

Suddenly without any warning, Monty leaped sideways.

"Shit!" I yelled, as I ended up on his neck. I grabbed hold of his thick black mane and tried to push myself backwards. "Fuck!" I shouted, when I found myself in the air after he bucked me off.

I landed with a thud on my back, which really hurt and I was very shocked. I think I even cried but more from the shock than anything else. Mel completely freaked out.

"Oh my God! Oh my God!" she shrieked.

"Ow! Bloody hell!" I gasped and stood up shakily. I forced myself to get back on because I knew that if I didn't I would never get back on again.

"I can't watch!" said Mel and she ran off to hide in the caravan.

"Are you sure you're OK?" asked Elise and Jack at the same time.

"Yes! I can't let him beat me," I replied and got back on.

"Excellent attitude!" smiled Elise. "On you get!"

This time Monty behaved perfectly and I honestly believe it was because Mel had removed herself and her fearful vibes so he could relax.

When we joined Mel in the caravan after the lesson, she was in a terrible state.

"I'm so sorry!" she wailed. She was more shaken up than I was. "I'm going to sell him!"

"No! Don't do that!" I exclaimed, shocked and very upset.

"He saw a rabbit in the hedge! That's why he jumped," said Elise, "and because Grace unbalanced him he threw her off. I doubt he'll do that again because it upset him."

Apparently, Monty had looked very worried when I came off. However, Mel was too upset to talk about it so she went home.

"You put too much effort into her horse and really you should just be having fun," said sensible Jack, who didn't particularly like Mel all that much. "She's taking advantage of you."

"Yes, she probably is," said Elise, "but you're learning a lot as well."

I didn't really know what to think except that it was quite ironic that I should come off when I wanted to display how good a rider I was. My ego had certainly been given a much-needed slap. Pride certainly does come before a fall.

When I hobbled into the house and told James what had happened, he was not impressed at all and agreed with Jack.

"It's too much for you to be dealing with an unschooled horse. You've got to think of Florence. Imagine if you'd broken your neck?"

He was right of course but I didn't want to stop riding Monty. Now more than ever I felt responsible for his welfare.

"But he's not *your* responsibility!" exclaimed Jack the following day as we leaned on the gate, idly watching the horses.

"She won't care who buys him, though, if she does sell him," I lamented.

"But that's out of your hands, Grace!" said Jack. "And even if you did buy him you would regret it."

"Why?" I asked.

"Because he's slow and ploddy. Soon you'll want something faster and more fun that you could jump with and do more stuff."

I pondered this but I loved Monty and couldn't bear to lose him.

My back and neck were killing me for days but eventually it eased off and on Jack's advice, I bought a body protector. It was such a ghastly thing, like wearing a terrible corset, but I knew it was better than breaking my back so I made myself get used to it.

Chapter 10

All was going well again with Monty so Elise decided we should have a lesson in the big field next to the donkey paddock. I had not ridden in any of the fields and I was very excited to give it a go.

We walked down the length of the field by the fence and ahead of us was a red water bucket. It was glinting in the sun and I had a funny feeling that Monty was worried about this item. I ignored the feeling and continued riding towards the bucket.

As Monty was young I should have dismounted and walked with him to let him see it was OK. At the very least I should have held the reins correctly to stop him from being able to spin and career off in the other direction with me clinging on desperately.

I flew off sideways and landed with a thud right on top of the only pile of turd left in that field. Typical. I was fine because I was wearing my body protector but I was very shocked because of the speed of the incident. I got back on but I had lost my nerve – mainly due to my inexperience and lack of understanding of the horse psyche.

This was the last straw for Mel when she found out what had happened, and she made her mind up to sell Monty. I was devastated. Everyone started bombarding me with numbers – the farrier costs this much, livery costs this much and so on – trying to help me see if I could afford to buy him or not.

Valerie wanted me to buy him because obviously she would benefit financially from that. Mel wanted me to buy him because then it would make her life easier. Jack was the voice of reason and encouraged me *not* to buy him.

All of it was irrelevant because James did not want to buy a horse. Half of me thought he was a selfish control freak but the other half of me could see his point. The expense of a horse would limit what we could do as a family and I didn't feel knowledgeable enough to confidently buy Monty anyway. But I was heartbroken at the prospect of losing him. I had begun to feel so much better about myself and my life – and that was all due to spending time with Monty.

"You know you could bring the little guy up to our field any time you like!" said one of my wealthy patients who owned land near Harewood. "It wouldn't cost you a penny because we aren't using the field."

This particular lady was a pretty, petite blonde Swiss woman who spoke very fast. She had a lovely big heart and the offer was genuine. Unfortunately, due to my lack of knowledge on horse care, I was under the illusion that a horse would need a stable, so I foolishly refused her kind offer of help.

I arrived at the yard the following day to a flurry of activity. Wagner was blaring out of the feed room where Valerie was preparing some medical concoction for the donkeys and Stan was trying to converse with a group of strangers.

"Have you an appointment with the owner to come and visit?" Stan sounded harassed. He turned round and shouted, "Valerie! For goodness' sake! Will ya turn the volume down? I cannae hear myself think!"

Just at that moment, a chicken got under his feet and sent

Stan stumbling into one of the visitors, which led to both of them doing a sort of dance in order to remain upright.

"Stanley! What the hell are you doing, man?" shrieked Valerie, who had stuck her head out of the door.

"I'm falling over one of your blasted chickens, woman!" shouted Stan, who was by now at the end of his tether.

"Don't use such vulgar language! They're very sensitive creatures. You could cause their feathers to fall out!" Valerie scooped up the chicken and smothered it with kisses. "Now, can somebody tell me what on earth is happening here? Who are these people?"

"They've come to visit Monty," gasped Stan, bending over on to his knees and having a mild asthma attack.

My heart sank into my boots.

"For God's sake, Stan, go and get your inhaler!" barked Valerie with absolutely no sympathy, as usual.

"Have you arranged to meet Carmel?" asked Valerie.

"Er... no, er... we just thought we'd pop in on the off-chance," mumbled the lady, clearly wishing they'd not come.

"Ah well, she won't be here today, but this is Grace who rides him during the week. She'll go and get him for you."

I felt sick as I walked to the field to collect Monty. He came to see me with a quizzical expression on his face, as if he could sense my upset.

"Some people have come to see you, Monty," I said, fighting back the tears. "Please do something naughty so they don't buy you!"

I led him into the yard and had a good look at the visitors. They consisted of a man and a woman, around the same age as me, and a very tall girl who looked to be about twelve.

"Hi, I'm Grace," I said unenthusiastically. "This is Monty."

They all said hello and they seemed quite nice but obviously I didn't want them to buy him.

"He looks lovely! How old is he?" asked the mum.

"He's five," I replied.

"Oh, that's great! We want a pony for pony club and something suitable that I could ride too. He looks ideal, doesn't he, love?" said the mum to the very tall daughter.

Valerie sucked her breath in loudly.

"Oh no no no! You cannae do that with this pony! Are you mad? For a start, he's only just being schooled and I dinnae think your wee lassie will have any idea how to do that – and you are far too heavy to be riding this pony. What do you weigh? It must be more than fourteen stone and that's a conservative estimate, I'll wager!" Valerie had her hands on her hips in quite an aggressive stance.

I was stunned and rendered speechless. I couldn't believe what I'd just heard. There was a moment of silence in which everyone froze, open-mouthed.

"Well, I think we'll be going," said the mum curtly. "You are a very rude woman."

"I am not rude, madam! I am merely speaking the truth. You are much too heavy for this pony and your daughter is too tall and too young." Valerie walked away to the feed room, ending the conversation.

The family marched off the yard without another word and I was left dumbstruck with Monty.

"Sometimes Valerie knows just what to say!" said Stan, who

had been listening to the whole thing from the safety of the caravan. We both laughed our heads off. I felt so relieved. "It's a real shame you cannae buy him. I can tell he loves you," sighed Stan kindly before mooching off to the Shetland paddock.

A short while after the incident I related the tale to Jack as we rode down the lane.

"Oh my God, I can't believe she said that! Actually, no I *can* believe she said it!" she laughed.

"You could have heard a pin drop. It was so uncomfortable!" I replied.

"I can imagine! Look, try not to worry about Monty," said Jack. "Everything happens for a reason and it will all turn out right. You'll find another horse, you know."

I knew she was right but it didn't make me feel any better.

A couple of days later I arrived to yet another scene at the yard. Stan was standing with an oldish-looking lady, holding on to Isolde's collar in a desperate attempt to stop her leaping all over the place.

"Oh, for goodness' sake!" came Valerie's voice from the caravan. "Why are people just turning up?" The door flew open and out she marched. "Yes?" Valerie looked the woman up and down with disdain. "How can we help you?"

"Oh, well, I... er... I've come to see the horse that's for sale," stuttered the lady.

"Oh, really? Well, the horse does not belong to me. Have you an appointment with Carmel?"

"Er... no, I... er... was actually just passing and thought I'd have a look, if convenient?" The lady seemed to be wilting under Valerie's glare.

"Grace! Go and fetch Monty!" commanded Valerie.

By the time I'd got back to the yard there was only Stan sitting in a deckchair, smirking.

"Where have they gone?" I asked, surprised.

"Ha! Dinnae ask! You dinnae want to know what Valerie said to this one!" Stan guffawed. "Oh dear, oh dear!" He shook his head.

"The ignorant woman wanted him for a ride and drive!" yelled Valerie, thrusting her head out of the caravan window. "She hasn't even had any riding lessons yet! Can you believe how idiotic some people are? I told her to get off my yard!" Valerie withdrew her head and the window slammed shut.

"Wow! That's mad!" I said to Stan.

"People are mad!" laughed Stan. "Especially horse people!"

I felt glad that Monty had had another reprieve and prayed that would continue.

The following week, Mel let me know that she would be meeting two sisters who were interested in seeing Monty and asked if I'd like to be there too. I arrived at the yard full of anxiety and presently the two sisters arrived. They looked very young – late teens, early twenties at the most.

"This is Grace. She's been riding Monty during the week for me," said Mel, introducing us.

Both girls looked down their noses at me and completely ignored me.

"We've got five acres of land in Barnsley so we can offer him a home for life if he's right for us," said the eldest sister.

"Yes, it needs to be right for our mam, really. That's who we're buying a horse for," chimed in the younger sister.

Mel went to get Monty and left me alone with the two snooty girls.

"I've been riding him most days for a few months and I'd really love to hear how he gets on if you do buy him," I said.

The elder sister glanced at me and said, "Yeah, sure," then turned away and looked at her phone.

It was very uncomfortable and I was beginning to feel very upset. Mel arrived with Monty and gave him a quick groom and tacked him up. All the while Monty looked at me with a confused expression on his face as if he was asking me what was happening. We all went into the school and the elder sister got on first. Monty was slow and steady, which was his nature, but the girl wasn't happy with that. She got him trotting before he'd even warmed up and then she asked him for a canter. Monty didn't fully understand the aids for canter so he just trotted faster. The horrid girl gave him a hard crack with her whip and eventually Monty went into a canter. The other sister laughed. I wanted to slap her.

"He's very ploddy, isn't he?" said the sister watching. "He'll be just right for our mam."

My heart sank and I wanted to cry. They paid for him there and then and arranged to return the following morning with a trailer. The rest of the day was just a blur of sadness. I walked the dog, cooked, cleaned and did some laundry, crying my eyes out. I was so upset I could barely breathe but I had to pull myself together because not only was it school pick-up time, it was also some kid's birthday party. I splashed cold water on my face, took a deep breath and collected Florence.

The dreaded birthday party was at a trampoline park and as Florence bounded around I bought a cup of tea and sat down to steady my emotions.

"Come on, Mummy! Come and have some fun too!" Florence came running over to me and grabbed my arm.

I just wanted some peace and quiet but there was no chance of that. I swallowed my pain and put on a cheery smile. I used to love trampolining when I was little so I decided to just go with it and hopefully it might make me laugh.

However, as it turned out, that was the moment nature decided to alert me to the fact that my pelvic floor muscles hadn't quite survived the pregnancy as well as I thought they had. I froze in horror as I felt the unmistakable warmth of urine oozing down my inner thighs. I was wearing light blue leggings and a T-shirt. There was nowhere to hide.

"It happens to us all! Come with me!" exclaimed one of the nicer mums who was bouncing nearby. "I always wear a thick sanitary pad when I come here!"

We dashed to the toilets and she very kindly lent me her cardigan so I could tie it round my waist and hide my wet bottom. She also offered to look after Florence and drop her back home so I could escape and clean myself up.

Can today get any worse? I asked myself as I drove home feeling completely at my lowest ebb.

I dashed up to the yard as soon as I'd dropped Florence at school the following day. I wanted to be there before Mel arrived so that I could have a last few moments with Monty alone. As usual he came straight to the gate to greet me and walked into the yard with expectations of going out for a hack. I led him into his stable so we could be alone.

"I'm so sorry." I buried my face in his thick black mane and sobbed. "I'm really going to miss you, Monty!"

Stan walked quietly into the stable and put a hand on my shoulder. He stood silently while I cried and then handed me a tissue. "Ach, it's a sad day," he said, wiping a tear of his own away. It was very surprising to see this sensitive side of Stan.

"I'm no rider but I do think all animals should have one owner for their whole lives. It cannae be nice to be passed from pillar to post, eh, lad?" He patted Monty.

Eventually Mel arrived and the two sisters turned up shortly after in a battered old horsebox. Monty didn't want to go up the ramp so Mel had to shove him in, which just added to the trauma of the day.

"I love Monty so if you ever need to sell him, here's my number," I said to the younger sister, handing her my business card.

She shoved it in her pocket and mumbled an acknowledgement.

I drove home completely heartbroken and phoned Jack. "It was awful!" I wailed. "They are a couple of total bitches!"

"Oh dear," said Jack kindly.

"I should have bought him!"

"But you couldn't and I promise you that in a few years you will see that he wasn't right for you anyway."

Jack was very sensible, which helped to calm my thoughts a bit. She came straight over and took me to the pub, which was very kind, and I drowned my sorrows with burgers and chips.

Just to add insult to injury, Mel heard from the sisters a few weeks later. Monty had bucked their mum off so they had sold him on to a dealer, who quickly resold him. The girls couldn't tell Mel where he'd gone because the dealer wouldn't tell them.

I was absolutely gutted, and furious that they hadn't bothered to call me to say they wanted to sell him. I know they probably assumed I still wouldn't be able to afford it but they could at least have let me know, considering I did actually care about him.

I still think of him to this day and wonder where he is. His freezemark is LSER, so if you know of him I'd love to hear about it.

Chapter 11

It was a few days later and I was walking the dog in the woods near my house. I was still feeling completely and utterly heartbroken about Monty and full of regret for not buying him, even though I knew we couldn't afford it. *I should have bought him. He could be having an awful time wondering where I am.* My mind tortured me with guilt.

But we can't afford a horse, replied the sensible side of my mind.

I loved him! I should have bought him! He must feel like I've abandoned him. Why did I listen to James?

Because we don't have the money to buy a horse.

I should have done it anyway, though! He was my responsibility!

No, he wasn't. He was Mel's responsibility and she should have trained him better and then she wouldn't have needed to sell him.

That seemed to stop my whirring mind because it was true. Mel should have put the effort in and Monty would have been a better horse for her. I sighed and brought my attention to where I was, in the woods with the dog. With no work booked in for that day I was looking forward to having a lovely long walk, enjoying the healing atmosphere of nature.

Suddenly my phone rang. It was Lucy's owner, Jan.

"Hello! Are you busy today?" she asked.

"No, I'm just walking the dog," I replied.

"Oh good," said Jan, "because Valerie has got a bit of a problem and needs help!"

"What's up?" I asked, intrigued.

Jan took a deep breath. "You know she keeps mentioning moving house?"

"Yes?" I replied.

"Well, an Italian developer has offered her a fortune and he wants to see inside as soon as possible! Valerie isn't fit enough to give it a proper tidy and Stan doesn't trust cleaning companies not to steal anything, so basically they're asking us lot to do it."

"Oh!" was all I could say.

I regretted answering the phone but Jan was such a lovely lady that I didn't want to let her down, so I said I would help.

"Oh, brilliant!" said Jan with relief. "I'll be round to get you in about half an hour!"

"Damn and bloody hell," I said to myself as she hung up. But it was too late – my fate was sealed.

I dashed home, fed the dog, changed my clothes and ten minutes later Jan was hooting her horn outside. Sukhi and Jack were with her too.

"Well, this is jolly!" greeted Sukhi as I got into the car. "Just what we all want on our days off... not!"

Sukhi had such an effervescent personality she could turn a funeral into a fun day out, so the prospect of cleaning Valerie's house didn't seem so bad. Also, I'd heard so much about it I was dying to see the place.

Valerie's Edwardian mansion was not that far away from the yard. It was a giant of a house set way back on the main road into the village and it had huge gardens at the front and back. My jaw dropped open in surprise at how ethereal it was. It was a Grade II listed building and made of Yorkshire stone. Beautiful wisteria draped over an archway above the front door, along with some dusky pink climbing roses. It was just wow.

"My God!" I exclaimed as we all got out of the car. "What an incredible house!"

"Stan's mum paid for it," said Jan. "She's loaded!"

"Wish I had rich parents," said Jack. "I'd be lucky to get a garden shed from my mother."

"Me too!" laughed Sukhi.

Jan was fumbling with a ridiculously large bunch of keys. "I can't flipping remember which key she said!" Jan had tried six keys already and it looked like there were around another twenty to try.

"Oh gawd, woman!" exclaimed Sukhi.

As is always the case, it was the last key that worked. The great big wooden door creaked open and out wandered a half-bald cat. It looked at us with great disdain as it slinked off into some nearby rhododendrons.

Of course, by now there was a barrage of painfully loud beeps as the alarm warned us it was about to go off. Jan scrabbled about in her pockets for the piece of paper with the alarm code written on it. "Shit! Where is it? Where is it?" she panicked.

"Oh my God!" we all said in chorus.

"I can't find it!" Jan wailed.

"I bet it's Susan's birthday," said Jack.

She tried it and miraculously it worked.

"Christ, woman! How on earth did you know Susan's birthdate?" asked Sukhi, totally awestruck, as indeed we all were.

"Valerie mentioned it last weekend and it stuck in my head!" laughed Jack.

"Bloody hell, that was an amazing piece of luck!" I said. "I had visions of the police turning up and arresting us all!"

"Thank God for Jack's brain!" said Sukhi. "Right then, chaps, let's get to work!"

"Crikey! Where to start?" I asked, surveying the scene.

We were standing in the *grand-entrance vestibule*. Or at least it would have been grand had it not been for the mountains (and that's not an exaggeration) of newspapers that were stacked impossibly high throughout.

Jack looked around and whistled. "That's a mental illness right there," she said.

"Valerie uses it for animal bedding," said Jan.

"Really?" I asked. "Which animals?"

"Goats!" shouted Sukhi, who had wandered off into a nearby room.

"Goats? Where do they live?" I asked, as there weren't any at the yard.

"In here!" shouted Sukhi.

"Oh my good God!" exclaimed Jack, as we all looked into the room where Sukhi was.

There were three nanny goats in what had once been a beautiful drawing room. It had a huge bay window with half-eaten plum-coloured, raggedy velvet curtains and a broken *chaise longue* covered in white hair. The stench of acrid ammonia was revolting and it stung my nose. Jack ran outside and was actually sick. Sukhi was laughing like a drain while Jan and I stood there, mouths open, silently shocked.

I looked down at the sticky, poo-stained parquet floor that was covered in newspapers and bits of straw. By this time, of course, the goats had wandered out of the room and were hobbling around the hallway, having a good sniff about.

"Bloody hell! Get them back in the room!" shouted Sukhi.

Unfortunately, even though all three goats were elderly and infirm they were still surprisingly nimble and seized the opportunity for adventure with great glee. One of them ran into the kitchen and leaped up on to the table to eat the remains of what looked like a bowl of muesli. The other two hopped straight up the very ornately carved wooden staircase that wound up and round and came to a long gallery.

Jack had recovered and was now back inside so we ran up the stairs while Jan went after the one in the kitchen. Sukhi was laughing so much she was doubled over on the floor.

"Oh my God, I've pissed myself!" she guffawed, holding on to her stomach. "Where's the bathroom?"

"Never mind that!" shouted Jan. "Help me get this bloody goat! It's firing poo everywhere!"

Goat poo is very comical. It sprays from their bottoms in little balls like a slot machine chugging out chocolate drops. Of course, it's not quite so comical when it's bouncing all over a kitchen table.

Meanwhile, Jack and I managed to corner one of the goats, who gave up the chase quite easily as she was probably exhausted from so much excitement. However, getting her to come back downstairs was another matter entirely. Although she didn't try to escape our clutches, she stubbornly refused to budge an inch. This left us with only one option – we had to carry her. I got the smelly back end, which kept spraying out poos and Jack got the front. Off we went down the stairs with the goat bleating loudly all the way back to the room.

"I don't know what she's complaining about," said Jack.

"That's bloody hurt my back! Right, let's get the next one!"

We dashed back up the staircase and found the second goat with its head in a washing basket eating a dirty sock.

"That can't be good for you," said Jack, pulling the sock out of its mouth. But the goat wouldn't let go so she was carried down the stairs with the sock swinging from her mouth.

Jan finally managed to entice goat number three back into the room with a packet of old biscuits. We shut the door and sat down, exhausted.

"We haven't even started tidying yet!" I complained.

"We need a skip," said Sukhi. "This place is an absolute nightmare!"

After a council of war, we realised we could only do our best so that's what we did. We also opened every door together in case any more herds of animals were waiting to escape. However, other than various cats, there were no more four-legged surprises.

But the house was full, from top to bottom, mainly with Wagner memorabilia. There were piles of old opera programmes and hundreds of books all about Wagner. I honestly don't know how Stan coped with it because he couldn't stand opera.

In the guest quarter, every room had stuff strewn all over the place – new clothes still with their tags on, magazines, newspapers, horse rugs, cat beds, dog beds, toys...

"Toys!" I exclaimed, picking up a train. "Do they have the grandchildren here?"

"Yes," said Jan. "They come at least twice a week."

"No way! I would never let my child come here!"

"I know! It's mental, isn't it?" agreed Jan.

"It's a health-and-safety nightmare!" Sukhi laughed. "One

wrong move and you'd get buried under a mountain of Wagner programmes!"

"I can't believe she has the nerve to look down her nose at me because I live in a council house," said Jack. "This is the maddest place I've ever seen in my life. At least you can see the floor in my house!" We all nodded in agreement.

All we could do was fold the clothes and rugs and make piles of things, then tidy up as best we could. There were so many rooms and passageways that by the time we'd finished we were all completely knackered, so we went for a well-earned drink in the village pub.

As expected, Valerie said a brief thank-you but didn't buy anyone any presents; nor did she offer to reduce anyone's livery bills that month. She really was, as Jack said, "tighter than a gnat's chuff"!

Chapter 12

Although I was now horseless, I still liked going to the yard, visiting the animals, especially Brunhilde the cuddly cow. She was so lovely and really enjoyed human company. Being with her was so therapeutic. She adored being groomed and would make rumbly moo sounds, especially when you brushed her ears – that was her favourite. Even when she was out in the field with the horses, she would stand for ages while being brushed, with no need for a head collar or any restraint. It was very soothing to hang out with her and it made my life feel fuller and more meaningful.

"Why don't you ride Lucy for a while to get your confidence back?" Jan suggested one afternoon while we were sitting in the field watching the donkeys.

Jan knew I had lost my nerve a bit since coming off Monty twice, so riding Lucy seemed like a good idea.

"Thank you," I said. "That would be really lovely!"

The following day I went up to ride Lucy. It felt weird, going there to ride a horse that looked like Monty but wasn't Monty. It was a peculiar combination of sadness and happiness that I'd never experienced before. Of course, Valerie immediately took charge of this new situation of 'me and Lucy'.

"You'll have to build her up steadily!" she called out as if from the heavens.

I looked over to see Valerie flailing her arms around as she toppled out of the caravan, only just saving herself from falling face first on to the ground.

"Stan!" she shrieked. "I told you to fix this step! I almost broke my neck just then!"

"Sorry, love!" replied Stan, smirking and not sounding remotely concerned. "I'll get on with it."

"Yes, do!" spat angry Valerie, as Stan shuffled off in search of some tools.

Valerie marched over to me in a very sergeant-major type of way. She just loved to be in charge.

"This is Lucy's head collar," she said, taking it off the hook that I could see was labelled LUCY quite clearly.

"You cannae ride Lucy the same way that you rode Monty," she began, arms folded and bust thrust forward in a very commanding stance. "She's not been properly exercised for ages so you'll have to stick to walk for the first few weeks."

Obviously, I was well aware of this as Jan had already explained everything about Lucy's stiff leg and so on.

"Yes, don't worry. Jan has filled me in on her needs," I said.

"She's got a stiff leg," continued Valerie, completely ignoring me. "She needs to build up gradually!"

Valerie continued to reel off instructions all the way to the field where Lucy was grazing but luckily her phone rang so she answered it and walked off mid-sentence.

Lucy lifted her head and looked at me expectantly. She seemed to know that I was there to see her but she didn't come over to me as Monty would have done. She stood, like the Queen, and waited for me to come to her. I sighed as I put her head collar on and led her slowly into the yard to give her a brush.

"I don't think I'll learn anything from riding you, Lucy," I said out loud as I untangled her raggedy mane.

Had I been more aware of horse body language I would have noticed the amused expression that flitted across Lucy's face in response to my ignorant comment. I continued grooming her when suddenly the gate clanged loudly as it swung open and hit the fence. I jumped and looked over to see Bossy Barbara marching into the yard with her arms full of tack.

Seventy-two-year-old Barbara was a retired English teacher. She was a very eccentric character, due to being so blunt and forthright, and she always wore her hair in an old-fashioned, tight bun with a hairnet. She was also exceptionally well-spoken, thanks to having elocution lessons as a child. Strangely, Barbara had fallen under Valerie's spell and had allowed her to choose an inappropriate horse.

Star, the pretty dun Arab, had been an unridden field companion for most of her life. Any sensible person would realise that there's a reason why a horse has not been ridden for years. However, "It's a free horse, Barbara. You'd be a fool not to take it!" insisted Valerie, waving the newspaper advert and almost hitting Barbara in the face with it. And as Barbara did not dare to argue with Valerie, she foolishly agreed.

Star was *free to a good home* because her ridden companion had died so the Arab was no longer needed. And it soon became clear why Star had only been a field companion. She was very strong-minded and wasn't thrilled at suddenly becoming a riding horse. Poor Barbara was forever being dumped in ditches when Star had decided she'd had enough for the day. She would merrily take herself back to the yard, leaving Barbara calling after her but to no avail.

Valerie wondered if Star's behaviour might be due to pain so she insisted that Barbara had her looked at by vets and physios and she even ordered several different saddles (paid for by Barbara) but it made no difference. Star just had her own plans. What originally was a free horse soon became the most expensive horse Barbara had ever owned. Thanks to Eva's help, Star became a lot better, although she was never reliable, riding out alone.

"Good morning!" shouted Barbara, like a cheery policewoman. "I thought I'd come and ride with you today!"

My heart sank a bit as I was looking forward to having a first solo ride to get to know Lucy. "Oh great!" I said, mustering up some enthusiasm.

I'd heard a lot about Barbara and how her voice tended to overshadow the entire ride for everyone else. I had never actually met her, though, but there was no avoiding her now. How would I cope with her alone, I wondered? Riding was my therapy time. It was the only part of the day that generated a feeling of joy and I felt dismayed at having that dashed by Barbara.

Barbara was soon back in the yard with Star and set to work very briskly with a dandy brush, all the while keeping up a very loud monologue that must have done poor Star's head in. She was literally giving a running commentary of everything she was doing.

"Right, we'll start with the dandy brush to get this mud off! Oh dear, you are dirty – have you been rolling? That's not very ladylike is it? Now, let's clean the brush with a curry comb. Where is the curry comb? Oh, it's here underneath the water brush! Goodness me, how did it get there? Lift your feet up! Oh dear, they are full of poo! What have you been doing? Yuk yuk yuk!"

She went on and on and on endlessly. I felt so jangled by the time I was ready to mount. Luckily, Lucy was not in the least bit affected by the relentless chatter and was calm and collected. I got on and immediately wished I hadn't. Lucy's saddle was horribly uncomfortable and I couldn't find a position that didn't feel awful.

"Crikey!" I exclaimed. "This saddle is awful!"

"I wouldn't say that in front of Valerie," said Barbara. "She chose it!"

"It's terrible!" I replied.

"Well, I think you need to sit up straight and lengthen your stirrups. They're much too short..." Barbara launched into a barrage of instructions, fully believing that she knew best. "Now look at your reins, they're like washing lines..."

On the contrary, Barbara had her reins so short that poor Star held her head unnaturally high to try to avoid the pressure on her mouth. Barbara would have continued interminably had it not been for Stan opening the gate and suggesting we get on with going out for a ride before it got dark. "Have fun!" he winked as I rode past.

"Ha! Yes!" I replied. Stan chuckled and closed the gate behind us.

Barbara took the lead and chattered the entire time. What amused me the most was how she would make comments to complete strangers as we passed them by.

"I'm not sure about that red front door!" she called over to an unsuspecting woman who was taking shopping out of her car. "It doesn't go well with your brown window frames!"

Luckily, we had gone past before the woman could respond but she didn't look happy.

"Good lord! That's a very untidy hedge, isn't it?" Barbara shouted to an elderly man who was doing a bit of weeding in his front garden. "I'd ask a neighbour to trim it, if I were you!" The man was too surprised to respond, thank goodness.

Barbara didn't seem to be aware of how odd she was and continued commenting to various strangers along the way. It was comical and embarrassing all at the same time but luckily, we didn't bump into anyone I knew. It really was impressive how she managed to maintain a constant stream of chat either to me, her horse or to random strangers.

After a while I realised I didn't need to respond because she didn't listen to my replies anyway. So, I turned my attention to the pretty village streets we were riding down.

Riding on a horse, even a small one like Lucy, provides one with a marvellous opportunity for looking into other people's gardens and front windows. It was very pleasant to have a good nosey into all those beautiful stone cottages. I sighed as I began to realise that I preferred country living to the modern home I had. Don't get me wrong, I was very grateful to have anywhere to live but the grass is always greener, isn't it?

Several days of riding Lucy helped to make me feel happy again. Although I still missed Monty, I looked forward to seeing her. She had an air of wisdom about her that intrigued me and I would have loved to have a conversation with her. However, I felt a bit concerned because she was so stiff and her strides were short and choppy. I wanted to help her to become more supple so that she could feel happier too.

As I said earlier, Lucy's saddle was horribly uncomfortable and she nipped when I tacked her up so I thought, *Bugger it! I will buy my own.* I figured if I couldn't have a horse, I could at least have a saddle, so I booked an appointment with the saddler.

"This saddle is awful," said Leon the saddle-fitter. "I'm not surprised she bites you. Look at how it restricts her shoulders!"

"There's nothing wrong with that saddle!" snapped Valerie, who as usual had to stick her nose in.

"There's nothing right with it, you mean!" laughed Leon good-naturedly.

"It's perfectly fine. I chose it myself!" Valerie harrumphed and folded her arms.

"Well, I can show you what's wrong with it, Valerie."

Leon was not in the least bit affected by Valerie as he'd known her for years and used to ride with her. He showed us how tight it was on Lucy's shoulders and how it was pressing too much further down her back. Valerie was very irritated to be shown up and refused to accept she had been wrong about the saddle.

"I think you're wasting your money, Grace," she said and flounced off for lunch.

Leon laughed and showed me how a saddle should fit, which was very interesting.

"This is probably the best saddle for both of you because it's cheap and you can alter it to fit other horses." The saddle was synthetic but it was very good quality. When Leon showed me the leather version I was amazed at how similar it was. The best thing about it was Lucy seemed instantly happier in the new saddle and her shoulders moved freely.

Thank God! she probably said, as I rode her round the school to try it out.

"Wow, this is so comfy! It's like an armchair!" I exclaimed as we marched past Leon, faster than I'd ever known Lucy to move.

"Good!" said Leon cheerily. "Lucy is moving better too!"

The next thing to go was her bridle. Every time I tried to get it on she would clamp her mouth shut and raise her head high so I had to grab her and force her mouth open, which I hated doing.

"Give her a crack – she's just trying it on! It's only a French-link snaffle," was Valerie's standard response to my struggles.

But I felt that Lucy was trying to tell me she hated it and I couldn't blame her. It's so medieval to put a piece of metal in an animal's mouth. Miraculously, fate intervened that very afternoon as I stumbled across an article in a horse magazine about Dr Cook's humane bitless bridle. It sounded perfect to me so I bought a cheap copy, which was OK but the leather was very stiff.

However, the transformation was amazing. Lucy was visibly happier the first time I used it, and the second time I went to put it on her, she voluntarily shoved her head into it for me.

Even Valerie was impressed and I caught her having a good look at it when she thought I wasn't noticing. I got the impression Valerie was annoyed that she hadn't invented it herself when she said, "Hmmmm... yes, well it's quite straightforward, really. Nothing particularly clever about it..."

After a few weeks of riding Lucy, I had begun to feel more confident as a rider, mainly because she was so easy. She was so laid-back, nothing ever unnerved her, so it was a very pleasant experience.

I had also discovered the Mark Rashid books, which helped me to understand horse behaviour and body language. His books are exceptionally interesting and informative. I highly recommend his book entitled, *Horses Never Lie*. It's amazingly eye-opening.

Lucy must have sensed the change in me because suddenly there was a big change in her. From being a sluggish, steady schoolmistress, Lucy transformed into a strong-minded pocket rocket. It began one sunny but chilly morning with an argument in the middle of the road about where we were going to go for our hack. I wanted to turn right and do a circular route through the village, past the old church and through some nice woods. But Lucy wanted to turn left.

"No, Lucy, we are going this way!" I commanded and turned her head to the right.

No, we are not! said Lucy's body language as she absolutely refused and turned her head to the left.

"Lucy!" I said sharply, pulling on the right rein.

Bugger off! said Lucy, yanking her head to the left.

This went on for some time and I am ashamed to admit that several swear words were involved. To my horror, I had to admit defeat and let her go left. Off she marched, head up and a jaunty swing to her stride as she laughed to herself, knowing that she was the boss. As I said earlier, there was an air of wisdom about Lucy so I didn't feel worried. I actually felt quite relaxed and curious to see where she wanted to go.

We went quite a way down the road until we came to a crossroads at which Lucy chose to turn right. She didn't care about such mere things as *right of way* and *waiting for our turn*. Oh no, she just continued on her way, causing brakes to screech noisily.

"Oh my God, Lucy, you've got to stop! What are you doing?" I yelled, sitting deep in the saddle, shifting my weight back, pulling on the reins and doing everything else that's meant to stop a horse. None of it made any difference, she just marched on.

Luckily the van driver had a sense of humour and didn't get cross but actually, we could have had a terrible accident.

"Lucy! We could have died then!" I shrieked at her.

Never mind! she seemed to say and I imagined her to sound like Hyacinth Bucket from *Keeping Up Appearances*.

We went down a lane I'd never seen before that was very pretty with the odd grand house set well back. In a field, with not much to offer in the way of grazing, were two beautiful warmblood horses. They pricked their ears up as we strode past and came cantering over, snorting with excitement. Lucy wasn't bothered one bit and continued, unruffled, even though they were prancing up and down the fence line. She gave them *a look* and they quietened down a bit.

Opposite the horses' field, on the other side of the road, was a hawthorn hedgerow that Lucy made a beeline for – and she had a lovely time stuffing her face. The two warmbloods looked on enviously. Lucy seemed to enjoy their jealousy and stood looking at them with her mouth full of hedge, chewing slowly.

When she'd had enough she sauntered on and we came to a farmer's field where the gate had been left open. Lucy stopped and looked around as if to check whether the coast was clear and I wondered what she was doing.

I didn't have to wonder for long because in she went – and suddenly we were off. I couldn't believe it – Lucy was cantering up a field. It was so funny and unexpected, all I could do was laugh. She went right to the top, then stopped, turned round and headed back towards the gate.

"Wow!" I exclaimed as she trotted out of the field and on to the road.

I was relieved that nobody was at the yard when we returned because I was so embarrassed that I'd been literally taken for a ride by elderly Lucy. I leaped off and untacked her and we stood for a few moments just looking at each other. No words were spoken but, like a game of chess, I realised I'd been checked.

"...and there was nothing I could do to stop her!" I poured out the sorry tale of my appalling lack of control to Lady Alexa that afternoon.

Lady Alexa guffawed as only the aristocracy can do.

"An elderly cob took total advantage of you? Oh dear, that's so funny!" She shook with peals of laughter. "You underestimated her, didn't you!"

"Yes," I mumbled, very embarrassed.

"Well, I think she is providing you with a wonderful opportunity to learn more from her. Horses have always been my greatest teachers. What do you think she's trying to teach you?"

Lady Alexa was right, Lucy was definitely teaching me something but what was it? I thought about it later that evening when I finally had a moment of peace. I figured I had to learn how to be more determined about where I wanted to go and be able to block Lucy from moving to where she wanted to go. It was easier said than done, though, because Lucy had a mind of steel.

A few days later, Jack and I were riding out together. Lucy was ambling along quietly, following Buddy, and it was very pleasant and relaxing.

"Ooh, look – that field has just been cut and the gate's open!"

said Jack excitedly. "Let's have a canter!"

"OK!" I replied, fully expecting Lucy to follow nicely behind Buddy, so I didn't bother to prepare myself or have any kind of contact on the reins whatsoever.

Zoom! Off she went like a firecracker, speeding past Buddy on the inside, and whooshed right to the top of the hill with Buddy snorting behind us, trying to catch up.

"Sorry!" I yelled but Jack just found it funny.

"Oh my God! What's happened to her?" she laughed.

There was no stopping Lucy after that. Sneaking into fields for a canter was her new favourite thing and I had to be on my guard each time we passed an open gate.

I grew to love Lucy despite being merely a passenger in her escapades. There was something so wise about her and so determined, I gave up the battle for control and just enjoyed her company.

"Where shall we go today, Lucy?" became my new greeting to her.

It was always a surprise where we ended up going and I loved every moment.

It was another bright but chilly morning and I was preparing my therapy room for work when my phone pinged.

"Hiya! Soz, can't make it today. Slept in lol!" texted the irksome client who was due to arrive in ten minutes. I stopped dead and reread the message on my phone. Anger welled up in my chest.

"Lol?" I said out loud. "You can just sod right off! I am not taking your shit behaviour any more!"

Finally, it had dawned on me that I deserved more respect.

There was no way that Lucy would put up with that kind of treatment, so why on earth did I? I didn't need this irritating woman any more. She was a dead weight. I silently thanked Lucy for the lesson she had been quietly teaching me for so long and replied to the client with a curt text.

"I will have to charge you for wasting my time, so please send a bank transfer."

"Oh yes! I'm so sorry, I will do! When can I book in?" came the instant reply.

"Unfortunately, I won't be able to book you in for the foreseeable future," I replied.

I never heard from her again and I could not have cared less. It was such a relief to get rid of a burdensome time-waster who had sapped my confidence for so long. I didn't need that in my life and I felt so much lighter for having spoken up for myself. I laughed out loud to think that it would have cost a fortune to have that sort of therapy with a counsellor but I had got it for free from a little old horse.

I thanked Lucy in person the following day for helping me to value myself – and gave her a handful of carrots. Lucy munched on them while eyeing me thoughtfully. I'm sure she understood every word I said because she let me choose where we went for our hack that day. Or maybe I had just become more determined?

Chapter 13

Lucy's owner, Jan, ran her own pest-control business and it was while she was working that she met the marvellous, yet spooky, Mrs Aurelius.

"I got a call yesterday from this really weird woman called Mrs Aurelius," said Jan, while we were both giving Lucy a bath in the warm autumn sunshine.

"That's an interesting name," I replied.

"Yes, it's unusual. isn't it? She called me because she has a cockroach problem so I went straight over and you'll never believe what happened!"

"Yuk! What happened?" I asked, expecting to hear something revolting about insects.

"Well, while we were chatting, she started looking at the ceiling and talking to the lampshade!"

"What?" I laughed, not expecting that kind of reply.

"Yes! It was so bizarre! She said, 'Not now – I'm too busy'. It was so weird! Then she apologised and asked me to carry on. Then she looked up again and said, 'What is it?' Oh my God! I was really freaked out. And then she said, 'They're telling me about your horse'!"

"No way? How weird!" I said.

"Completely weird!" agreed Jan. "But that's nothing. Wait until you hear what else she said!"

"Go on!" I said, fascinated.

"She said. 'It's the little black one, not the big brown-and-white one'!"

"Oh my God!" I couldn't believe my ears. "How did she know you had two? And how did she know their colours?"

"I don't know!" said Jan.

"So, what did she say about Lucy?" I was dying to know.

"Well, she said, 'She's OK now, but she will be ill soon. She's got a poorly leg and her foot's not quite right.' How weird is that?"

"Bloody hell!" I was amazed.

Lucy's leg was much better for being exercised more regularly but it would never be right. She also had navicular syndrome in her front feet that she regularly needed to rest. She had special shoes for it but she lay down for hours during the day, which is not normal for a horse. They generally only lie down for two hours per day to get a full brain sleep. I was worried about riding her initially but the vet said exercise would help and it definitely did.

Mrs Aurelius had given Jan a rose quartz crystal Buddha to hang in Lucy's stable.

Valerie, of course, was not impressed in the slightest by Mrs Aurelius. She fancied herself as the next *Mystic Meg* and belonged to a psychic development group that held meetings every week. It was hard to keep a straight face when Valerie regaled me with her latest psychic instalments. The maddest was when she randomly came up to me one day while I was grooming Lucy and said, "I've got a message for you from Bernard."

"Pardon?" I replied, furiously trying to think who Bernard was.

"Yes, he came to me just now and asked me to say that he isn't cross any more but that you will see that he was right."

"Oh!" I said. "Erm... I don't really know what that means."

We had an old family friend called Bernard who was dead but

he had never played a significant part in our lives.

"Yes, I get the feeling —" Valerie continued, obviously on a roll — "it was something that happened at a family gathering. A big fallout."

"Right…" I said.

I didn't really know what to say as there had never been a big fallout at any family gathering. However, Valerie looked very pleased with herself and strode off to feed the donkeys.

Sure enough, Mrs Aurelius turned out to be right. Less than a week later, Lucy was hopping lame.

"Stan!" shrieked Valerie, huffing and puffing from the exertion of running back to the yard from the field. "Call the vet! Lucy's on three legs!"

I had just arrived so I phoned Jan to let her know and I waited at the gate for the vet. Fifteen minutes later, the vet shot past the yard, screeched to a halt further down the road and then reversed at top speed back to the gate and wound his window down.

"Now, is this the right place for Lucy?" he asked, with a lovely southern Irish lilt.

"Yes!" I replied, opening the gate for him.

The vet, a very overweight and rotund man, heaved himself out of his car wearing full Highland dress. "I'm on my way to a wedding," he explained, looking slightly embarrassed as he strode into the yard. "I feel like a total *eejit* in this outfit! Now, where is this lame horse?"

Lucy was standing by the caravan, looking very sorry for herself, surrounded by the chickens who were being particularly noisy, squawking and scratching the ground.

"Good heavens! This place could do with a clean-up couldn't it?" said the vet with his hands on his hips looking around the yard, grinning. "It's reminding me of that programme from yesteryear. Now what was it called? Ah yes, *Steptoe and Son*, I do believe!" He threw his head back and laughed so loudly and with such force his sporran shook madly.

This comment did not sit well with Valerie, as the yard was her pride and joy. She was just about to launch a scathing attack when suddenly nature stepped in and lodged a bit of biscuit in her throat. She made a noise like a strangled cat and while Stan thumped her back I took the vet over to the stables so he could see Lucy.

"Walk her up and down, my love. Let's see the little horse moving!"

I encouraged Lucy to walk and she snorted in protest and gave me a very dirty look.

"Oh dear! She's a bit of a drama queen, now, isn't she?" The vet laughed. "Come on, now, little lady. I can't help you if you don't walk for me!"

Lucy snorted again but agreed to hop a few steps and then she glowered at the vet.

"Probably just an abscess," he said, grabbing her foot and bending over to look, which was a comical sight. It's not every day a vet turns up wearing a kilt and sporran and it was impressive that such a large man could actually bend forward without falling over.

"Ah yes. Now here's the little feller just peeping out from under the shoe."

The vet whipped Lucy's shoe off in the blink of an eye and

chucked it down without looking. It narrowly missed landing on one of the chickens.

"Mind my chickens, for goodness' sake, man!" Valerie exploded.

"Oh, you're Scottish!" said the vet, standing up and stretching his back out. "You'll appreciate my outfit, I'm sure!" He laughed.

Valerie was not amused in the slightest. "Not really – it's a MacDonald tartan. A very common clan. I wouldn't even dress my chickens in it," replied Valerie curtly.

The vet just laughed even more and I was wondering if he'd had a bit to drink. His cheeks were red and the blood vessels on his nose were all broken.

"Well, now would you believe I'd never heard of the MacDonalds? I just grabbed the first kilt I could find and this was it! Now getting back to this little horse here. She's got an abscess. Nothing to worry about but she will need to be stabled to keep it clean. Have you got a hoof boot, my dear? And might I compliment you on your beautiful pink hair? You look like you should be in a magazine, not here in a stable yard!" The vet stared at Valerie's pink hair, smiling sublimely as if it was the most beautiful thing he'd seen in his life.

Valerie instantly melted and patted her hair coquettishly. "Oh, well, that's very kind. I did do a spot of acting in my youth you know," said the blushing Valerie.

"I can imagine you did!" smiled the vet.

Stan was hovering in the background and he smirked as only Stan can smirk.

"Go and fetch the nice vet a cup of tea, Stan, for goodness' sake!" barked Valerie, and Stan shuffled off to the caravan.

The vet cleaned and dressed Lucy's foot and I led her into her stable. She looked very annoyed but perked up when I brought her a large armful of hay. While Valerie and the vet walked away, I called Jan to update her on Lucy's foot.

It took a few weeks of intense care to get HRH Lucy's foot better. She stood in her stable, like the Queen, and her facial expressions were so comical. She had me running around bringing her extra hay when Valerie wasn't looking. She also demanded carrots and apples and on top of that I had to clean her wound and change her dressing twice a day. This, of course, meant that Florence had to come with me in the afternoon. I felt a bit anxious about taking her up to the yard as I had no idea how she would behave with the horses. The thought of her running around and being silly really stressed me out but I had no choice, she had to come.

"Now I need you to really listen to what I say when we go to help Lucy," I said to Florence as we walked to the car after school.

"OK, Mummy," replied Florence very earnestly.

"Lucy has a poorly foot and Mummy has to clean it and put a bandage on it," I continued. "So you will have to be very sensible in the stable yard and stand quietly while I'm doing that."

Florence hadn't been up to the yard before. In fact, her only interaction with equines had been with donkeys on the beach. I hadn't wanted to take Florence or James to the yard because it was my escape from the pressure of parenting. It was the place where I could forget about responsibilities and have fun. So I wasn't particularly looking forward to going to my *secret place* with Florence.

"Let's get Lucy some carrots, Mummy. She will need them to get better, won't she?" asked Florence.

"Good idea," I agreed and we stopped at a shop on the way.

Luckily all was quiet at the yard when we arrived. Valerie and Stan had gone home and there was only Lucy and the donkeys in the stables.

"Looooseeee!" Florence called out. "We've brought you some carrots!"

Lucy's head appeared over the stable door and Florence marched over with the bag of carrots.

"Now Lucy," said Florence, showing her the carrots. "This is your medicine so you must eat it up very nicely or you won't get better!"

Lucy nodded her head as if in agreement.

"Good girl, Lucy!" said Florence and she opened the bag and gave her a carrot. Lucy took the carrot gently and Florence looked extremely pleased with herself.

"Excellent! Well done!" I was impressed. "Now you wait out here while I go in and clean her poorly foot."

Amazingly, Florence stood and waited quietly while I sorted Lucy's foot out.

"Can I brush her hair?" she asked when I'd finished.

"Yes, of course!" My anxieties melted away and I felt pleased that she was taking such an interest.

Florence brushed and plaited Lucy's hair, and all the way home she could talk of nothing else except ponies. It was so lovely. For the first time ever, I was able to enter into a conversation with her, wholeheartedly, with no pretences.

The following day after school, she rushed out and insisted we go straight to the shops to buy carrots and once again we had a fun-filled afternoon feeding and grooming Lucy. Lucy was very patient and gentle with Florence as if she knew she had to be careful with her. It was wonderful to watch a bond growing between them.

"Mummy, are you crying?" asked Florence as she noticed a tear falling down my cheek.

"No, I've just got some hay in my eyes," I replied, rubbing my cheek and swallowing the urge to cry. Something had clicked in my heart. I felt a huge wave of love for Florence and that was not something I had ever felt before. Of course, I had felt fondness and a desire to take good care of her but not actual emotional love.

But there it was. Love pouring out of my heart like a fountain and all because Lucy had re-connected our spiritual umbilical cord. I had to steady myself against the wall but luckily Florence was too busy cuddling Lucy to notice.

I had only ever seen James (and his mother) in Florence's face but something shifted in my vision. All of a sudden, I could see me as a little girl, cuddling the ponies I had loved so deeply at the riding school.

"Bye bye, Lucy!" said Florence, giving her a kiss. "See you tomorrow! Be a good girl!"

I drove home choked with emotion, thoroughly enjoying listening to Florence discuss her ideas for a get-well party for Lucy. Every day Florence seemed more and more interested in Lucy and when Lucy was finally all healed, Florence asked if she could have a ride. Luckily, Jan was there at the time.

"Of course you can have a ride!" said Jan enthusiastically. "I've even got a little hat that should fit you. Let's try it on."

The hat was a bit too big but it was fine for just a little ride in the school. Florence had a grin as wide as her whole face as Jan led her round and round.

"Well, I think I know where you'll be going this weekend," laughed Jan. "To the tack shop to get you a hat and some jodhpurs! What do you think, Mum?" She winked.

It was such a wonderful experience to take Florence to the tack shop and get her fitted for a riding hat. She also chose some pink jodhpurs and a pair of boots. James waited in the car throughout as he didn't want to know how much money we were spending but he was very glad that Florence and I had something we both enjoyed doing together. Then we all went to visit Lucy so Florence could show off her new hat and riding clothes.

Lucy looked approvingly at Florence as she chattered away, telling her about her new riding clothes and I am certain she glanced at me with a knowing look. She knew that she had helped me and it felt so good to be genuinely enjoying doing something with Florence. I wasn't pretending to be a *fun mum* anymore. I was being myself and I was having a really good time watching Florence having fun with Lucy.

Chapter 14

Note to self – never listen to Bossy Barbara when she says, "Don't be ridiculous! It'll be all right, it's only a bit of snow!"

Winter had arrived suddenly, like a sharp slap on the face. I looked out of the window and noticed the road was white. For most sensible people this would have been enough information to decide not to ride that day. However, I ventured up to the yard anyway because I had no work booked in and I wanted to give Brunhilde a brush. I had neglected her for a while, looking after Lucy so much, so I was feeling a bit guilty.

The chickens were busying about around the stable yard wearing an assortment of gaily coloured tabards. Even though by now they had regrown their plumage, Valerie still insisted they needed to wear them because "It's too cold!" or "It might rain!"

"They don't really need them any more," a young vet had said during a routine check-up.

"Well, you're wearing a jacket!" Valerie replied, folding her arms defensively.

"Er… yes, but that's not really the same thing, is it?" laughed the vet nervously.

Valerie pushed her chest out and drew herself up to her full height. "What do you mean, *It's not the same thing?* You're too young to know anything about chickens and I bet you've only just qualified! Well, let me tell you, laddie, I've been caring for animals since before you were born so don't tell me what my chickens should or should not wear!" With that she marched off into the feed room, leaving the bemused vet standing in the yard, scratching his head, not quite sure what to do. He wandered away eventually when he realised Valerie was not coming back.

So the chickens were still in their tabards, which they appeared to enjoy wearing. I did a double take because one of them looked like a duck. In fact, yes it was definitely a duck – also wearing a knitted tabard.

"Where did the duck come from?" I asked Jack, who had also just arrived.

"That's Elsa!" announced Valerie, as usual appearing from nowhere. "I rescued her from a very cruel woman who had clipped her wings!"

"Oh, poor Elsa!" I said. "Why is she wearing a tabard?"

"Because she'll feel left out if she isn't the same as her new family, of course! Honestly, Grace, you do ask ridiculous questions." Valerie huffed and scooped up the duck. "Say hello to Elsa."

Jack and I said hello to Elsa and tried not to laugh at the sight of a fully feathered duck wearing a pale blue knitted tabard with pink hearts.

"Won't she need a pond?" I asked innocently.

"Yes, she will. Jack can get on with that tomorrow. I'll show you where I want it later."

Before Jack had time to register and protest about what had just been said, Valerie's phone began ringing from the caravan so she walked off to answer it.

"Oh, bloody great! That's all I need!" said Jack. "You can help me make it."

"Are you kidding? I'm crap at things like that. I've never made a pond in my life!"

"Neither have I but it can't be that hard." Jack was capable of making anything and would win a gold medal if there was a DIY Olympics.

The gate swung open with a resounding metallic clang and in marched Bossy Barbara.

"Good morning, ladies! Nice day for a ride!" she called out.

"It's freezing!" I said, pulling a face.

"Nonsense!" said Barbara in her brisk manner. "It'll remind us of our pony club days! Didn't you ride out in the snow as a child?"

"Um... yes, I suppose I did."

I had to agree I had done that many times as a youngster, when I didn't feel the cold. Funny – or actually not funny at all – how you change when you get older and suddenly need thermals.

"Right then – come along, ladies!" said Barbara enthusiastically.

"I don't think Jan would be happy about me taking Lucy out in this weather. Her foot's playing up again," I said, not enthusiastic about sitting on a horse in cold weather.

"You can ride Vera. She needs some exercise!" shouted Valerie through the caravan window. "Barbara, get Vera's tack out of the shed for Grace!"

"But isn't it a bit dangerous to ride in this weather?" I asked.

"Don't be ridiculous!" replied Barbara in her school-teacher manner. "It'll be all right, it's only a bit of snow!"

Jack pulled a face but went to get Buddy anyway. Barbara handed me Vera's extra-large head collar and I went into the paddock to collect her. She looked at me as much as to say, *Oh, it's you today*. She wasn't remotely bothered. She was so laid-back she never really reacted to anything or anyone. Lucy looked up from eating the hedge but seemed glad not to be going out.

Vera was a very big, heavy-weight cob with the thickest, longest mane I've ever seen in my life. I certainly got a sweat on while grooming her and ended up hurling several layers of clothing on to the floor. She was very docile, though, and stood happily throughout and didn't complain about being tacked up. I'd never seen such a long girth in all my life and it only just fitted as Vera was so massive. When I was mounted it felt so weird because she was so wide it was like doing the splits.

"Oh my God! My legs are coming out of their sockets!" I said as I sat down.

"You won't be able to walk tomorrow!" Jack grinned. "I couldn't move for days after I rode her. I'd never ride her again, that's for sure!"

"*Tch! Tch! Tch!*" said Valerie, clucking around like her chickens. "Don't be so mean to poor Vera, you'll hurt her feelings!"

As usual there was a litany of instructions from Valerie about how to ride Vera.

"Keep her at the back. She doesn't like other horses behind her! She likes to walk with her head down but don't let her – it's a bad habit! She doesn't like sheep so be careful because she'll jump into the other side of the road!" (This turned out to be a ridiculous exaggeration. When we did go past a sheep field all she did was veer ever so slightly into the middle of the road.)

Finally, everybody was mounted and off we clattered into the village, which really did look beautiful with its dusting of snow. Vera walked out nicely. She certainly wasn't a slug, but she had the peculiar habit of holding her head very low. I pondered on this as we walked down the lane.

Of course, Bossy Barbara had something to say about it when

she looked back to check on how I was riding. "Bring her head up, Grace!" she commanded.

"Why?" I asked.

"Because it's a bad habit!" replied Barbara, as if she knew best. Her attitude irritated me somewhat.

"I'm wondering why she has her head like this," I said.

"It's because she's being naughty!" said Barbara.

Jack looked round and raised her eyebrows at me. She found Barbara annoying at the best of times.

"I disagree. I think it's a bit silly to say she's being naughty," I said. "It seems to me she's uncomfortable somewhere in her body and she's holding her head down to ease it."

"Stuff and nonsense!" scoffed Barbara. "She's just being naughty!"

"I agree with Grace," said Jack. "She knows about bodies. Vera isn't a naughty type of horse, it's pretty obvious. Maybe you could give her a massage?" She laughed.

"Not a bad idea!" I agreed.

It struck me that for the first time in years, I'd spoken up about my opinion. I felt pleased that I had been able to voice my views and not feel inferior. Also, I'm sure it gave Barbara something to think about. She wasn't a bad person by any stretch of the imagination. In fact, she had a very kind heart, but like a lot of horse owners, she believed everything was due to naughtiness. I expect she probably mistakenly viewed horses in the same way as she viewed her old school pupils.

For a while we rode on in peaceful silence and I enjoyed looking at the pretty cottages, with their snow-covered gardens perfectly untouched except for delicate little v-shaped birdy footprints. I was in a bit of a daydream enjoying the views, so I didn't notice that Barbara, in her wisdom, had decided to take a left turn off the main village road down a steep single lane track.

I was just thinking what a beautiful old stone house we were passing when suddenly we hit ice. All three horses started skidding out of control. Star was like a cartoon character with her legs crazily going in four different directions at top speed.

"Mary, mother of God!" shrieked Barbara as Star literally spun round and round in terrifying circles, desperately trying to stay upright.

"Steady! Steady!" yelled Jack in her lowest voice, trying to stop the snorting Buddy from freaking out. His legs slid from under him and he sailed sideways down the endlessly long hill.

I cannot describe the horror I was feeling. I was almost sick. I grabbed hold of Vera's thick mane and sat as still as possible. Terrible visions of falling over and being crushed under her mighty weight flashed across my mind. But I should have known this docile, super laid-back cob would not give a shit about such irrelevant things as ice.

Vera lifted her head up, ignored all the chaos around her and simply locked her knees so we slid elegantly down the hill. Faster and faster we went, my heart jumping out of my throat. But I needn't have worried. Vera kept her body still and just allowed the experience to happen and when the track levelled out she calmly sailed into a bush and came to a stop.

"Oh my God!" I panted, looking round to see if the others were OK.

Miraculously, all was well. Star and Buddy had managed to remain upright and had also crashed into the hedges at the bottom. Barbara was slumped on Star's neck, sobbing, while Jack took her hat off and mopped her steaming brow.

"Jeeeez!" said Jack eventually. "I knew we shouldn't have come out today! I'm getting off!"

"Good idea!" said Barbara and I in unison and we all leaped off with very jelly legs.

We walked home slowly, fully aware that we were lucky not to have broken our necks, and silently vowed never to ride on a snowy day ever again. Obviously, I did not relate this tale to my husband for fear of him going berserk and putting a stop to my riding.

"Why are you all walking?" asked Valerie in great surprise as we came into the yard.

"It was too cold so we thought we'd warm ourselves up by walking!" replied Jack with superlative presence of mind.

"Yes, I suppose it is a bit too cold for riding," agreed Valerie and she wandered off to look for something or other.

"Crikey that was quick thinking!" I said to Jack, in admiration of her amazing mind.

"She'd explode if she knew what had just happened!" laughed Jack.

We all smiled innocently as we untacked the horses and turned them out.

"We shall never speak of this again!" announced Barbara rather dramatically. We all agreed and never mentioned it again – until just now, of course.

Chapter 15

The following week the snow had disappeared and I was grooming Lucy outside her stable.

"Jack!" yelled Valerie, bits of spit flying out of her mouth. "Bring the donkeys in at four pm, no later, and remember to put their jackets on! It's going to be freezing tonight!"

Before Jack had a chance to reply, Valerie marched off to her car and drove away.

"For God's sake!" muttered Jack as she began grooming Buddy.

Out of the kindness of her heart, Jack had made the fatal error of offering to help with the donkeys when Valerie had a bad cold, and ever since then Valerie had expected her to continue.

"I'm sick of those donkeys!" exclaimed Jack as we rode out of the yard and headed for a particularly pretty village lane.

"I'm not surprised," I replied. "What are you going to do? You can't continue being an unpaid servant."

"I know. Whenever I say I don't have the time, Valerie starts wheezing and coughing so then I feel guilty and end up doing it anyway."

"Nightmare!" I said.

"Total nightmare," sighed Jack.

We clattered along the road in thoughtful silence for a while and ended up in the heart of the village by the fish and chip shop.

"Let's get some chips – I'm starving!" said Jack as she slid off her horse and handed me his reins. She came back moments later, holding two big steaming packets of chips.

"Don't tell any of the others but I'm actually leaving," whispered Jack conspiratorially.

"No! Really?" I was stunned.

Jack had become such a good friend and was so fun to ride out with. I was shocked at the thought of her leaving.

"Where will you go?" I asked, trying to get my head round what she had just said.

"I don't want to say until I'm there in case it jinxes it, but as soon as I've gone I'll text you. I'm not even telling Valerie or Stan. I'm going to go up after they've gone home for the day, clear all my stuff out and leave them a note!"

I munched sadly on my chips.

"I can see why you want to leave but I'll really miss you!" I said, feeling terribly sad.

"I'll miss you too but hopefully we'll still be able to meet up for rides," said Jack. "I won't be too far away."

"Why aren't you going to let Valerie know? She'll be so upset!" I asked.

"Because, to be honest, I daren't! I know that sounds pathetic but I just can't tell her. She'll go mental after all the help she gave me but I just can't stay anymore."

I can't really remember much about the rest of that ride because I was too busy feeling sad but suffice to say Jack followed through with her plan a couple of weeks later.

"I've done it!" she texted one night.

"Oh my God!" I replied. "Hope it's nice. Let me know when I can come and visit!"

"Will do!"

The hoo-ha at the yard the following day was unbelievable.

Valerie was crying and Stan was furious.

"Why didn't she just tell us she was going?" demanded the usually quiet Stan.

"I think she was too worried," I replied, feeling extremely uncomfortable.

"Worried about what, for goodness' sake?" asked Stan.

"About Valerie being really cross." I just wanted the ground to swallow me up.

"But why would she think I'd be cross?" asked Valerie between sobs. "I was very fond of Jack – and the donkeys will miss her terribly!"

I daren't mention that the donkeys were actually the reason why she left. "I have no idea, Valerie," I replied, feeling guilty for lying. "She's such an impulsive person. I don't think she meant any harm by it. She just wanted to go. The new yard is closer to her house so maybe that's why she went there?"

It was the most awkward experience, especially because Stan had to go to the dentist, so I was left alone to comfort poor Valerie. Luckily, her CD player was in the caravan so I put some Wagner on and that seemed to soothe her.

The following day I drove over to see Jack at her new yard. It was a big place and had a very impressive outdoor arena but it had a weird atmosphere. Even though nobody else was there, the place felt uncomfortable and after kisses and cuddles with Buddy I was keen to leave.

The yard was just a bit too far away from Valerie's for us to meet up for regular hacks and I felt deeply sad about that. Jack had been instrumental in my healing up to this point. She had been instantly friendly, encouraging and tremendous fun. Her easy-going, honest manner had burned away a lot of my sadness and brought great joy into my life.

My rides with Lucy became quite silent without Jack's stream of chatter but I still loved going. The silence opened up a new dimension in our relationship. I became aware of a constant, non-verbal communication between us and I felt more attuned to her body and how she moved. Being with Lucy made my heart open and feel love, not just for her but in general. It was a love for nature and the wider world. I had not felt this very much since becoming a mum due to the awful circumstances of the birth. However, just being with the horses and the rest of Valerie's menagerie, seemed to be healing this part of me.

It was an extremely ghastly morning. My beloved cat, Princess, had been looking rather bedraggled for a few weeks which was unlike her. She was usually very fastidious about grooming. I knew in my heart she was unwell but it was still a shock when the vet ran blood tests which showed her kidneys were failing. With a heavy heart I made the executive decision that all pet owners hate to make but it was the kind thing to do. Princess flew away to realms unknown to me and I sobbed a world full of tears. I'd been her unpaid servant for eleven years and I loved her more than words could say.

After a few hours of crying, I felt that a ride would help take my mind off my misery so I dragged myself out to see Lucy. Luckily nobody was at the yard as it was lunchtime so I had much-needed peace and quiet.

The horses were in the largest of the fields and Lucy was all the way at the far end, which was a very long walk. I sighed, opened the gate and entered the field. To my surprise, Lucy stopped grazing, lifted her head to look at me and whinnied really loudly. I was amazed by this greeting and it stopped me in my tracks. Lucy stared at me and then began walking purposefully towards me. I was stunned. I could not believe what was happening. She stopped just in front of me, stared into my eyes for a few moments and then put her nose on my heart. I howled from the depths of my soul. It was so moving. It was as if she knew that I needed her matriarchal wisdom and love.

Eventually, my tears subsided and Lucy nudged the head collar I was holding it as if to say, *Come on now. Let's get going!* We had a really lovely ride around the village and I felt very happy and peaceful. Just being with her was like a therapy session. Without words she had let me know she understood my pain and had given me some love that was like no other love. I was filled with gratitude that the universe had given me the opportunity to have spare time that I could spend with such a special horse and have such a genuine heart connection.

Winter came and went as winters do and Lucy began to get slower. Instead of sneaking into fields for a canter, she took to sneaking down driveways to eat bits of garden. It was horrifyingly embarrassing as I tried to turn her, shouting, "No! Lucy, stop it!" with no success. I would end up having to dismount and drag her away. Fortunately, most people found it amusing and one person really enjoyed our visits and kept a bag of apples by the door especially for Lucy. I was very aware that Lucy was coming to the end of her time, though.

"I had to visit Mrs Aurelius again last night," said Jan one frosty spring morning.

"Oh no! What did she say this time?" I asked.

"Well, she said that it was time for Lucy to go very soon. She said she's tired and is ready to move on. How has she been on your hacks out?"

"I didn't want to mention it but, actually, Lucy is feeling very tired. She's much slower and won't go any faster than a walk." My heart felt very sad at what seemed like the inevitable.

"Hmm. She's been lying down even more than normal too, which is worrying," sighed Jan. "I think I'll get the vet to take a look."

Lucy had had a bad start in life but had been very well cared-for by Jan and was loved by all of us. Each member of the gang had ridden Lucy at one time or another and we all had our own funny stories to tell about her.

The vet confirmed Mrs Aurelius's prediction. Lucy was in pain from her navicular syndrome and she was old and tired. He said, "When it comes to putting an animal to sleep, it's better a day too early than a day too late."

So Jan made the difficult decision to let Lucy go. It was heartbreaking to say a final farewell but Lucy was more than happy to go. She was put to sleep on a cold but bright spring day and was eating right up to her last breath.

I will never forget her or the lessons she taught me. Thanks to her I was becoming a much better mother and my daughter had started having riding lessons. We had a shared interest. I was also more assertive with clients and no longer accepted being messed about by them. There are many fields that will always bring a smile to my face as I remember how Lucy used to nip in and zoom off regardless of my feeble protestations.

Chapter 16

Life felt empty without Lucy. Other than the occasional ride on Vera, I was horseless and felt very sad about that. Vera was too wide for me to ride her often. I always ended up with sciatica afterwards, which was no good at all, and Siegfried's back had gone bad again so I couldn't ride him either. For some reason I felt a bit powerless to change the situation. Maybe I was feeling so low about Lucy's death that I didn't feel up to searching for horses to loan on the internet. I just vainly hoped that something would turn up.

A short while later it was Easter weekend. I was sitting on the North Beach at Bridlington with my husband and Florence, when I received an interesting text from Jack.

"There's a horse at our yard that needs a rider. She's about fifteen hands. Do you want to try her?"

"Ooh yes!" I replied with great excitement.

It really perked me up to think of riding with Jack again so we fixed a date for me to go over and see the horse the following week.

I felt very nervous driving up the long driveway to Jack's new yard and hoped it wouldn't be full of people. It all seemed so much bigger than Valerie's little place and it had such a peculiar atmosphere. However, I was very much looking forward to riding again. Jack knew me well so I was confident the horse would be similar to Lucy, a steady cob that just needed hacking out a few times a week. You can imagine my surprise, therefore, when I walked into the stable yard and was greeted by a very tall and sleek 16.2hh chestnut sport horse.

"Hello!" said Jack.

"Hello!" I replied.

"This is the horse," said Jack unnecessarily, pointing at the massive animal.

"Right!" I replied.

I had no idea what to say or do. Jack introduced me to the owner of the horse and I smiled nervously as she shook my hand. All the while I tried to avoid eye contact with the horse.

"I thought you said she was only fifteen hands!" I hissed at Jack through my false smile.

"I just guessed!" she whispered back and then conveniently disappeared.

Suddenly I was alone with the horse's owner, her niece, her niece's mum and her niece's mum's mum. A handful of other terrifyingly horsey women, who all had horses at the yard, appeared as if from nowhere and wanted to watch the proceedings. They looked at me with such disdain it made me feel exceedingly uncomfortable beyond measure.

It was a nightmare – I wanted to vomit. I'd never ridden anything like this horse in all my life. I was only used to pootling around on Lucy, for goodness' sake.

"Right, let's get cracking! I'm in a bit of a rush," said the owner before I could make an excuse and leave. She led the horse out of the barn towards the arena and I followed in a daze.

"My niece will ride her first so you can get a look at her," she continued, giving the girl a leg-up.

I was horrified. The horse was like a racehorse – very nervy and stressy, snatching at the reins and she could really shift. Round and round she went like a train at top speed, sweat shimmering on her golden shoulders.

"Slow down! Whoa!" growled the niece, pulling hard on the reins.

It made no difference except to curve the horse's head to the inside while she still zoomed round the ring. I wanted to run away but I was too embarrassed to admit my fears – and where the hell had Jack gone?

The word has yet to be invented that could fully describe how I was feeling in that moment. It was worse than being told I needed an emergency caesarean.

"She's a beauty, isn't she?" said the owner, hands on hips and smiling proudly.

"Er... yes," I mumbled, feeling sick. The horse was indeed very beautiful but she wasn't the sort of horse I had ever wanted to ride.

However, the moment of doom finally arrived. The niece somehow managed to stop the horse without flying off, which was very impressive. She dismounted and invited me into the arena. I realised I genuinely understood the meaning of the saying *my heart was in my mouth* as I walked towards the horse. My heart was thumping like a bass drum in my throat and my legs had turned to jelly. How I managed to get on is a mystery to this day because the horse certainly did not stand still at the mounting block. She jogged around on the spot and kept spinning her bum out to the side.

But then all of a sudden, I was on and I had to *do something*. My throat felt like it was full of marbles and I was finding it difficult to swallow. It was awful.

Calm down! instructed the sensible part of my brain.

Calm down? Are you mad? I'm about to die!

Take a deep breath and relax. You can do this!

I took a deep breath and did the opposite of what the fearful part of my mind would have suggested – I gave the horse a loose rein. Miraculously she instantly took a deep breath too, lowered her head and relaxed. She began walking very calmly. I couldn't believe it. The relief washed over me like a very pleasant cool shower and I was able to feel more in control of the situation.

Round and round we walked, nicely and quietly. Excerpts of Mark Rashid books sprang to mind – *bring your energy down to your feet.* So I visualised my feet being on the ground, walking slowly, and it seemed to work because the horse began to walk even more slowly. That helped me to feel quite brave so I did some figures of eight and a serpentine. It was really funny to hear the comments from the spectators:

"Ooh look at that!"

"She must be a very experienced rider…" and other flattering yet untrue comments.

I looked around and, in the distance from the safety of the yard, I could see Jack grinning and she shot me a thumbs up. I could have murdered her. What had she been thinking of? She knew I had zero experience of a horse like this.

I decided it was time to get off the horse so I halted and leaped off. I racked my brains to come up with an excuse to leg it back to my car and get the hell out of there. But fate had other plans.

"I've decided you're the one!" exclaimed the owner, striding into the arena, the gate clanging shut behind her. She grabbed my hand and shook it hard. At six foot, she towered over me and all I could do was smile weakly.

"I can tell our Poppy likes you, so I won't bother trying anybody else." She smiled.

"Oh! Er... ahem... well," I spluttered, desperately thinking of what to say in order to escape. Of course, all I needed to say was, *This horse is too scary for me! I'm not experienced enough!* but the words wouldn't come out because I was so embarrassed.

"I can tell you're a very experienced rider," continued the owner, completely oblivious of my shocked expression, "so I'm confident you'll look after her and do a great job!"

"Oh... erm... thanks!" I mumbled. I was like a rabbit in headlights, completely immobilised. *Oh my God, nooooo! I can't deal with a horse like this!* I shrieked in my head.

"So I'll pay for everything and you'll look after her and I'll see you in a few months' time, OK? I'm just in the middle of moving house, and my mum's not too well, and I'm helping my cousin through a nasty divorce –"

"It's a really nasty divorce!" nodded the niece's mum, grimacing.

"He's a bugger!" added the niece's mum's mum and then almost toppled over, she was so doddery.

"It's a godsend you've turned up. A real godsend!" smiled the owner, shaking my hand again. "I can't thank you enough. Oh blimey, look at the time. I've got to go! I'll see you later."

And with that, she was off. She just walked away. I was literally left standing in the arena, mouth open in shock, holding on to the type of horse I never ever wanted to have anything to do with.

"I'll show you to her stable," said the niece briskly.

The journey from the arena to the stable was like a terrible video game. First, we had to cross a large swathe of field that had suddenly become full of ponies. They hadn't been there on the way to the arena so I had no idea where they had come from.

"You need to be careful with the two feral ponies!" warned the niece.

"The what?" I replied.

"Some mad woman fancied learning how to ride so she bought a young Fell pony straight off the moor. The seller could obviously see her coming a mile off so he convinced her it would be better to buy two! Anyway, she never did learn to ride so the pair of them just run riot here."

"Oh my God!" I stuttered.

"Watch out, Mum, they're coming for you!" shouted the niece.

"Ooh, Mum, be careful – they're coming! They're coming!" shouted the niece's mum.

"Get back, you buggers!" panted the niece's mum's mum, waving her handbag at them and tottering dangerously from side to side.

The niece flapped her arms about to keep the ponies away. They snorted and reared, waving their legs around in a very threatening way that set the rest of the ponies off running, bucking and farting like nutters. How I kept hold of Poppy, who was also up in the air, was nothing short of a miracle.

It took an interminable amount of time to open the gate on the other side of the field, mainly because it was totally crap and tied shut with several bits of frayed bailer twine. Finally, we managed to open it, keep the band of lunatic ponies back and get through to the other side.

"Those two buggers want shooting!" scowled the niece's mum's mum.

"Ooh, Mum, that's not very kind!"

"It's bloody true, though! And the owner wants shooting too!"

"Mum!"

They continued to bicker as we walked across the yard to the American-style indoor stable block. The niece showed me where everything was and I sort of listened but none of it went in because I still couldn't believe what was happening. I felt like I was in a very bad dream.

"Right, I'll be off now. I've got my own livery yard to look after," said the niece – and I suddenly came round with a jump.

"Oh! How come Poppy isn't at your place?" I asked, which was the first coherent thing I'd managed to say all morning.

"We're full and she's a bit too crazy for me to cope with! Haha! Well, it was nice to meet you. Come on, Mum, come on, Gran, please hurry. I've got to get the horses in! I'm late!"

The niece's mum gave me a hug – she was a very sweet lady – and then they all walked away. I felt absolutely sick with responsibility and fear. I looked around and realised everyone else had disappeared too so there was just me and Poppy standing in front of her stable, staring dumbly into each other's eyes.

As if by magic, Jack suddenly popped up from behind a stable door. She almost sent me and Poppy into orbit from the shock.

"Oh my God!" I exclaimed as Poppy spun round, knocking me sideways. "What are you doing in there?"

"I thought I'd hide until everyone had gone!" Jack grinned, brushing straw (and what looked suspiciously like poo) off her jacket. "I can't believe you had the nerve to get on that mad horse. She's so fast! No way would I ever ride her!"

I couldn't believe what I was hearing.

"Then why did you set me up to ride her? What were you thinking? This horse is way too much for me!" My voice had risen an octave due to fear.

"To be honest, I just wanted you to come so we could ride together again. I really miss our hacks and everyone here is a bit nutty," said Jack, looking sheepish.

"I miss our hacks too, but bloody hell, what a horse! Couldn't you have found me a cob?"

Poppy sidestepped into a bucket, squashed it flat then danced about for a few moments and bashed into a stable door. Jack dived out of the way and unfortunately fell into a wheelbarrow laden with muck. She looked so funny that I laughed and that must have helped Poppy to settle down because she suddenly relaxed, which was a huge relief. I had visions of the whole place being smashed to bits.

As Jack cleaned herself off for the second time, I told her the sorry tale of how I was too embarrassed to admit that I was scared of Poppy, and how the owner had been so pleased with my riding she now trusted me with her horse and wouldn't be back for months.

"Blimey! What are you going to do?" asked Jack.

"I don't know! I'm stuck now!" I wailed.

Suddenly there was a loud crash and in staggered a middle-aged woman wearing a leopard-print onesie with her face smeared in make-up.

"Oh, good afternoon!" she said in a terribly posh voice, her breath heavy with gin. "Whom do we have here, Jacqueline?" (She pronounced *Jacqueline* with a French accent.)

Jack managed not to laugh as she introduced me to the bizarre lady, whose name was Veronica. Veronica worked for Leeds Central Library and lived in a very ordinary semi-detached house but she liked to fantasise that she was an heiress with a massive fortune.

"Welcome to our yard, dearest Grace!" she said with a flourish of her hand. "If you require any dressage coaching then do be sure to ask me. I would be terribly happy to help."

Veronica lurched off into the tack room, singing the national anthem very loudly in an operatic style.

"Is today really happening?" I asked Jack. "Or am I having the maddest dream I've ever had?"

"That's nothing. You've not met the rest of them yet." She grimaced.

"I don't know what the hell to do with this horse," I said.

"Well, you could either turn her out or put her in her stable?" suggested Jack.

There was no way I was going to do battle with the mad wild ponies again so I decided on the second option. It took several attempts (and many expletives) to get Poppy into her stable as she kept leaping sideways at the last minute. It was very stressful and more than a bit scary but finally we managed it, miraculously all in one piece.

Luckily, once Poppy was in she immediately settled down. She looked over her stable door with a thoughtful expression on her face. She was definitely sizing me up and I wished I could hear her thoughts. *Oh my God, what am I doing with this horse?* I wondered.

I drove home almost in a stupor. My brain was whirring with thoughts and fears. What on earth was I going to do? The owner hadn't given me any contact details so I felt completely stuck and unable to get out of the situation. Horse riding was meant to be fun and therapeutic but this was the total opposite.

I'll call Alexa. She'll know what to do! I suddenly thought.

I called Alexa as soon as I got home. She laughed and came straight over to see me because she was actually driving nearby, which was a stroke of luck.

"Oh dear, let's have a cup of tea!" She laughed as she waltzed into my kitchen. It was usually me who made the tea but I was very grateful Alexa was taking charge.

"Now, calm down and tell me all about it!" she continued, filling the kettle.

I poured out the whole story and Lady Alexa listened intently.

"Hmm," she said, "this sort of thing happens a lot, you know. I know several people who have ended up with horses they didn't want. But don't panic. Give it a go! Remember you're a much better rider than you were and it could turn out really well. Stop doubting yourself! If you managed to calm her down in the school, that's excellent work and there's no reason why it shouldn't continue. It sounds like the horse felt very comfortable with you so there's no need to worry as much as you are."

Alexa gave me much to think about. She highlighted my propensity towards self-doubt and she helped me to see it was OK to give it a go. She also pointed out that the yard owner would have the owner's details if I decided I wanted to stop. This made me feel much better about the whole thing and I almost looked forward to the challenge.

I told my husband all about it that evening and surprisingly he said pretty much the same things as Lady Alexa. I was amazed at how encouraging James was so I went to bed feeling much less worried.

Chapter 17

The following morning, I arrived at the yard early in order to avoid seeing people. I wanted to have an opportunity to see if I was capable of handling Poppy alone. I was focused and determined to succeed – and that felt good. It was like the old me. However, as soon as I drove through the gate, a wave of nausea welled up in my stomach. "Oh my God!" I said out loud to myself.

I walked into the indoor barn where all the stables were and realised that Poppy was the only one stabled. All the other horses were out 24/7 because it was spring. I looked at Poppy; she looked at me. I didn't have a clue what to do. I had never had the responsibility of looking-after a horse since being a child. Monty and Lucy had been on full livery so my only duties had been to groom, tack up and ride. "Oh my God!" I said once again.

"What's up, luv?" said Jack in her Yorkshire accent, as she walked into the barn with her saddle over her arm.

"Oh, thank God you are here!" I said. I was so relieved I could have cried. "I don't know what to do! I've never had to look after a horse before!"

"Are you serious?" laughed Jack.

"Yes! I have literally no idea! I can't remember how to muck out or anything like that – it's been years!"

"Bloody hell, you big lump!"

Poppy kicked on the door and gave me a very meaningful stare.

"She's hungry. You'd better give her a hay net," said Jack matter-of-factly.

"How do I do that?" I asked, feeling like a total imbecile.

"Oh my God, Grace! Have you never made a hay net?"

"No!" I almost squeaked. "I just used to dump piles of it in Lucy's stable."

"Wow!" Jack was very amused by my ineptitude.

She laughed and took me over to a bale of hay on a pallet that had a sign next to it saying POPPY.

"Each horse has its own hay so this is Poppy's," said Jack. "Now you need a net. You can borrow one of mine."

I am embarrassed to admit that at the age of thirty-five I had my first lesson in filling a hay net. And then came the dreaded moment of having to go into the stable to tie it up – again, something I had no clue how to do because I had never had to do it at Valerie's.

As soon as I was back in front of the stable with the hay net, Poppy started kicking the door and stamping her feet, flailing her head around very expressively. It was terrifying.

"What happens if I open the door and she runs out?" I yelled. "You go in! You're tougher than me!"

"No way! I'm not going in there – she's your horse now!" exclaimed Jack, stepping backwards.

"But *you* got me into this mess!" I replied.

"Go on! I dare you to just do it!" said Jack with a malevolent grin.

There was no other option. I took a deep breath, decided that I was the boss, slid the bolt and opened the door. Poppy stepped backwards and allowed me to go in, which was a surprise and a relief. Then suddenly she sprang forward and dived into the hay, eating hungrily, pulling at the net madly. It was a battle to keep hold of it and tie it up while Jack shouted instructions.

I dashed out of the stable, relieved to be in one piece. "Phew!" I said, and just at that moment, in came Veronica. She was wearing pink silk pyjamas covered in silver stars, and muddy, green wellington boots. It was a very interesting look.

"Good morning! Good morning!" she greeted cheerily in her posh voice and then she tottered off to the tack room, singing 'The Long and Winding Road' in an operatic style.

"Quick!" said Jack excitedly, "Let's tack up and follow her!" and before I could reply, she dashed out of the barn to get Buddy.

"Oh my God!" I said to myself yet again.

I was not relishing the thought of grooming and tacking up, let alone actually riding Poppy. However, the realisation dawned on me that I had no other option. Nobody else was going to come and look after this horse, she was my responsibility now. I took a deep breath, set my mind to it and walked into the stable with determination. Fortunately, she just ignored me and continued eating.

Poppy had one of the few *posh* stables that had its own tack and feed room at the back, and her owner had left her with everything she needed, thank goodness.

Step one: get her head collar on. That felt so weird because I just wasn't used to dealing with a) such a giant horse and b) such a sporty horse. Luckily, she wasn't bothered as she was so busy eating that she didn't really notice me putting the head collar on.

Step two: groom her. That proved to be quite a difficult experience because she seemed to hate it and came at me with her great big scary teeth. I was shocked. I'd never been threatened like this by a horse.

Step three: clean her feet. I was very nervous about doing

that. I had visions of getting my head kicked in but thankfully she understood what I wanted to do and gave me her feet very politely. They were massive, like dinner plates.

Step four: tack up. This was not so easy as she had all sorts of faffy gadgets that I wasn't used to. Her bridle had a weird-looking bit and an extra strap thing to keep her mouth shut, which she clearly didn't like at all. She waved her head around, rolling her eyes, and cracked me in the face.

"Ow!" I yelled, rubbing my cheek. I was cross, but in her eyes, I could see she was very unhappy, so I unbuckled that strap and she relaxed.

The next bit of kit was a martingale, traditionally used to stop the horse from throwing its head up. I didn't have a clue how to put that on and I didn't like the thought of it anyway, so I didn't bother with that. I didn't like her saddle either. It was like a cross between an English saddle and a western saddle and was massive and very heavy. Poppy bit my bum when I put it on so I figured she also didn't like it.

"I'm sorry!" I said to her. "I'll get you a nicer saddle but today this is all we've got."

Poppy stared at me and nipped me again as I tightened the very stiff leather girth. It was a gentle nip so, again, it felt like a communication of *I'm not happy*.

Eventually she was ready and that in itself felt like a huge achievement. Jack was ready with Buddy, standing quietly in his usual zen kind of way. She tied him at the bar in the middle of the barn and helped me lead Poppy over to the mounting block. Poppy was very nervy and wouldn't stand still. She danced around like a young racehorse and it took several attempts (with both of us holding her) to get her to stand near enough to the mounting block for me to get on.

The first attempt was going well. Jack was standing near her head and I put my foot in the stirrup. But just as I lifted up, Poppy did a wide sidestep, leaving me doing the splits in mid-air, followed by a terrible flop on to the ground. *Ouch.*

Looking back, I am amazed I got on her. I must have gone into autopilot mode. Something inside me made the decision that it would be OK and that I could do this, so I did. As soon as I was on she immediately settled, which was a huge relief. Jack leaped on to Buddy in her usual cowboy style and off we went.

"Oh my God, this feels so weird!" I said.

"She's massive, isn't she? Are you OK up there?" asked Jack.

"I think so!" I replied.

Poppy was very forward-going, unlike the chilled-out cobs I was used to. She was also very nervy, looking around at everything, which I found a bit unsettling.

Opposite the yard, on one side, was a road that led into beautiful countryside and a very pretty village with quaint stone cottages. On the other side there was a large and quite bleak council estate. This is where we were heading.

"Why are we going this way?" I asked as Poppy decided to do a little jog on the spot for no apparent reason. I took a deep breath to settle myself and that settled her.

"This is where Veronica will be going," Jack replied, "so we'll hide in the bus terminus and then we'll follow her!"

"*The bus terminus?*" I couldn't believe my ears. It sounded completely insane but we literally pulled into a large bus shelter and waited for Veronica. I was terrified at the prospect of being near buses with Poppy in case she went berserk and ended up killing me. I could feel my throat tightening up and my heart began booming in my chest.

Calm down and breathe deeply, commanded the sensible portion of my brain.

Calm down! I could die any minute now!

Are you afraid of buses? it asked me.

No! I replied.

Then calm down!

I had to force my mind to remain in control. I took a deep breath and reminded myself that buses are nothing to be afraid of. I focused on where I wanted Poppy to stand, relaxed my hands and legs… and miraculously she didn't turn a hair. Buses came and went and she stood quietly, even though Buddy was a bit on his toes. Poppy watched people coming and going and enjoyed the attention from passers-by. This helped me to relax and I began to feel slightly more confident.

"There she is! Oh my God, she's still in her pyjamas!" Jack guffawed and nearly slipped off her horse.

I was gobsmacked. Veronica was riding along on a very pretty black horse, wearing pyjamas and still singing 'The Long and Winding Road' very loudly in a terrible operatic style. Every now and then she would call out a hearty, "Good morning!" to amused onlookers. Strangely, she didn't appear to notice us. Jack was in orange hi-vis, I was in pink and we both had large horses. How she didn't see us was a mystery.

We followed at a distance on the wide grass verge of a very busy road and I focused on my breath and letting my legs relax. Lorries and buses sped past and Poppy was absolutely amazing.

She literally was not bothered at all, it was incredible. I was so busy thinking *Wow!* that I didn't notice we were turning into a large shopping centre until we were in the car park.

"What the hell are we doing here?" I asked in surprise.

"She's going shopping!" Jack laughed her head off, tears streaming down her face.

Sure enough, Veronica got off her horse, tied her to a dog ring in the wall, and went into Tesco.

"Oh my good God, what is she doing?" I couldn't believe what I was seeing.

"She's bloody mad! Oh no, I think I've peed myself! That's what comes of having three kids!" She laughed even more as a streak of wet travelled down her jodhpurs.

A group of kids flocked round Veronica's horse and patted her. They all thought it was wonderful to see a horse outside the supermarket. A few elderly shoppers enjoyed making a fuss of her too and it was lovely to see how the presence of a horse created so many smiles.

After a while Veronica came out of Tesco with a bag of shopping and got back on her horse. Obviously, she was still wearing her fancy pyjamas, which rendered the audience dumb with shock. She smiled and waved at the onlookers, like royalty, then rode back to the yard, still singing and still apparently unaware of our presence. It was the weirdest hack I had ever been on.

Once back at the yard Veronica suddenly seemed to see us and she asked if we'd had a nice ride. It was beyond peculiar. However, by that point I didn't care about mad Veronica because I was so full of joy at the fact that I'd successfully ridden scary Poppy through a busy council estate to a shopping centre, in heavy traffic, and not ended up in A and E.

I gave Poppy a kiss and she almost smiled. She looked me in the eye and (probably) said, *Well, you've passed today's test but you're still on probation.*

I drove home feeling like I had wings and I told James all about the ride.

"She went riding in pyjamas? To Tesco?" He thought I was making it up.

"Yes! She's absolutely mad but that's not the point! The point is I rode Poppy through a busy estate to Tesco and she was great! Can you believe it?"

"That's great, love! But I didn't think you would have a problem anyway. Sounds like she trusts you. Now, where did I leave my spanner?" James wandered off. I felt surprised that he wasn't surprised.

I called Alexa to see what she had to say.

"Why are you so surprised?" She laughed. "I don't think you realise how relaxing you are to be with. It must be your massage-therapist aura – that's why Poppy was relaxed! Really, Grace, you do need to stop doubting yourself. Riding a horse isn't rocket science, it's mainly common sense."

I thought about what she said earnestly. Lots of people did say that they found me very relaxing – friends and massage clients alike. Could that really be why Poppy was so relaxed, I wondered. I didn't have much time to ponder, though, as *mum jobs* were beckoning, as usual.

Chapter 18

The following day began with a gloriously sunny and still morning. I wasn't working until after lunch so my plan was to drop Florence at school, walk the dog and then spend some quality time getting to know Poppy.

I arrived at the yard, relieved to find I was alone, and had a good look around for the first time. I'd not noticed before but the whole place was completely dilapidated. Worse than Valerie's, incredibly. I could see that once upon a time it had been, without a doubt, a beautiful farm, surrounded by rolling meadows. But life is never static and the barns were crumbling, the fences were broken and there was a lot of sad, old machinery lying rusting in various corners. Such a shame no one bothered to maintain it, I mused.

The atmosphere was peculiar too and I couldn't quite work out why that was. Valerie's place always felt very pleasantly welcoming even when nobody else was there. But this place felt distinctly unwelcoming. I decided not to think too much about it so I grabbed Poppy's head collar, took a deep breath and headed down the path.

I leaned over the gate, trying to work out several things. Firstly, how to untie all the ridiculous bits of orange bailer twine to open it. Secondly, how to get past the dangerous feral ponies alive. Thirdly, how to get Poppy, who was out in the horse field at the far end of the yard. I had yet to do this journey alone and I wasn't relishing the prospect.

"Ha! I bet I know what you're thinking!" said a voice behind me.

I looked round to find a friendly-looking, middle-aged blonde woman. She was wearing bright purple jodhpurs and a bright yellow T-shirt, emblazoned with a JUST DO IT slogan.

"I'm Sally and I'm guessing that you are Grace?" She smiled.

"Yes, I am! Hello!" I was very relieved to see a friendly face.

"Don't bother opening this gate until you need to get your horse through it," said Sally, who then executed a perfect handspring over the gate.

"Wow!" I was taken aback.

"I used to be a gymnast but now I teach contemporary dance in a young-offenders institution," said Sally, matter-of-factly.

"Oh!" I replied.

The dreaded ponies had begun to wander over, glowering menacingly as if to say *Get out of our territory!*

"Now personally, I like to use dance to keep myself safe going through this field," continued Sally.

Before I had a chance to ask what she meant, she launched into the most insane Flash Dance style routine. I watched, open-mouthed, as she cavorted, cartwheeled and spun herself around. She fell over several times but it didn't put her off and amazingly she managed to remain on a straight trajectory up the path to the next gate. But even more bizarrely, it actually worked and the ponies bolted to the other end of the field. I was lost for words as I clambered over the gate and jogged after Sally, who was bent over puffing and blowing, leaning forward on to her knees.

"You see dance is actually a life skill," said Sally, once she'd recovered her breath. She said it in such an ordinary way as if that sort of comment was completely normal.

"I'm actually gobsmacked!" was all I could utter. I'd never

witnessed anything like it in my life and had no idea what to say. It seemed that each time I arrived at this livery yard, something mad happened.

We walked to the horse field and Sally chattered away about various people at the yard – who was nice and who wasn't – and presently we arrived at the gate. Luckily, this was a very straightforward gate that opened easily with no skill required. Sally went to get her skewbald cob called Malcolm and I went to get Poppy, who was eyeing me with suspicion from afar.

Now, usually when I went to collect a horse from a field it was no big deal. I would walk up to it, put the head collar on and off we'd go. But Poppy preferred to do things differently. She stood quietly and allowed me to come close. Then just as I reached out with the head collar, she snorted large amounts of snot on to my arm and trotted away, swishing her tail… which in her language probably meant *Bugger Off!*

I wiped the snot off my arm, feeling a bit wound-up, and walked after her. She stopped and looked at me. As I drew close she let out a loud whinny and trotted off.

"For God sake!" I exclaimed and marched after her.

Eventually, Poppy stopped again and stared at me. I reached out to grab her and she snorted and trotted off again.

"I haven't got time for this nonsense!" I sighed and jogged after her again.

This continued for quite some time until I was feeling infuriated and very tired as it was such a large field. All I could think about were the one hundred and one jobs I had to do at home, yet here I was wasting my time with a horse I didn't really want to ride anyway. I don't know what made me continue trying but I did and finally, I managed to catch her. As soon as I had the head collar buckled on, she walked with me calmly, which was an unexpected relief as I assumed she would behave madly.

Sally was waiting for me at the gate with Malcolm, who seemed to be a very laid-back horse. "She's a bit of a bugger, isn't she?" She laughed.

"Yes, that's one word for her!" I agreed, not laughing.

"You'll soon get the hang of her. Malcy was a total turd when I first got him but he's great now, aren't you, Malcy?" Sally smothered him with kisses.

"Now we've got to get through the pony field," she continued, "so if you take Malcy then I'll sort them out."

Oh my God! I thought to myself, terrified that Sally would launch into another dance and send Poppy running for the hills with me flying after her. But Sally did not perform another dance routine. Instead she reached into her pocket and pulled out a party blower (one of those things you blow in and it uncurls and makes a terrible noise). She blew it several times in the direction of the ponies.

"I got this from a party last night!" said Sally. "Look – it's working!"

She was right, it was indeed working. The ponies cantered away and stood in a group under a tree with pricked-up ears, no doubt wondering what on earth this woman was going to do next. Miraculously, Poppy was not in the least bit bothered by the crazy party blower. She was far too distracted by Malcolm even to notice what had just happened.

"Oh my God!" laughed Sally as Poppy lifted her tail and squirted a jet stream of stinky wee at poor Malcolm.

"What's she doing?" I asked, shocked and embarrassed.

"Aww! She's in love, aren't you, Pops?" Sally found the whole thing hilarious but it was so awkward trying to get down the path, out of the pony field. Poppy kept swinging her bottom round and stopping to spray wee at Malcolm every few steps.

"Poppy! Stop it! The ponies are coming!" I implored, but she wasn't listening. She was too infatuated with Malcolm to care about anything else. Malcolm looked confused and was clearly not feeling any love back for Poppy. Sally continued blowing the party blower and somehow, I managed to drag both horses out of harm's way and we made it through the pony field. Sally took Malcolm into the stables while Poppy and I headed for the arena.

The arena was large and although the fencing was a bit broken, it was a good place to do schooling. I had learned a bit of rudimentary lunging with Monty and thought I'd give it a go with Poppy, just to create some sort of relationship. Poppy stood quietly and allowed me to check her feet and get the lunging gear on her, and she walked very nicely when I asked her to. She walked round and round in a large circle and stopped immediately when I asked. She changed direction and again walked round and round very nicely. I decided to go up a gear and off she went, trotting round and round, very nicely in both directions.

Hmm, I thought. "Let's try a canter." I asked and she immediately went into a very nice canter. Round and round, round and round. She moved absolutely perfectly. I brought her back to a walk. Round and round she went like a machine. There was no eye contact, no rebellious snorts. No looking at me as if to say *Do I have to? I can't be bothered!* like Monty often did. There was nothing but cold, mechanical perfection.

"That horse has been badly treated. I'd put money on it!" I turned to find Sally leaning over the fence. "She's like a robot, isn't she?"

"I was just thinking that too," I replied as Sally hopped over the fence and came to have a closer look.

"She reminds me of some of the kids where I work. Look, no eye contact." Poppy was standing very nicely and not looking at either of us. "I reckon it's from her first home, whoever it was who actually backed her," Sally continued.

"I'll ask her owner if she knows anything about them. I don't think she'll know, though, because Poppy was a gift to her daughter. I think an uncle bought her? That's what Jack told me anyway."

Sally reached out to stroke Poppy's shoulder. She shivered and sidestepped into the fence, then rebounded with a snort.

"Poor thing!" said Sally. "You'll have to work hard to get her to trust you. I'd better get back to Malcy." And with that, she was off. Sally leaped back over the fence towards the stables, leaving me alone with Poppy.

Poor Poppy. I felt sadness welling up in my heart and I gently put my hand out towards her nose. She turned to look at me and her head lowered to touch my hand. It wasn't much but it was a start – a moment of connection. In that moment, I felt more than ever that I wanted to do my best for her.

As usual, there wasn't much time to immerse myself in any further thoughts because I had to get to work. Luckily, the journey back to the field was uneventful, thanks to some activity on the neighbouring farm that kept the feral ponies entertained.

My first client of the afternoon was Lady Alexa. She hobbled through the door wearing a great big orthopaedic boot on her leg. "Don't ask!" She grimaced and promptly took herself up the stairs to my therapy room, on her bottom.

"What's happened?" I asked when we were in the room.

"Bloody Tony's ridiculous girlfriend is what happened!"

"His girlfriend?" I was shocked. Had she attacked Alexa?

"She's a first-rate imbecile of the highest order!" exclaimed Alexa, flinging her clothes off and collapsing on to the therapy couch. "Would you mind putting a cushion under my knee, there's a dear?" Then she launched into the story.

That morning, a top showjumper had arranged to come and view one of Tony's horses. The horse was fairly young and had come first in some basic competitions. Alexa was riding the horse in the arena and everything was going well until Tony's girlfriend decided to take the dogs for a walk. Tony's dogs are very strong, energetic Rhodesian Ridgebacks. Tony's girlfriend is just shy of five foot and weighs not much more than a chicken feather.

"What was she thinking? God only knows!" exclaimed Alexa.

I waited with baited breath for the rest of the story.

"So there we were doing a lovely canter when suddenly it was as if the world exploded! All three dogs leaped over the fence into the arena, barking their heads off. Tony's girlfriend was screaming blue murder but not actually doing anything about the dogs. She was *literally* standing and screaming. So, of course, the horse went berserk and started bucking all over the place, which was tremendous fun for the dogs! They thought it was a super game and chased us round and round. God only knows how I had managed to stay on thus far. Anyway, suffice to say I wasn't on for much longer. I've wasted all bloody morning in Wharfedale Hospital!"

I was dumbfounded. Firstly, I couldn't believe how idiotic Tony's girlfriend was and secondly, I was amazed at Alexa's tough attitude. She really was incredible. She'd had that terrible experience and broken her leg yet she still came for a massage.

"Why ever would I not?" asked Alexa, aghast at my thoughts. "It's only my left leg and my car is automatic."

"I'd be in total shock if that happened to me!" I exclaimed.

"No, you wouldn't. You'd just be annoyed like I am. And anyway, I am badly in need of a shoulder massage now!" She laughed.

It wasn't until later that day, when Florence was in bed and I was sitting with the dog, that thoughts of Poppy and her mysterious past filtered into my mind. I wondered if I would ever know her history. I realised it would have to wait until I saw her owner again in a few months' time. That thought in itself was very stressful. I had so much to do every day and looking after a horse like Poppy just wasn't something I wanted to do.

My mind began spiralling again. *I'll call her owner and tell her I don't want to do this. I can't cope with a horse like this! I'm not experienced enough for a horse like this! But who else will look after her if I don't? What if she ends up in the hands of someone who treats her badly?* I remembered Sally's words.

I was exhausted from thinking about Poppy and I collapsed into bed.

That night I dreamed about Poppy being beaten by a horrible man. It was such a graphic dream, featuring close-ups of Poppy's face with terrified eyes. I woke up in a hot sweat, feeling sick.

I'll give it a go for another few weeks, I decided. *And if I still can't cope then I'll call her owner.*

Chapter 19

It was a Saturday morning and my mother-in-law took Florence out. James was on a course so I had a rare opportunity to go and see Poppy without feeling guilty for wasting time. For some reason, riding mid-week felt like a luxury that I didn't deserve to have, but riding on a weekend felt acceptable. I have no idea why my mind chose to view it in that way.

I felt quite relaxed when I went to get her from the field and even though she gave me a good run around, I didn't feel too annoyed. I suppose that was because I wasn't feeling pressured to do housework.

Poppy finally allowed me to catch her and we walked in a leisurely manner down the track. Luckily, the ponies had been given a large bale of hay so they were too interested in that to bother with us.

"That's too much horse for you!" greeted a complete stranger as I walked into the stable yard with Poppy. As you can imagine I was rather taken aback by this comment and so my response was short and sweet.

"Oh, right?" I replied.

"Yes, I know all about the yard where you've come from. You used to ride little ponies, didn't you?" continued the strange, unfriendly woman in a very patronising way.

"Yes, I did... and who are you?" I was beginning to feel extremely irritated by this woman for several reasons. Firstly, who the hell was she and how did she know about me? Secondly, her authoritative tone was triggering all my self-doubts about my ability to deal with Poppy. And thirdly, why was she so perfectly presented? The mysterious, rude woman was dressed in immaculate cream breeches with a beautiful sapphire-blue, silk shirt. She had shiny, black-patent leather boots that hurt my eyes to look at them and of course her hair was perfectly coiffured. She even had manicured nails, for God's sake.

In contrast, I was wearing a pair of scruffy jeans, slightly muddy brown boots, a faded pink T-shirt and a green fleece jacket that was fifteen years old.

"I'm Louise and I do dressage," said the unpleasant, snooty woman, full of self-importance. "I expect you'll just be hacking if you can get to grips with that type of horse? She's a big step up from a cob so you'll have to have some lessons, if you can be bothered to stick with her of course."

I was stunned and rendered speechless by her absolutely appalling manner so I couldn't reply. I just walked into Poppy's stable and luckily Poppy walked in with me without any embarrassing nonsense. Louise sauntered off and came back a few moments later leading her unfortunate horse, a 15.2hh dapple-grey thoroughbred. She mounted, rather heavily, and trotted off in the direction of the arena.

"All the gear and no idea!" came the laughing voice of Sally, who had just walked in. "She's a right cow, isn't she?"

"Yes! I can't believe what she just said!" I was so relieved to see Sally.

"Oh, that's nothing. You should have heard what she said about Malcy being too scruffy to come here! She actually asked the yard owner to bar me, silly cow! She did the same to your friend Jack."

"Never? What an awful woman!"

"She's not even that good a rider, either. She's never won anything and she's always banging on about dressage competitions. I think the best she's ever got is a fourth prize – and that was because there were only four people in the class, so actually she came last!" Sally laughed her head off.

"She made me feel really crap just now and I've got the saddle fitter coming this morning," I said, feeling anxiety welling up in my chest.

"Don't let that evil witch put you off, love. Just ignore her! You keep doing what you're doing and bloody prove the silly hag wrong!" I loved Sally's attitude and it rubbed off. I suddenly felt very determined to prove the evil witch wrong.

"Yes, you're right. I bloody well will!" I laughed.

"That's the spirit!" grinned Sally and off she went to get Malcy.

"Right, madam," I said to Poppy, "time to give you a hairbrush." As usual, this involved many a black glare from Poppy and several nips.

"You shouldn't be such a pushover," said horrible Louise, who had come back to get something from her stable. "You should give her a firm smack on her nose and a crack with your whip. My horse would never dare to treat me like that!" Before I could reply she marched off back to the arena.

I was boiling with rage. "Who the hell does she think she is?" I shouted out loud. I looked at Poppy; she looked back at me. In her eyes I saw no malice, just fear and sadness.

"What good would it do if I gave you a smack?" I asked her. "Nothing," I continued. "It would just make you worse, wouldn't it?"

Poppy remained silent and continued to look at me. I'd like

to think that she had understood the conversation that had just happened and that I had chosen not to hit her. I will never know, but I did make some interesting observations. Poppy was fine when I groomed her left side. However, she hated her right side being touched, mainly behind her shoulder and mostly where the girth would be. So I brushed her more gently and she breathed a sigh of relief and began to eat her hay. I felt that this was a good step forward so I continued, still very gently, and she wasn't bothered at all by the time I'd finished.

When it came to brushing her face, that was a whole new ballgame. She became very nervy and snorty and stretched her head up high, like a giraffe.

"Hmmm," I said. "Did somebody hurt your face, I wonder?" I put gentle pressure on her head collar and eventually she lowered her head. "I'm going to brush your face gently," I told her and I brushed her cheek twice.

Her eyes were wide with fear and she pulled away so I stopped and stood back.

"That wasn't such a terrible ordeal, was it?" I asked her.

Poppy looked thoughtful but happy and that made me feel happy too.

"OK, that's enough on your face," I said. "We'll work up to that slowly."

"Grace! I'm here!" called a voice, making me jump. I looked over the stable door to see Leon, the saddle-fitter. "Well, this is a step up for you!" he greeted (in a friendly way, not patronising like horrible Louise).

"Yes! Oh my God, I can't believe I've ended up with this horse!" I replied and then poured out the whole sorry tale.

Leon laughed his head off and told me I was an idiot. "Never mind!" He chuckled. "I'm sure it'll work out OK and if not, run for the hills! Bring her out and tie her up here; let's have a look at her," he said cheerily.

I led Poppy over to the long bar in the middle of the indoor stable barn, where most people tied up their horses to groom. For some reason, Poppy took an instant dislike to Leon and she refused to stand still.

"OK, Poppy," said Leon. "Let's have you nice and still." Leon attempted to stroke her neck but she was having none of it. Poppy snorted, rolled her eyes and jogged sideways. She came to the end of her lead rope and leaped back towards us, knocking me off my feet. Leon pulled me up with a sympathetic smile. I was very embarrassed as it showed me up for the inexperienced person that I was.

"It's OK, Poppy," I said in my most soothing voice. "Leon is a friend so you can settle down."

Obviously, that made no difference whatsoever. She was too wired.

"Let's lead her around a bit to get the adrenalin down," said Leon and he bravely untied her and walked her round the barn a few times very quietly. It seemed to help as Poppy relaxed for a few moments and allowed Leon to get the first measurement. But then she reverted to jiggling around. It was like she was doing a tap dance and I had to hang on to her lead rope with all my strength.

Amazingly, despite the dancing, Leon managed to get her measured and luckily the saddle I'd bought for Lucy fitted Poppy really well with only a few minor adjustments. It was very interesting to watch Leon take bits out of the saddle and add other bits – and then it fitted her nicely.

"Right, I'll get on," I said, leading the prancing Poppy over to the mounting block.

"You're not seriously going to ride that horse, are you?" asked Leon, his eyes goggling in disbelief.

"Yes, I am!" I replied. Even though Poppy was behaving like a stressed young racehorse, dancing around and bashing into things, I instinctively felt that she would be quiet as soon as I was sitting on her. I also felt it was now or never to take the plunge and ride out solo – obviously not a decision I would have made if I'd had more time to think it through.

Leon waited, his face a picture of horror, while I tried to line Poppy up at the mounting block and get on. It took several attempts and I was feeling increasingly embarrassed. However, my intuition served me well. As soon as I was mounted, she instantly relaxed and walked out of the barn like a seasoned trekking pony.

Leon was astounded by the transformation and waved me off with relief. I felt like sticking a finger up as we passed Louise, who was on her way back into the barn, but I kept my dignity and ignored her. The look of surprise on her face was enough pleasure for me and we wandered at a leisurely pace down the long driveway.

Oh God! What am I doing? Terror suddenly pinged into my head as we approached the road outside the safety of the yard. *Oh my God, I am riding this massive horse on my own!*

We managed to cross the road and I realised we were heading for the council estate. Stress caused me to unconsciously grip more tightly with my knees and my hands. Of course, this transferred instantly to Poppy. She grew several inches taller as she raised her head in fear of whatever it was I was scared of, and her strides became quick and choppy.

Oh my God, this is terrifying! My brain was exploding with all the millions of things that could go wrong. By now I was also aware that I didn't have a clue where we were, as we had ventured quite far into the busy council estate. Poppy went up another gear, marching along at top speed, snorting, ears pricked, looking for danger. The veins in her neck and shoulder became prominent and beads of sweat began to form on her smooth hair.

I looked at my hands and suddenly understood what the term *white-knuckle ride* actually meant. *Breathe, Grace! Breathe!* instructed the sensible part of my brain. So I breathed deeply, relaxed my legs and relaxed my hands. Thank God, after a few moments, Poppy responded. She began to slow down and I continued to breathe deeply.

"Now that's a fine-looking horse!" said an old man who was walking along the pavement nearby. "Had a mare similar many years ago!"

There was a nice energy about the man so I asked Poppy to halt and miraculously she did. The man came over to see her. "You were looking a bit worried!" He laughed. "New horse, is she?"

"Yes!" I squeaked, relieved to talk. "And I'm only used to little cobs!"

"Ah well, you'll be all right, lass! It just takes time to adjust. She's a beauty! What's her name?"

The pleasant chatter soothed my nerves and we walked along together. The old man, who was called Jim, told me all about his life as a traveller and horse breeder. It was fascinating to hear about his experiences. He eventually tired of travelling so now lived in a house on the council estate. He certainly knew a lot about horses and presently we arrived outside his house.

"Come and have a look at my wagon!" he said, and without thinking, I dismounted and led Poppy down his drive. I don't normally wander into strangers' gardens, but the man had made me feel so relaxed, I felt it was OK.

In Jim's back garden was the most beautiful, traditional Gypsy caravan that he was very proud of because it had been in his family for generations. He held Poppy so I could have a good look inside. It was absolutely gorgeous and I wished I could have one. Jim's wife came outside to see what was going on and she was very taken with Poppy.

"This lass has just got this horse and she's a bit nervous!" Jim informed his wife.

She laughed but in a kind way and brought me a piece of cake that Poppy ate before I could get a mouthful. The old couple found that very amusing and they made a big fuss of Poppy. It was really very lovely and Poppy clearly enjoyed the attention. I was seeing a side to her that I had not previously seen. She was relaxed and engaged very happily with Jim and his wife, clearly sensing their deep connection with horses.

"This is really amazing," I said. "Up to now, she's been such a bag of nerves. She hates being groomed, especially on her face, and she never stands still at the mounting block!"

"*Tch tch tch*," said Jim, shaking his head. "Now that's very sad. Has someone been a bully to you, eh, girl?" He stroked Poppy's cheeks and she didn't flinch. She obviously could tell he was a good man.

"I'm absolutely stunned that she is so relaxed with you!" I exclaimed.

"Well, I am very honoured!" laughed Jim as Poppy put her nose on his cheek and breathed deeply. "There are a lot of ignorant bastards, excuse my language, who don't know anything about horses," he continued. Jim spoke very calmly and quietly, all the while stroking Poppy's face. It was as if he was uncoiling some deep sadness within her and allowing her to feel safe.

"They just want to make quick money and they think that training is about breaking the spirit of the horse. I hate the words *breaking-in*. I like to use *backing*, which I think is much kinder," Jim continued. "This type of horse is very sensitive and they're clever buggers an' all. She just needs respect and understanding and you'll succeed."

"She's come to you for a reason." Jim's wife smiled. "You'll end up a better person for knowing her."

I almost cried when she said that because it was as if she had some psychic ability. She seemed very worldly and wise.

"Is there any more cake, love?" Jim asked his wife.

"There is!" She winked and went to get some.

"Now when I was a boy, my grandad used to breed traditional Gypsy Vanners. My job was to keep the buggers clean and tidy!" Jim laughed his head off as he remembered the hours he spent ensuring their thick, long tails and manes remained free of knots. "That was a never-ending task, I can tell you! But I learned a lot about horses just by grooming them. In fact, I think I can honestly say I learned more by watching them than riding them. Do you ever watch Poppy while she's in the field?"

"Yes, I have done," I replied.

"What does she do that has stood out to you?"

"Hmm, that's a good question!" I thought deeply about what I had noticed. "The thing that has struck me the most is how she's usually on her own when I go to get her. The other horses are closer to each other in groups. And when I put her back she never goes up to any of the other horses – she goes off to graze alone."

"OK." Jim nodded. "So what do you think that might say about her?"

"Well, at first I thought she was a bit uppity. But now I think she's just not very comfortable with other horses."

"Horses are never uppity." Jim smiled. "They don't think like we think and they have different rules too. I think she is probably a sensitive soul who doesn't want any trouble. She wants to keep herself to herself so she remains unharmed. That's the feel I get from her. It's as if she's come from quite a hard place and I'd put money on the fact she was probably taken from her mam too young."

My heart filled with sorrow as I imagined the physical and emotional pain Poppy may have experienced in her first home. "How can I help her to feel better?" I asked, my eyes welling up.

"Well, just be you. The fact you even asked that question shows you are a good-hearted lass. You can't change her past and we can only guess it was harsh. But you can make things nice for her by being fair."

Jim's practical and level-headed answer helped me to feel much calmer.

"Remember she's a very intelligent animal," he continued. "So don't be soft and baby her. Just be kind and clear with your requests. She needs to work or she'll be bored. So long as you know you aren't hurting her, that's the main thing. She will feel happier in time when she realises she can trust you."

I pondered on his words as we ate the delicious cake and Jim regaled me with more tales of his boyhood. Then I realised I had to be getting home as my mother-in-law would be back soon with Florence.

"I suppose I'd better be heading back," I said, nerves rising again as I remembered I was lost.

"I'll walk with you, if you like? It might help your nerves!" said Jim.

"Oh God, yes, please! That would be great because I haven't got a clue where I am!" I admitted, feeling embarrassed.

The walk back to the yard was lovely and relaxing thanks to Jim's stream of chatter about horses. Poppy was relaxed because I was relaxed and I felt so much better.

"Right, lass, here we are. Now don't get lost again!" laughed Jim as he went on his way with a cheery wave.

Poppy and I meandered calmly up the driveway to the yard and it was perfect timing as Louise was just leaving. I smiled sarcastically at her and she pulled a face like a bulldog chewing a wasp, which gave me tremendous satisfaction. Of course, I knew I owed it all to my new friend, Jim, but Louise didn't know that.

"We survived!" I said to Poppy as I led her into the stable to untack her. She lowered her head and blew on my face, which made me cry with relief and happiness. It felt like such a huge achievement to have gone out alone and come back alive.

Thank God for Jim, I thought to myself. *How many people are lucky enough to meet a person like that?* It really felt like fate had intervened and had brought the most perfect horseman to help me just at the right time. I was now even more curious to know about Poppy's history and wondered if I would ever find out where she originally came from.

As usual, though, as soon as I got home, life drowned me in a tidal wave of responsibilities so all thoughts about Poppy had to be shelved.

A few days later, Poppy's owner randomly turned up at the yard to check on her. I was filling a hay net when she suddenly appeared next to me.

"Hello, luv!" she greeted.

"Oh! Hello!" I almost fell over from the surprise.

"I can't stay long as I'm on my way somewhere. Just thought I'd see how you're getting on."

I was so taken off guard that I didn't feel able to say how overwhelmed I actually felt by the whole thing. "It's going OK!" I found myself saying.

Although it was a great opportunity for a chat about Poppy's history, sadly her owner knew nothing. She said she would try and find out as soon as she had any spare time, which didn't sound too hopeful, and then she told me all about her own horsey history.

She had spent her twenties on a ranch in America, learning how to drive cattle with cowboys on large open plains. She fell in love, got married, came back to England and forgot about horses until her daughter started asking for a horse. An uncle bought Poppy for her but – typical teenager – she lost interest almost immediately, hence the need for someone to help.

Before I had a chance to reply to the fascinating story she had to dash off. She was very much like a whirlwind and I was left none the wiser about Poppy.

.

Chapter 20

Spring was almost becoming summer. The hedgerows were bursting with life and were ablaze with colour. My life felt like it was also bursting as I now had even more to do than usual, thanks to Poppy.

Florence was keener than ever on riding and had joined a pony club at a lovely riding school, which of course involved a lot of to-ing and fro-ing. However, I loved watching her enjoying her riding because it reminded me of myself at her age. She was a natural at riding so watching her was a tremendous joy and it was wonderful to feel proud of her.

Although it felt good to have such a full life that didn't just revolve round household chores, I was aware that once again, I was putting a lot of heart into a horse that did not belong to me. I wouldn't have minded so much if it had been an easier horse like Monty or Lucy. Poppy was harder in so many ways. She was so big that grooming took ages, she was so nervy I was always worried I'd end up getting injured and she was so fast it terrified me.

"Why am I putting so much effort into somebody else's horse?" I asked Jack and Sally as we leaned over the gate, watching the horses. Buddy was lying nearby, lazily flicking flies with his tail as it was a particularly hot day.

"Because that's what you always do," answered Jack with perfect insight into my character.

"What *do* you mean?" I asked haughtily. My ego was annoyed by the fact that she was totally right.

"Well, you always feel responsible for every horse you loan and end up doing too much. You can't help it – it's in your nature," she said matter-of-factly.

"You're right," I sighed, "but at least the others were easier horses!"

"Well, why is that so bad, anyway?" asked Sally. "It's a free horse and you'll be learning loads from her. It sounds like a pretty good deal to me!"

"I'd love a free horse," said Jack, "but not one like Poppy. I honestly don't know how you dare ride her!"

"I don't know either – I must be mad." I grimaced.

Just at that moment, Poppy, who had been quietly grazing, decided something was terrifying. She squealed, leaped into the air and galloped off madly, holding her tail high like an Arab and snorting like an absolute nutter. This set all the other horses off, except for Buddy and Malcolm, who couldn't be bothered to move. I wished I had a Buddy or a Malcolm.

"Oh my God, she's so fast! Look at her go!" exclaimed Sally, laughing.

I wasn't laughing. I was feeling nauseous, thinking, *Christ, I hope she doesn't do that while I'm sitting on her!*

"Where is her owner?" asked Sally.

"Oh, she's so busy she doesn't have time for horses," I replied. "I actually saw her recently and she said she would try to find out where Poppy came from."

"Well, I think it's a brilliant opportunity and you should make the most of it!" said Sally enthusiastically. "Come on, let's go out for a ride while there's nobody else around."

It was a strangely quiet day due to the fact that a local horse show was on, so most of the yard had gone either to compete or watch. Needless to say, we were all hoping that horrible Louise would come last in everything she had entered. Sally was the only one honest enough to say it out loud, though.

Poppy came trotting over, more relaxed now that she'd had a good run, and I felt quite elated to see her coming to me. However, as soon as I attempted to put the head collar on, she did her usual thing of blowing large globs of snot on me and trotting away again.

"Haha! She's such a turd!" laughed Sally.

My heart dropped as I realised that, once again, I was going to have to follow Poppy around for ages, wasting time when I had loads of jobs to do, with no real idea of how to encourage her to stop. She trotted round the edge of the field and I was too annoyed to chase after her. Instead, I stopped and admired her paces. She had a lovely flowing action that was truly beautiful to watch.

As soon as she realised I'd stopped following her, Poppy stopped. So I walked towards her and off she went again but this time much more slowly. I stopped and she stopped. I walked and she walked. I took a deep breath and relaxed and she walked more slowly.

"Whoa," I said in a long, low voice as I stopped walking. And can you believe it? She stopped and stood as still as a statue.

"Good girl!" I said, quietly walking over to her. "Whoa," I said again and she didn't move.

"Would you like to go out for a walk with Malcy?" I asked her. I'm sure she understood because her ears pricked up and she happily let me put her head collar on. Poppy sashayed towards Malcy like a catwalk model, flapping her eyelashes at him.

"Take cover!" I called out to Sally.

"Oh my God, I should have brought an umbrella!" laughed Sally as Poppy jetted a gallon of smelly, steaming wee in Malcy's direction.

"Oh, yuk, that stinks! I'm glad she's not in love with Buddy!" laughed Jack. "Quick, let's get to the yard before we're all covered in it!"

Luckily, the ponies had been moved into another field so this time the walk from the field to the yard took moments instead of half the morning. I tied Poppy to the bar, next to Buddy, to groom instead of going in the stable. She still pranced around a fair bit but there was definitely an improvement. She didn't appear to be as stressed as previous times. Her behaviour seemed more like a habit than anything else.

"Do you think it's because she's young?" asked Jack.

"I don't know. I've not found out how old she is," I replied.

"She seems young, though, doesn't she?" asked Jack, stepping back to have a good look.

"I suppose she does," I stood back to observe too.

Poppy lurched sideways and crushed my grooming kit box. Brushes scattered all over the floor.

"Oh, for God's sake!" I exclaimed, gathering everything up quickly and narrowly avoiding getting stood on myself.

Finally, we were ready to go and we discovered that each of us had exactly the same pink hi-vis tabard, which looked ridiculous but we found it really amusing.

"Louise wouldn't be seen dead wearing this stuff!" said Sally.

"No, she'd just be found dead because drivers couldn't see her. But at least she'd be looking stylish in the ambulance!" Jack smirked.

We went a different way out of the yard this time, down a farm track, past a beautiful white mansion and along the side of a sheep field. It was sunny, the sky was blue and the birds were chirruping away happily. It was so perfect.

"Oof, what are you doing now?" I asked Poppy, who suddenly began dancing sideways, snorting.

"She doesn't like the sheep!" laughed Jack. "Can't blame her – I don't like them either. Don't you think they have weird eyes?"

"I can't look at their eyes! I need to settle this lunatic." I wasn't used to riding a horse that was so sensitive, nor one that danced. Whenever Lucy hadn't liked something she just used to walk slightly faster and would give dirty looks to whatever it was. Luckily, an excerpt from a book sprang to mind about scratching the withers to help calm the horse so I tried it and it worked.

"Good girl!" I said as Poppy lowered her head and walked normally again.

After crossing a terrifying A-road, we ended up in a very pretty village and Poppy suddenly remembered she was in love with Malcy. She reversed her big bottom into him, lifted up her tail and weed all over Sally's leg. It was dripping wet.

"Oh my God! I am so sorry!" I was mortified.

Luckily, Sally had a tremendous sense of humour because she just laughed her head off. "It's fine! I get worse from the kids at work," she said, prodding Poppy's bum with a stick to move her away.

Every few steps Poppy would reverse and spray wee at poor Malcy (who didn't understand what the hell was going on) until she had no wee left. But she still kept trying to swing her bottom into him. I'd never in my life experienced this sort of behaviour from a horse. It was exhausting to deal with and very embarrassing too as there were people walking along the street watching us.

Finally, she became more manageable and walked forwards instead of backwards. I flattered myself that it must be my riding skills... until I realised she was just being distracted by the activity that was going on around us. The village was bristling with people and was beautifully decorated with bunting and floral arrangements everywhere. Banners proclaimed VILLAGE IN BLOOM FLOWER FESTIVAL and the whole neighbourhood was out admiring all the displays. Children smiled and waved at us and wanted to pat the horses, so we stopped to let them.

"Ooh, he is a very pretty horse! What's his name?" asked a little girl.

"It's a she!" I smiled. "She's called Poppy."

The little girl looked at me blankly and continued to refer to Poppy as *he*. Luckily, Poppy wasn't bothered either way.

"Oh my God! Malcy, no!" shouted Sally suddenly.

I looked round to see Malcy with a mouth full of roses and a not-too-pleased-looking woman with a watering can in her hand, muttering her displeasure.

"Sorry!" said Sally and we hurriedly walked on.

"Oops!" I laughed.

"Oh, wow, look at that!" said Jack, pointing to a life-size donkey made of orange flowers. "That's so clever!"

"Maybe we could buy it for Valerie?" I laughed.

"Malcy, will you stop it!" exclaimed Sally.

I looked round again to see her yanking at the reins, attempting to get Malcy's head out of a flower bed on the side of the road.

"Oh, bloody hell, Malcy!" shouted Sally, exasperated, as Malcy looked up with another mouthful of flowers. "I'm so sorry!" she said to a cross-looking man.

"I should think you are!" he replied. "Do you have any idea how long –"

Unfortunately, we never got to hear the end of his sentence because Malcy, overcome with excitement, marched off to another display on the other side of the road.

"Malcy! Stop it!" yelled Sally, desperately trying to steer him away from the smorgasbord of floral delights. A group of young children were posing next to the display for a photo with the local newspaper photographer. It was a clever seaside design but Malcy couldn't care less and walked right into the middle of it. My jaw dropped open as I watched in horror at the unfolding events. Everything got completely crushed under Malcy's enormous hooves while the children shrieked and scattered in all directions.

"Malcy, will you get off!" shouted Sally, pulling at his reins, red-faced with embarrassment.

"Oh my God!" I gasped.

Unfortunately, Malcy, who was like a small tank, completely ignored all of Sally's attempts to control him and thrust his head down to eat. The movement was so sudden and strong that it pulled Sally over his head and she tumbled to the floor, completely destroying what was left of the children's entry for the competition.

"Oh no!" said Jack, biting her hand to stop herself from screaming with laughter.

I couldn't speak. I was so embarrassed I just wanted to disappear. After a moment of shocked silence, the children began to cry. Fond parents began telling Sally off in a very restrained and polite way that only middle-class people are capable of doing.

This was too much for Jack, who began shaking with laughter. She laughed so much that she lost her balance and somehow managed to fall off sideways into somebody else's display – a beautiful rainbow of flowers surrounding the word WELCOME spelled out in wild oats. Buddy copied Malcy and began to snatch mouthfuls of oats as if he'd been starved of food for years, until all that was left was OME.

"I'm so sorry!" I squeaked to the Lord Mayor, who was there to judge the competition. He was standing with his mouth open, dumbstruck, and clearly not amused.

Nobody was amused except us and I don't know how I managed to keep it together but luckily, I did. Sally grabbed Malcy and Jack grabbed Buddy and somehow, we managed to get out of the village flower fiasco before collapsing with laughter by the wall of the fish and chip shop round the corner and out of sight of everyone.

"I can't believe what just happened!" I said, crying with laughter.

"Poppy was the only well-behaved horse!" said Sally, also doubled over with laughter.

"I can't believe I fell off! How did that happen? My shoulder is killing me," said Jack, rubbing her shoulder.

"Let's get chips. I think we need some!" said Sally and she ran into the shop.

They were really delicious chips but unfortunately Poppy snaffled up most of mine quicker than a Labrador. "Why can't you eat flowers like a normal horse?" I implored, pulling the paper bag out of her silly mouth.

We clattered back to the yard, laughing the entire way. The driveway was full of horseboxes as everyone had returned from the competition.

"It was fixed! Nobody stood a chance!" shrieked a red-faced Louise as she unloaded her horse. Of course, she was still immaculately presented.

"Oh, did you not do well? That's a shame." Sally cocked her head to one side, comically feigning pity.

Louise ranted on about how the judge only gave prizes to people he knew and it was disgusting. When we were out of earshot, the three of us laughed like a coven of witches as we led our horses back to the field to turn them loose.

It felt so good to laugh with Jack again. I had really missed riding with her and I was so happy that I had met Sally too. She really was excellent company.

When I took Poppy's head collar off I expected her to zoom away like she usually did. However, for the first time since I'd been riding her, she put her nose on my cheek and stood for a moment before turning to walk calmly away. It made me feel very warm inside and I realised she was definitely worth the effort.

Chapter 21

A few days later I was clearing up after work and feeling stressed about Poppy. I wanted to feel more in control when I was riding instead of feeling so fearful. So I thought it would help to do all the correct sort of riding I had done in my youth... but I couldn't remember how to do it. I had been able to walk, trot and canter with varying levels of impulsion. The levels were called *collected*, where it's quite slow and very controlled; *working*, where the pace has a bit more oomph with an upward motion; and *extended*, where the horse is faster and really stretches out its legs.

"Mummy! What are you grumbling about?" asked Florence. She was sitting in my massage room doing some colouring while I cleaned.

"Grumbling?" I asked.

"Yes, you keep muttering and grumbling!" she replied without even looking up from her book. I was amazed at how much Florence noticed.

"I was just thinking about how I wish I could ride Poppy as well as you can ride," I sighed.

"Well, why don't you have some lessons?" asked Florence very sensibly.

"Of course!" I exclaimed. "Why didn't I think of that? You are absolutely right. I need some lessons!" I was a bit embarrassed at the fact that it took my very young daughter to state the obvious and remind me about Elise, the wonderful riding instructor from Valerie's yard.

That evening I gave her a call. Elise was very amused to hear all about Poppy and our adventures thus far, and said she would love to help and could see me the following day.

For some bizarre reason, I felt really nervous about having a lesson with Poppy. I was worried that she would behave so badly it would show me up for the ignorant novice I felt I was. Not for the first time I wondered what the heck I was doing with a horse like her when I should really just have an elderly plod. However, there was no going back now so I got my riding gear on and set off to the yard.

When I stepped out of my car at the yard I was greeted by a strange, thunderous, deep bass rumble. *What on earth was that?* I wondered, looking around.

The noise happened again. I walked past the stables and scanned the whole area and to my surprise I realised that it was Poppy. The car park was at the front of the yard, near the indoor stable barn. The horse field was up a very long track that was at least a couple of hundred yards away. Yet there was her big ginger face poking through the hedge, greeting me with an incredibly loud nicker.

I stood for a moment, stunned. I felt very emotional but in a nice way. How did she know that I was there and how did she create such a loud noise?

I grabbed Poppy's head collar and hurried to get her. Unfortunately, the mad feral ponies were back in their usual place so the first obstacle was to get through their field in one piece. Damn those ponies! They were so annoying when you were in a hurry. It was a great game for them to come snorting at anyone who dared trespass into their territory. They would spin around and threaten to kick out with both barrels.

I wasn't as athletic as Sally so cartwheels and 'Flash Dance' were not in my toolbox… but I did have some of Florence's maracas, which worked a treat. I shook them vigorously and the ponies turned tail and bolted off to the far end of the field. I was very pleased.

I jogged up the track to the horse field and there was Poppy, standing by the gate as if she knew I was coming to collect her. It was so peculiar. As usual, though, she moved away as soon as I attempted to put her head collar on. However, there was an improvement because this time she just walked away – she didn't trot.

"It's like a dance!" called Sally, startling me. I hadn't noticed her doing yoga on the inside edge of the field. "Life is actually like a dance when you think about it," she continued, stretching up on one leg with her hands clasped behind her back. She wobbled, then fell over, but credit to her, it didn't stop her stream of chat. "Sometimes you're close with your family and sometimes they piss you off so you step back for a while. Think of you and Poppy like a dance!"

Sally was completely bonkers but at the same time it was actually good advice so I considered her words as I followed Poppy around the field for the umpteenth time.

"Whoa," I said quietly but firmly, and once again that worked. I had to say it a few times and keep standing still but I managed to get her head collar on more quickly than previous attempts.

As I led Poppy down the track to the barn, I examined my general feeling towards her – which was mainly anxiety. She was so big and athletic, unlike all the horses I'd ridden recently at Valerie's. I was aware of her ability to run very fast and I was aware that we barely knew each other. The newness of a horse had never bothered me before and I had been able to connect quickly with Monty and Lucy. But with Poppy there was some invisible barrier and I couldn't put my finger on it.

I was jolted out of my thoughts when suddenly a loud whinny heralded the return of the feral Fell ponies. They ran straight up to us, snorting. Poppy started spinning around as I shook my maracas at them but thank God that worked again and they went haring off. It took a few moments to settle Poppy but finally we got through the ridiculous broken gate and into the safety of the yard.

Grooming and tacking up was, again, a stressful experience. It was slightly better than before so I felt a bit more positive as I led Poppy to the outdoor school for our first lesson together.

"Well, this is a bit different for you, isn't it? She's a beauty!" greeted Elise, my wonderful riding instructor, who was waiting for me in the school. Elise had been a racehorse trainer and was very *old school*. She was actually retired but did the odd lesson now and again. She was very tough, straight-talking and brisk but she had a lovely soft centre and always knew how to help you to get through your fears.

Elise was, as always, very smartly dressed in dark corduroy trousers and her signature tweed jacket. The weather had turned a bit cold so she had also decided to wear what I can only describe as the maddest hat I have ever seen in my life. It was multicoloured fleece with several protrusions that made it look similar to a jester's hat and it was completely incongruous with the rest of her outfit.

"That's an interesting hat!" I said, unable to stop myself from laughing. It was such a zany hat, quite the opposite of Elise's military-style manner.

"It's fun, isn't it?" agreed Elise. "I love it! It keeps my ears warm!"

Luckily, I didn't have much opportunity to be distracted by the crazy hat as Elise asked me to start walking with Poppy so that she could see how she moved. I led Poppy around the school and she became very nervy at the top end, which was flanked by a tall, thick hedge line. It was difficult to keep hold of her and I found it quite scary as she snorted and leaped about, but then she settled again when we turned the corner and came back down.

"Right, well we know where the hotspots are. I thought she wouldn't like that hedge," said Elise and she asked me to walk round again. "Be ready for the hedge! Just ignore her behaviour; talk to her and tell her she's brave!"

Without officially starting the lesson, Elise had taken us both into her capable hands and was teaching me how to gain Poppy's trust in such a simple way. Just by walking together.

We walked round and round while I spoke to Poppy and soon enough we were able to stop by the hedge and have a little chat. Eventually, Poppy wasn't nearly as worried about the hedge and I noticed she was much more relaxed. She still gave it a look but no other reaction.

"Right! Time to get on!" called Elise. She was standing in the middle of the school with her legs akimbo and hands on her hips rather like a sergeant major except for the mad hat that kept bobbing around.

Mounting Poppy was a whole world easier thanks to that simple exercise of walking around together. "Wow!" I exclaimed. "This is the first time she's stood still while I got on!"

"You're lucky to be alive then, aren't you?" Elise pulled a stern face.

I'd not really thought of it that way before but I realised she was right. Unfortunately, I couldn't take her seriously due to her hat, so I just laughed.

"OK, let's see a walk on a nice loose rein."

The thought of 'a nice loose rein' brought fear into my veins even though that was precisely what I had done during the test ride. "I daren't do that!" I squeaked.

"Why not?" asked Elise.

"Because she might run off with me!" I felt sick at the thought of it.

"Well, she won't run far in here, you big muppet! Look at the tension in her neck. Can you feel how short and choppy her strides are? She's telling you you're holding on too tightly."

Elise was absolutely right, of course. I took a deep breath and reminded myself that I'd done it before so I could do it again. I let go of the reins. Poppy instantly relaxed, lowered her head and took longer, more comfortable strides.

"You see! Now that's better, isn't it? Well done!" Elise clapped her hands.

We walked around the school several times and everything was going well so I wandered into a bit of a daydream. Suddenly, Poppy lurched into a canter, turned sharply across the centre of the school, galloped straight for the fence and, just as I was thinking, *Oh my God, she's going to jump!* she stopped dead. I shot forward out of the saddle. In front of me were the two menacing faces of the ghastly feral ponies, who had come to spectate without me noticing. I snatched hold of Poppy's sparse mane and ended up on her neck and, thankfully, she froze so I pushed myself back on to the saddle, still clasping her neck for dear life.

"Oh my God!" I was so shocked – and I was amazed I'd managed to stay on.

"Well done!" said Elise, quickly grabbing hold of Poppy's bridle. "Where on earth did they come from?"

I was a gibbering wreck for a few minutes but I calmed down eventually. In the meantime the ponies had a sniff of Poppy and she had a sniff of them and then they all lost interest in each other. The ponies went back to grazing and Poppy appeared to be ready to continue with the lesson. Meanwhile, I needed a shot of brandy.

"Right, let's do some walking again and this time be relaxed but alert!" said Elise.

The fact that I'd managed to stay on helped to give me confidence and I realised that in future I needed to remain focused and not let my mind wander, which was the usual thing for me.

"Now, let's get rid of those stirrups – your legs are gripping too tightly."

"What?" I was horrified.

"Come on, you can do it. Get those feet out!"

I glanced at the ground.

"Yes, it's a soft landing!" laughed Elise. "Feet out!"

"Oh my God!" I looked around for the ponies, who were now busy grazing and not interested in us. I took a deep breath and slid my feet out of the stirrups.

"Great, now just relax and keep walking. Stay in the bottom half of the arena so you don't need to go past the hedge. I'll make it easy for you!" Elise walked next to us, which helped me to feel more confident (not to mention amused by the funny hat). I allowed my legs to let go and relax. This was a big step for me and it took a lot of courage.

After a few circuits, Elise gradually walked back to the centre of the school and silently observed us. The transformation was incredible. Poppy walked quietly round and round in both directions, while I relaxed more deeply into the saddle. I began to feel much more at ease and happy (with one eye still on the ponies). I was very proud of myself because although it sounds a small thing to do it felt like a huge thing to me.

"Perfect! Now come towards me and halt," called Elise.

Poppy turned into the middle of the school and halted easily.

"Give yourself and her a pat for being so good!"

"Good girl, Poppy!" I said, leaning forward and giving her a big cuddle.

"Right, you can dismount now."

"Is that it?" I was surprised.

"Yes! That's enough for today. Look how far you've come, and she's only young."

"Is she? I actually don't know how old she is," I said as I jumped off.

"She looks about five to me. Didn't her owner tell you her age?"

"She doesn't know. Her brother-in-law bought Poppy and there's no age written on her passport. She said she thinks she's nearly ten."

"Rubbish! She looks very young to me but a dentist will be able to tell from her teeth. I'll have a quick look."

Elise expertly removed Poppy's bridle and put her head collar on in two seconds flat. She opened her mouth, moved her tongue out of the way and had a good look at her teeth. I was very impressed. There was no way I'd voluntarily put my hand inside Poppy's bitey mouth.

"Yes, she's definitely around five from what I can see. But get a dentist anyway – some of her teeth look a bit sharp."

I was dumbstruck. "Five! I'm riding a five-year-old massive, fast horse?"

"Yes! She's between four and five, probably closer to five."

"Oh my God! What am I doing? I'm not experienced enough for this!" My brain began firing off all the terrible possibilities of what could happen.

"Nobody is experienced until they've had the experience. Remember Monty was only five and he didn't even know how to walk in the school. You've done well with Poppy so far. You're still alive!" Elise laughed heartily.

"Only just," I muttered. "She's totally different from Monty!"

"Look, of course she's different from Monty so don't bother to compare. Remember that groundwork will be the key to creating your relationship with her. Let's do a bit of lunging to see how she moves."

Elise was forever capable of encouraging me to see what I could do rather than what I couldn't. I took Poppy's saddle off and Elise attached the lunge line to her head collar and started her off at a walk. I was wondering if Elise would think Poppy was mechanical. I said nothing and just stood quietly next to her as she worked Poppy in walk, trot and canter.

"Well, she certainly doesn't need to be told what to do," said Elise. "She moves very nicely."

I watched Elise as she observed Poppy going round and round perfectly.

"I think I'll just try something," she said as she asked Poppy to halt, which she did immediately, like a machine.

Elise walked up to Poppy and moved her lunging whip close to her. Poppy snorted and leaped sideways into the fence, then rebounded and pranced around for a few moments, her eyes white with fear.

"Hmm, that's a bit sad, isn't it? What a reaction! It seems as if Poppy hasn't been started in a particularly nice way. She shouldn't be so scared of the whip at any rate."

"I lunged her a while ago and noticed she was very mechanical," I replied, feeling a bit sick at the thought of what sort of home Poppy had started out in.

Elise was very sympathetic yet practical, and quietly put the lunge whip near Poppy's shoulder, speaking calmly all the time. At first, Poppy was quivering and she flinched when the whip touched her body. It was horrible to see and it made me feel sad and angry that someone could have been so nasty to her. Elise stood quietly but kept the whip on her. She then ran it over her back, all the while telling Poppy what a clever girl she was. Everything she did was slow and calm and it wasn't long before Poppy settled down and stopped jumping and quivering.

"She needs to know that this whip is just an extension of your arm and not something to be afraid of. I suggest you do this for a couple of minutes each time you bring her in here, until she takes no notice of it. Don't overdo it, though. You don't want to stress her. It's about doing it gently so eventually it becomes nothing."

"OK." I nodded.

"To be honest, I think that right now you're a bit over-horsed but if you put the time in, it really won't be long until you can have some fun together," she continued.

Elise gave me some exercises to do for homework and made a

plan of how to progress. I felt so relieved that I almost cried.

"Don't look so stressed!" laughed Elise. "I wish I was twenty years younger. I'd love to ride her! She'll be excellent at dressage. Let's aim for that because it'll be great for your balance."

"Dressage? There's a really bitchy woman here who does dressage."

"There always is!" Elise pulled a face.

"And coincidentally, here she comes now." I grimaced.

Louise had a lesson booked immediately after mine and as usual she looked down her nose at me as we walked past each other. I couldn't care less, though, as I was feeling so much better about my progress with Poppy.

"Right, practise what I've told you every day. Remember, no more than twenty minutes and I'll see you next week. And keep hacking, it's good for both of you," said Elise, giving me a cheery wave as she walked away, her crazy multicoloured hat wobbling madly.

I felt very satisfied as I looked at Poppy. She looked back at me and I noticed a faint smile in her mouth. We walked quietly up the track to the field and stopped by the gate. The feral ponies were eyeing us with suspicion but from afar thankfully.

"You were very good today and I hope that you enjoyed it," I said to her. She looked at me thoughtfully so I gave her a kiss and scratched her shoulders. She looked very happy and relaxed as she walked away to graze and I felt very happy too. I walked back down the track with my head held high, feeling more confident and lighter in my step. That feeling remained all the way to the school gates at pick-up time.

The bitchy mums were all in a group, gossiping about various people. They looked me up and down in their usual sneery fashion and for the first time I didn't give a stuff about any of them. In fact, I suddenly found them amusing and I stood back to observe them. They were all wearing black (they always wore black), they all drove expensive, perfectly clean, black 4x4s and, as usual, they were perfectly made-up and manicured with neat, straight hair. In contrast, I was wearing slightly muddy, blue-denim jodhpurs and a purple fleece and I had several bits of hay in my wild, curly hair. My car was a ten-year-old gold Honda, splattered in mud from the yard and I loved that the inside smelled of dog and horse.

My feeling towards the bitchy mums became pity. It was suddenly so clear that their monochrome lives revolved round appearance, shallowness and gossip. Whereas, my colourful life was full of fun, excitement and challenge.

I smiled at the group of sad, self-obsessed (and probably bored) women and felt thoroughly grateful that I wasn't one of them.

Chapter 22

In hindsight, shouting "Yee-haa!" at the top of her voice probably wasn't one of Jack's better ideas. The day had started off well. It was sunny, warm and the sky was blue – perfect horse-riding weather. When I arrived at the yard, there was no one around so I took the opportunity to practise some of the homework Elise had set.

Step one: get through the dreaded pony field alive. This was a constant source of irritation that never seemed to improve due to the two feral Fells being completely bored out of their minds. I had forgotten to bring my maracas so I had the bright idea of using fly spray. Historically, every horse I'd ever known had always tried to run away from being sprayed with insect repellent. It worked, thank goodness. The two crazy ponies took one look at the bottle, turned tail and ran for their lives.

Step two: collect Poppy. She was trotting around the field for no apparent reason, so I resigned myself to accepting that this might take some time. It was a challenge to try and stop feeling uptight as my mind reeled off a load of chores that I should have been doing instead. I stood and watched Poppy and presently, after doing a whole circuit of the enormous field, she came trotting over to me and stopped. This was a new and welcome improvement.

"Hello!" I greeted. "Would you like to go and do some stuff together?"

Poppy breathed deeply and flared her massive nostrils.

"Is that a yes or a no?" I asked and took a step forward. "Whoa,"

I said in a deep voice and Poppy stood still. I took another step and said "Whoa," again and managed to get the head collar on. "Well, that's getting better, isn't it?" I smiled and off we went towards the gate.

I almost forgot to pick up the bottle of fly spray that I'd left by the hedge but the sound of cantering pony hooves was a helpful reminder. The feral ponies had murder in their eyes as they came hurtling towards us. Poppy froze and lifted her head high and snorted.

"For God's sake, will you bugger off!" I shouted at them and held up the bottle and sprayed it. The ponies snorted, spun round and ran off. Not for the first time I wished the livery-yard owner would step in and remove the two hooligans. It just seemed so mad to allow two dangerous ponies to cause such a nuisance all the time.

We made it to the yard and it was still silent, which was nice, so I groomed, received a few nips (reduced in severity) and tacked up. Poppy did not easily accept the bit, even though it had been changed to a snaffle so it was by no means harsh. Still, she would clench her jaw and hold her head up high, which made it awkward for me as I am somewhat vertically challenged. I had to stand on my grooming-kit box to reach. I sighed and realised I needed to consider trying the bitless bridle I had used on Lucy, but Poppy's head was so large I was doubtful that it would fit.

Finally, we were ready to get schooling. I say schooling in the loosest sense of the word because, obviously, I didn't really have a clue what I was doing with this type of horse but I was determined to do my best for Poppy.

I walked her in-hand around the school and it was very good

to see that she had remembered not to be scared of the hedge. That was a result. We walked and halted, changed directions and attempted a figure of eight. All the while I chattered to her about rubbish and she seemed to relax into my voice. It was very gratifying to observe her standing calmly by the mounting block, and such a pleasure not to have to leap on hurriedly but get on slowly and correctly. That in itself felt like a tremendous achievement for me and I could feel my confidence growing.

When I got on board she stood quietly until I asked her to walk. Poppy immediately took off at top speed and my automatic response was to tense up. However, in my head, I could hear Elise's sergeant-major voice calling out, *Relax!* so I relaxed and loosened the reins and Poppy slowed down.

The feral and non-feral ponies ambled over to watch, which was quite amusing as they all stood in a line staring at us with great interest. Poppy had spotted them but luckily, she wasn't bothered, she just kept walking. I felt sublimely happy going around the school. I know it sounds such a little thing to celebrate but it was a significant step forward for us as a team. It was very invigorating to feel competent at something that had worried me so much.

"Do you fancy going for a ride out?" called Jack, walking towards the fence.

"Oh, hello! I didn't see you arrive. I'd love to go out but I've got so many things I need to do today," I replied sadly.

"Like what?"

"You know. Shopping, bedding changes and other boring things."

"Bugger that, Grace! You need to have some fun too!" grinned Jack.

"Oh, I know you're right!" I sighed, furiously working out in my head if I could do all these things later in the day.

"Great!" said Jack as if that was decided.

I asked Poppy to halt, which she did, very smoothly, and I dismounted. It was only a short session but I felt that I had gained a lot from it in terms of connection and building a relationship. I gave Poppy a pat while Jack shooed the ponies away by doing star jumps.

"Sally's on to something with this! Look – it works!" She laughed before crumpling forward on to her knees, puffing and panting. "God, I'm so unfit!"

I led Poppy back to the yard without a terrible pony battle, while Jack walked off to get Buddy. In the stable barn were Sally and two new friendly faces. A young student vet nurse named Ije and a middle-aged mum with long, bright green hair named Alex.

"Hi there!" greeted Alex and I warmed to her immediately. "We're going to the old Roman fort if I can get this big lump saddled up! Will you stand still, please? Preferably not on my feet, thank you." Alex was grooming the biggest horse in the yard, a Clydesdale x cob called Jenny, who was built like a tank.

Poppy rather liked Jenny because she had such a calm energy about her, so for once Poppy stood without prancing about, which was a pleasant change.

"I'll keep Malcy in his stable until we're ready so we don't all get covered in Poppy's pee!" laughed Sally as she wandered past with the kettle. She disappeared round the corner and I noticed she filled up the kettle from the water trough, so I politely declined when she offered everyone a cup of tea.

"Ooh, don't you look pretty?" said Alex, standing back to admire the pink ribbon she'd tied in a bow in Jenny's very thick forelock. "She's my magical unicorn, aren't you, Jenny-Wenny-Doo-Daa? Kisses for Mummy!" Alex pressed her cheek up to Jenny's enormous nose. Jenny looked blankly into the distance, half asleep but clearly very contented. I laughed. Alex was mad but very likable.

"Those bloody ponies!" chuntered Jack, walking in with Buddy. "They do my head in! They nearly kicked me!"

"You need to boogie!" laughed Alex, doing a crazy Seventies-style disco dance.

"I did and I bloody fell over and almost died!" exclaimed Jack, rubbing her bruised arm.

Finally, after lots of chatter, we were all ready to go. Ije, the young student, had a very cute chocolate-brown Welsh Section D pony called Buttons. She was trying out a new treeless saddle because Buttons didn't seem to like his usual saddle. (A treeless saddle is flexible and moves with the horse. The *tree* in a tree'd saddle is like a skeleton that creates rigidity and is designed to fit the shape of the horse. These saddles are meant to spread pressure evenly over the horse's back. Unfortunately, some horses are very difficult to fit with a tree'd saddle due to their shape.)

"Right, everybody!" said Alex dramatically, shaking out an ordnance-survey map. "Let's go and find the old Roman fort!"

"That sounds interesting. Why are we going to an old fort?" I asked.

"It's for our Michael's homework," Alex replied. "He's got to research some local history but he's too lazy to do it himself!"

"He's not daft, is he?" smirked Jack. "He knows you'll do it for him. You always do!"

"I know. I'm a big softie!" laughed Alex.

We clattered out of the yard and headed for the track that would take us to the village. Alex led the way, wearing a hi-vis yellow tabard emblazoned with DOES MY BUM LOOK BIG IN THIS? The map was propped up against Jenny's massive neck and, amazingly, it stayed put all the way there. The village was beautiful to look at as ever. There's something so relaxing about riding along village lanes past pretty stone cottages with gardens full of chickens and apple trees.

Presently we arrived at a derelict farmstead that had amazing views over rolling hills and in the distance, through some woods, was the old Roman fort that went by the funny name of Pompocali.

"Hang on! Let me get some chickweed!" exclaimed Alex suddenly. She hurled herself off her massive horse, stumbling sideways as she landed. "Ooh, my knees!"

"Chickweed?" I asked in surprise.

"Yes, it's for my hot flushes. It's great stuff!" replied Alex as she stuffed handfuls of chickweed into her saddlebags.

"Do you eat it?" asked Ije, looking slightly perplexed.

"No, I make a tincture. It's a full moon tonight so it'll be a good strong batch!" Alex climbed on to a handy drystone wall and heaved herself back up on to Jenny.

"Right!" said Jack, raising her eyebrows. Sally laughed heartily.

Off we went again but it wasn't long before Alex was leaping off her horse once more. "Oh my God! Look at that!" she exclaimed with great glee before tripping over Jenny's trailing reins and landing in a heap on the dusty old farm road that led to the woods.

"What is it? Are you all right?" I asked with great concern.

"It's vervain! I can't believe it! It's really rare to find it up

North. It must be chalky here." Alex pulled some up to inspect it.

"Vervain?" asked Ije. "What's that?"

"It's excellent for cleansing your aura and directing magical energy, which I will obviously need to do before making my chickweed tincture," replied Alex matter-of-factly.

"Well, obviously, everybody knows that!" said Jack but her sarcasm was lost on Alex. Sally and I just grinned. Watching Alex was hugely entertaining. Ije, who was quite scientifically minded, was very interested to know what the chemical properties of the plants were.

"Ooh, now there's a good question!" said Alex. "I have absolutely no idea but they definitely work. When you're older I'll make you some!"

"That's all she needs," said Jack, rolling her eyes. "I'd stick to paracetamol if I were you, Ije."

"My grandma always talks about her witch doctor back in Nigeria using herbs for this and that. She swears by it. I bet you'd love to meet her, Alex!" laughed Ije.

We continued on our way along the dusty old road that was flanked on both sides by enormous, undulating fields full of tall crops waving gently in the breeze. A hare popped its head up and zoomed off, startling the horses. It was amazing to watch how fast it could run.

Finally, we came to a wide, bubbling stream at the entrance to the woods and all the horses splashed through, except Poppy, of course. She took one look at it and said *No!*

"Come on, Pops, you can do it!" called Alex from the other side of the stream. But Poppy was having none of it. She reversed up the bank, took a sharp left and walked smugly across the bridge with her head held high as if she was the Queen.

"Well, she can't get her tootsy-wootsies wet now, can she?" laughed Alex.

On the other side of the stream was a long, soft-surfaced bridle path that wound its way through the woods.

"This is a great place for a canter!" said Jack "Shall we have a little blast?"

"I've not cantered with Poppy yet!" I felt a bit uneasy.

"Well, now's your big chance!" said Jack, grinning. "Go on, you can do it!"

"And the map shows there's a gate at the end of the path so she can't go far!" added Alex.

"OK." I realised this was as good a time as any to try it but I was a bit apprehensive to say the least.

"You go first because Poppy's definitely the fastest horse," said Jack and then everyone arranged themselves behind me in order of speed.

My heart was thumping hard in my chest, threatening to leap out of my throat. I took a deep breath to calm my nerves. I had no idea what I was about to let myself in for and Poppy had very little in the way of mane for me to grab hold of if the worst happened. I focused my mind on Mark Rashid, the cowboy whose books I had been reading. I actually visualised myself as being him – relaxed, calm and in control. I imagined that I was a very experienced cowboy and this was my new horse that I was training and all was well.

We set off at a walk, then I asked for a trot, which was extremely fast, and then I asked for a canter. Wow! I have never felt such a smooth and comfortable canter in all my life – it was so breath-taking. Poppy was like a top-of-the-range sports car, if I had to compare her to a car. She was impressively fast. Her strides were so long and the power and athleticism were unlike any horse I'd ever experienced.

"*Yee-haaaa!*" called out Jack behind me, and Poppy shifted up a gear but still perfectly smoothly. It felt like we were flying. I vaguely heard a bit of a commotion happening behind and suddenly realised someone was yelling "*Stop!!*" It was all a blur.

I looked round to find that Ije's pony, Buttons, was next to me but with no Ije – and the saddle was almost underneath him. Without thinking, I reached over and caught hold of his reins. "*Whoaaa!*" I called out and both horses slowed and then stopped, thank goodness.

Poppy was surprisingly aware of what needed to be done. Without asking, she manoeuvred herself and Buttons round and we headed back down the path to the others. Ije was in a crumpled heap on the ground next to a tree, not moving. Jack was leaning over her and Sally had hold of Buddy's reins.

"Oh my God! Is she dead?" I asked, shocked.

"No, but my bloody head is killing me!" snapped Ije crossly.

"Oh, thank God for that! What happened?"

Unfortunately, when Jack called out "*Yee-haa!*", Buttons had jumped into the air, the new saddle slipped sideways because the girth wasn't tight enough, and Ije flew off head first into the tree.

"I'll make a cooling compress with some docks!" said Alex as she jumped off Jenny.

"No! Don't touch her head!" Sally commanded. "I'm a first-aider! Don't move her at all. We need to call an ambulance!"

"OK! I'll give her some reiki then." Alex knelt down next

to Ije and put her hands on her back, while Jack rolled her eyes skywards.

"I'll call for an ambulance!" I said. "Damn, I've got no signal!"

Nobody had any signal.

"Go to the end of the path and you'll get to a road!" said Alex. "You should get signal there!"

I turned Poppy and urged her into a gallop. She flew to the end of the path, her feet barely skimming the ground. It felt amazing… and it suddenly dawned on me I was galloping alone on Poppy for the first time. Luckily, Poppy spotted the gate and slowed down and stopped, thankfully. I didn't relish the thought of flying over that on to a road.

Still no signal.

"Oh my God!" I leaped to the ground, dragging Poppy along the road until we got a signal. I don't know if you've ever had to call the emergency services before but it was quite a stressful experience. Obviously, they need to ask questions but when you've got someone with a possible head injury you want to be as quick as possible. It seemed to take an eternity to get to the point where I was asked the dreaded question…

"Where are you, love?" asked the operator kindly.

I didn't have a clue. "Erm… Er… Oh, damn, I'm not actually sure! Where am I? Oh my God!" I stuttered.

"What part of Leeds are you in?" she asked with amazing patience.

"I'm near Thorner! I think? And it's near a Roman fort!" I exclaimed.

"A Roman fort near Thorner? OK, I'll just google that," said the operator with great presence of mind.

Suddenly I noticed a dog walker ahead so I ran over to him, with Poppy trotting behind me.

"Where am I? What is this place?" I shouted, like a total mad woman. The dog walker looked very taken aback as you can imagine.

"Er... I don't know! I've not been here before!" answered the man.

"Bloody hell! How can you not know where you are?" I shrieked.

"I know we're near Wetherby Road, if that's any use?" he offered, stepping backwards to get away from me.

"Is it Pompocali?" asked the operator.

"*Yes, that's it!* Oh my God!" I was so relieved.

"What road are you on? I'll get the ambulance to meet you there," she asked, once again throwing me into a panic as I didn't have a clue what road I was on.

"I don't know! It's the road at the end of the bridle path!" I looked around desperately in search of a road sign.

"It would really help to know the name of the road if you could have a look for a sign."

I ran down the road, dragging poor Poppy along with me, and finally found a road sign half hidden in a hedge.

"Ambulance is on its way – you wait there!" said the operator and I collapsed on a drystone wall, puffing and panting. Poppy looked at me quizzically, then began to graze on the various weeds by the side of the road. I realised how amazingly calm she was being under the circumstances, considering I'd ridden her away from the herd and was asking her to wait by a road we'd never been on before.

Obviously that realisation immediately pinged into Poppy's

brain and she suddenly decided she wanted to go back to the others. She began dancing around, snorting and prancing, spinning in the middle of the road like a hooligan.

"Stand still!" I commanded with the loudest, deepest voice I could muster and amazingly it worked... more or less. She stopped pratting around and became quieter but she wasn't overly happy.

Thankfully, the ambulance was very quick to arrive and the two paramedics followed me down the bridle path to where Ije was still on the ground.

"Hello, love, can you hear me?" said the male paramedic, bending down next to her.

"Yes, my ears are still working," replied Ije rather crossly.

"Ah good, that means you're not dead then!" He looked round at us, pleased with his observation.

"Really? Well, thank goodness for that!" said Ije sarcastically.

The paramedic laughed like it was the best joke ever and gently checked Ije for broken bones and so on. "You're OK, lass. Let's get you to hospital for X-rays though, anyway."

"I used to ride horses," said the female paramedic, stroking Buttons. "I really miss it until I have to come to accidents like this."

"Do you go to many horse-related accidents?" I asked.

"Luckily, no. But we do find that most head injuries are because the rider's hat was already damaged."

"Really?" asked Sally.

"Yes, you've got to be so careful. Not many people know they get damaged rolling about in your car, for example, or if you just drop them on the floor. Check your hats, ladies – they could save your life!" The paramedic showed us how to do it.

We all took our hats off and gave them a squeeze. It was quite shocking hearing the strange creaking noises as we discovered we all had broken hats.

"You must replace them immediately!" insisted the paramedic. It was very sobering.

Poor Ije was whisked off to hospital while the rest of us stood around looking at our hats.

"What the heck should we do about Buttons?" I asked. "I don't fancy riding and leading him all that way, especially in my broken hat!"

"Oh God, the first thing I'm going to do tomorrow is buy a new hat," said Alex. "This one must be at least twelve years old!"

We decided to ride to the road so we could get some phone signal and call for help.

"I feel so bad!" said Jack as we walked up the bridle path.

"Why?" asked Sally.

"It's all my fault for shouting out *Yee-Haa!*" Poor Jack looked very miserable.

"No it isn't! It was just one of those things. The saddle obviously didn't fit Buttons so it slipped," said Sally pragmatically. "You didn't shout it on purpose to cause an accident. And at least now we all know we need to buy new hats – so you've done us all a favour really!"

Luckily, another girl from the yard answered our call and taxi'd over to help us out with Buttons.

"Did you ever get to the fort?" asked the girl.

"Bugger! No, we didn't!" exclaimed Alex. "We'll have to come again."

By the time we got back, the yard was very busy and everybody was asking what had happened. Mercifully, Ije was absolutely fine and just had mild concussion.

A week later, when Ije's head was feeling better, we all went to Pompocali for a picnic – with no yee-haa's. The Roman fort was a very peculiar place full of enormous, grassy mounds and winding paths. It had a very strange atmosphere about it that was hard to describe. Not unpleasant, just odd. The horses sensed it too and walked faster with their ears pricked up.

While we ate our sandwiches, Alex collected some herbs and performed a ritual, sprinkling them at the site of the accident to "clear the negative energy". It was actually quite fun and even Jack joined in with great enthusiasm, which was very unlike her.

Of course, a group of walkers had to turn up at that very moment. They found it most amusing to watch us chanting and dancing while sprinkling herbs. I often wonder if horses can feel embarrassment because I'm sure that could have been quite a mortifying moment for them. However, it was such a liberating, life-enhancing experience to do something as mad as that. It was the sort of thing you do when you're very young and believe in magic and fairies and so on, but then age and responsibilities take over and life becomes quite humdrum, doesn't it?

I took the idea of *magic ritual* home with me and suggested to Florence that we collect some flowers and do some spells. She wanted to do a spell for extra sweets and it was really good fun and totally silly. I genuinely enjoyed having fun with her and I laughed my head off just like my mum did when she was playing mad games with Florence.

Chapter 23

As I mentioned earlier, Poppy had a deep loathing for her bit. She made it perfectly clear each time I approached her with the bridle by clenching her jaws and holding her head up high like a giraffe. I hunted through my garden shed to find the bitless bridle I'd used on Lucy but was dismayed to find it mouldy, stiff and completely unusable. I wasn't really surprised because it was a cheap copy of a Dr Cook bridle and the leather was very poor quality. So I decided to try and find an official one.

This wasn't easy as they aren't very common in the UK but thanks to the magic of the internet I located a riding school in Wales that specialised in official Dr Cooks. After several emails with Marjorie, the lady who owned the place, I realised I'd been talked into actually going up there to stay for a weekend.

How did that happen? I wondered. *I only wanted to buy a bridle!*

However, I was very intrigued to meet her and learn all about how to fit the bridle correctly. My only wish was that she lived a bit closer.

My husband was very enthusiastic about my trip as he knew I needed to stretch myself out of my comfort zone to help me get over the postnatal depression. Obviously, horse riding had done me a power of good and I was beginning to return to my usual bold self but I had yet to travel any real distance alone.

I felt a strange combination of excitement and fear as I packed my case, typed the postcode into the satnav and set off. I'd not been anywhere on my own for several years so it felt like I was embarking on a great adventure.

A huge burden of responsibility lifted off my shoulders as I joined the motorway and left Leeds behind. The satnav decided that the most direct route would be really boring and that we should take the scenic route instead.

Five and a half hours later, my back shrieking at me in pain, I finally arrived at the destination, which was on the top of a large hill, seemingly in the middle of nowhere. A feeling of trepidation filtered into my body when I drove into the gravelled yard, as I realised how secluded the place was and that I had no phone signal.

"Welcome! Welcome!" called a jolly voice as I stepped out of the car. I looked around and there was Marjorie smiling and waving in such a friendly way that my worries instantly melted. She was accompanied by a medium-sized, very fluffy pink pig, who snuffled at my feet waggling his bottom.

"This is Arnold! He's frightfully friendly and extremely intelligent, aren't you, little man?" Marjorie was very well-spoken and had originally lived in the south of England.

"Hello!" I said to Arnold, who was nibbling the handle of my suitcase.

"Let's drop your stuff and I'll give you a tour!" said Marjorie very enthusiastically.

Marjorie, who was about fifty, looked quite similar to Barbara from *The Good Life*. She was wearing denim dungarees and her long, grey hair was tied up in what looked like a tea towel that declared WELCOME TO BRIDLINGTON. (At least I think that's what it said – I could only actually see OME TO BRID and pictures of seagulls.)

A winding path led to a wonderful olde-worlde cottage with

a traditional thatched roof, surrounded by various outbuildings scattered around haphazardly.

The inside of the cottage was fascinating. There were large pot plants and colourful crystals everywhere, creating the feel of an Aladdin's cave. Dusty old paintings of horses hung on the walls, and here and there a photograph of Marjorie with various animals.

"We'll park your stuff here for now and I'll show you around," said Marjorie, putting my case near the kitchen table. I noticed that Arnold had followed us into the kitchen but Marjorie didn't seem to mind. A very fluffy tabby cat sprang off the window ledge and followed us outside.

"Come on, Percy, you can come too!" laughed Marjorie, referring to the cat.

Marjorie led me through her farmyard and up a hill to a beautiful pasture. "I've always loved Wales. The land here is perfect for horses. Look and learn, my dear girl!" She knelt down on the ground in the middle of a paddock full of ponies. "Come along, kneel down! You can't see from up there! Or I can't, anyway, not without my glasses. Where are my glasses?" Marjorie fumbled in her pockets. "Found them! Oh dear, they seem to be in a crisp packet. How did that happen? Oh well, never mind. Look around and tell me what you can see!" She put the glasses on regardless of the fact that the lenses were a bit smeary and speckled with bits of old crisps.

I looked around. "Er… well, I can see a field!" I said, not really knowing what more to say.

"Not just a field, my dear! Is it full of grass?" asked Marjorie, head cocked to one side.

"No!" The field was definitely not full of grass. Unlike the perfect billiard-green field at Poppy's livery yard, this pasture was teeming with various weeds.

"*Tch tch tch! Weeds* is a very negative word for these marvellous herbs!" Marjorie exclaimed. She then proceeded to point out several types of 'weeds' and explained the health benefits they presented for horses. It was so fascinating and eye-opening.

"To be honest, I've never really taken any notice of Poppy's field," I admitted.

"Sadly, not many people do." Marjorie heaved herself back on to her feet. "They generally think *Is there enough grass or is there too much grass?* But that's only a very small part of what a horse needs to eat. You wouldn't just eat potatoes and nothing else, would you?"

"No!" I laughed.

"Right! Oh, hello! Where did you come from?" Marjorie was suddenly surrounded by a flock of alpacas. "Have you escaped again, you cheeky devils?"

The alpacas lived in an adjacent field but had decided to leap over the drystone wall to see what we were doing. Arnold the pig didn't seem to like the alpacas so he trotted off back to the gate.

"They love visitors," said Marjorie, biting her lip and looking slightly concerned. "But they are a bit naughty! We must get them back into their own field."

Rounding up the alpacas was reminiscent of a Benny Hill scene, beginning with Marjorie flailing her arms behind them. This resulted in the whole flock running around in circles, followed by myself and Marjorie trying to herd them towards the gate. It was such a ridiculous farce because they kept splitting into two groups at the crucial moment. We then had to start all over again, trying to encourage them to move in the same direction together. I was almost collapsing from exhaustion when they decided for themselves to leap back over the wall and wander off as if bored with the game.

"Phew!" said Marjorie, doubled over and gasping for breath. "Well, that's our exercise for the day, or indeed the whole week! Now we'll just grab some milk and then we'll go and have dinner."

I could barely get my legs moving but Marjorie had recovered her strength remarkably quickly and was marching off towards the yard so I had to run to keep up.

'Grabbing some milk' did not involve a trip to the local shop. No, it involved actually milking a goat. Marjorie had five goats and they could all roam freely around the yard and fields. Similar to the alpacas, really, as they had just demonstrated that they could go wherever they fancied. The goats were very amenable to being milked and it didn't take long before Marjorie had filled up a jug.

"Right, let's have dinner!" she trilled and led me back to her cottage.

Dinner was out of this world as it was all her own produce and tasted divine. We dined in the lovely old kitchen, which had traditional oak beams covered in horse brasses.

We were also accompanied by Arnold. who ate his dinner out of a large ceramic bowl next to the fireplace. "He's like a dog really!" said Marjorie, eyeing him fondly. "He was the runt of a litter born just down the hill at the farm. Poor little chap wasn't strong enough to get any milk because his brothers and sisters kept pushing him off the teat! So I took him in and hand-reared him and we've been together ever since. Haven't we, little man?"

It was a lovely story and I couldn't help feeling wistful about Marjorie's life. It seemed perfectly idyllic up there in the beautiful countryside surrounded by so many marvellous animals. Totally different from my ordinary life. Although it had, of course, become 1000 watts brighter since engaging with horses once more.

The best experience of the day was yet to come as Marjorie had a wonderful home-made, wooden hot tub overlooking the most incredible view of wild hills, untouched by humans. She lent me a swimming costume that was bright orange and covered in purple butterflies. Luckily, no one was there to see me wearing such a garment. It was truly the most amazing feeling to sit in the gloriously hot water while being entertained by a beautiful peacock who strutted around, showing off his fantastic tail feathers.

"I don't know where he came from," mused Marjorie. "He turned up last summer and never left, so he obviously feels at home!" I couldn't blame him for making it his home – it was such a special place to be.

Finally, the adventures of the day caught up with me and I couldn't stop yawning.

"It's all the fresh air!" laughed Marjorie as we clambered out of the hot tub into the garden.

My bedroom turned out to be a conservatory at the back of the house, separated from the living room by a large flowery curtain.

"Arnold sleeps in the spare bedroom, I'm afraid," said Marjorie apologetically, "and he would be most upset if I turfed him out!"

I didn't mind at all. I was so tired I would have slept anywhere. I wondered if Arnold slept on a bed or if the room was filled with straw like a stable. Sadly, I never got to know the answer as I didn't want to appear completely nosey. Anyway, the bed in the conservatory was perfect and I had the best night's sleep I'd had for years.

I was woken at 7am by the extremely loud, ethereal sounds of the peacock, and the smell of cooking breakfast got me out of bed very quickly.

"Today you will meet my partner in crime," said Marjorie, waving a spatula around. "Bloody flies get everywhere! Get away from our breakfast!" A big fat bluebottle managed to escape out of the window. "What was I saying? Oh yes, Julie is coming to give you a wonderful day of training! She's absolutely marvellous," Marjorie continued.

Julie arrived shortly after breakfast and turned out to be a very friendly, easy-going woman of around the age of forty. She was dressed very simply in jeans and a pink checked shirt and had long blonde hair tied back in a ponytail.

As I had no idea what to expect, the day unfolded into the most magical experience.

"Usually, we do this work in groups but you're very lucky because a one-to-one is so much more effective," said Julie, as we walked to the horse field. "Now, have a look at the herd and without giving it too much thought, choose three horses that you like and one that you don't."

I looked at the herd and instantly chose three that I liked. Each one reminded me of the ponies I had loved over the course of my life. Marjorie quietly collected them and led them over.

"Now the one you don't like?"

One horse stood out immediately to me. He was a large bay sports horse that made me feel uneasy. Marjorie let the three ponies run loose into her indoor arena and then she collected the sports horse, whose name was Andy. As they walked past me, Andy stopped and put his nose on my heart very gently.

"He's telling you that you don't need to be afraid," said Julie – and with that I promptly dissolved into tears.

Julie led me into the indoor arena and handed me a tissue. "Talk to me about your fears," she said kindly, as the big horse came over and put his nose on me again.

"I wouldn't know where to start," I sniffed.

Julie remained quiet, allowing me time to process my reaction and thoughts. I took a deep breath. "I don't really know what I'm afraid of. I just feel fear. Fear of Poppy spooking and galloping and me falling off from a great height and ending up paralysed. I've never been afraid of falling off before. I don't know why I am now."

"Come and stand next to Andy's side and put your hands on him," said Julie very softly. "Now close your eyes and just feel his energy."

I stood with my hands on Andy's warm, powerful shoulder, feeling his large muscles. His skin was soft as satin, just like Poppy's, and he was very tall, just like Poppy. He stood so still and so calmly, breathing very rhythmically. I began to breathe in time with him. My fear began to melt away and was replaced by a sensation of love. Andy curved his neck round and put his large nose on my head, very gently. More tears poured out and Julie and Marjorie stood in perfect silence, holding the space.

I suddenly felt calm and no longer afraid. I could see that there was no malice in Andy and no malice in Poppy. They were just horses but also, more than *just horses*. They were alive and had their own emotions and they needed to give and receive love just like I did.

Time seemed to stop moving while I stood with my hands on

the big horse, sharing his space as if we were one unit. Eventually, it felt like whatever it was that happened had been completed, so I took a step back and looked around. Marjorie and Julie were quietly waiting in a very calm and unhurried manner.

"So, tell me what just happened for you," said Julie.

"Well, at first I felt terrified of Andy because he reminds me of Poppy but then when I put my hands on him and allowed my mind to calm down, the feelings changed," I replied. "The fear disappeared and I felt a lot of love instead and I knew that everything was OK."

Julie and Marjorie smiled.

"You know, horses are just horses and they only run fast if they're scared. And to be honest, they would prefer not to waste their energy if they don't need to! You can help Poppy to be brave by tapping into the confidence within yourself," said Julie as she led me into the indoor arena where the three ponies were wandering around.

Such simple, yet profound words.

"Can you tell me an example of something that you've done that involved you being confident?" asked Julie.

"Starting my own business. I had to be confident when I first became a massage therapist. So many people thought I was too silly to be successful at anything and I decided I would show them they were wrong!"

"Excellent!" smiled Julie. "Can you tell me more about what you did?"

"Well, basically, I got a Yellow Pages and just rang round loads of companies to see if they wanted any on-site massage for their staff. Loads of people were really rude to me but I didn't let it get me down. I continued and ended up landing a few contracts with nursing homes, and that's where I really learned how to be good at what I do."

"Excellent!" nodded Julie. "Just excellent! You must have oozed confidence to get those contracts!"

"Yes!" I hadn't thought about it at the time but, looking back, I was amazed at my tenacity.

"You can tap into that ability to be confident when you are riding because it's an intrinsic part of who you are. Visualise yourself as that calm, confident and happy person. That will give Poppy confidence in you as her guide and partner when you are with her. It will make her more inclined to listen to you, instead of running away if anything scary happens."

Julie gave me a few moments to digest what she had said. I could feel it sinking into my mind as if doors were opening in my subconscious. I remembered my childhood riding lessons in which I only ever felt happiness and excitement – even if I did fall off. The ponies generally did what I asked them because I never doubted that they would.

Marjorie led Andy back to his field and then came to join us. We all sat down and observed the three ponies interacting quietly for about half an hour to allow my mind to process, digest what I'd learned and calm down. It was very relaxing just to sit and watch.

"Now one thing you mentioned was your trouble catching Poppy," said Julie after a while. "Tell me a bit more about that."

"Well, when I go into the field to get her, she always walks or trots away and it's so annoying because it takes ages to get her to stop!" I exclaimed.

"Right!" agreed Julie, getting up and walking towards the

ponies. "Because who's got time for that?" The ponies looked up and started moving away from her. "I mean, listen, I'm in a rush and you guys are really messing about!"

The ponies started trotting.

"I'm really getting annoyed with you lot!" shouted Julie, waving a head collar around. "I've got so many things to do today! I've got the shopping to do, the washing to do and I've got to do the school run! I haven't got time for this!"

By now the ponies were trotting really fast round and round and Julie was running after them. "Stop, you little gits!" she called. "Stop immediately!" It was hilarious to watch.

"Do you know what? Bugger it! I'm just going to sit down," panted Julie, out of breath. She sat down on a mounting block, crossed her legs and fanned herself, ignoring the ponies. Almost immediately, the ponies calmed down, and after a few moments they wandered over to Julie as she sat looking away from them. Quietly she stood up and stroked their heads and then easily put the head collar on one of them and led him over to me, followed by the other two.

"You know, it's a funny thing about horses!" said Julie, grinning. "They naturally enjoy being with humans so long as our energy is calm."

I laughed. She had taught me a valuable lesson in such a comical way that it really needed no explanation. It was suddenly very clear that I had been inadvertently sending Poppy away from me with a combination of fear, exasperation and a belief that *I am in a rush*.

"That was so funny and such an eye-opener! Every day I have a list of things I need to do and I'm always thinking about the next job. I'm never in the moment. Everything is always rushed and it's stressful because I feel like there isn't enough time."

Julie nodded and smiled but remained silent, allowing me to delve even deeper into my subconscious. There was an air of peace and calm around Julie, and the ponies were peaceful and calm too as if there was no such thing as time. It made me realise that I was missing living because I was always rushing to do the next thing. I wanted to be calm and peaceful like the ponies and like Julie.

"I'd really like to be able to just enjoy time with Poppy," I sighed.

"What's stopping you?" enquired Julie in a curious, non-accusatory way.

"I suppose guilt. I feel guilty for enjoying myself when I should be working more or cleaning the house more. Or... oh, I don't know... just more sensible things rather than fun things!" I replied. "I feel like I don't deserve to have leisure time."

"Where does that belief come from?"

"I don't know." I looked down and picked some hay off my leg. "No, I *do* know. It's because my mum never had time to do fun things... and she really loved horses. She always had to work so she never had the time or the money to have a horse. And she helps me now with Florence, which she loves, because she loves being a grandma. I just find it so hard to be a mum! I'm crap at being a mum! Well... no, that's not totally true. I'm a lot better than I was. I do fun things with her and I love her but I just really need to have my own time with horses. It's where I feel like myself again."

More tears streamed down my cheeks as the deep pool of sadness I'd been carrying for so long finally overflowed.

"I feel so guilty!" I sobbed.

Julie put her hand on my shoulder in a non-intrusive yet very supportive way, which made me cry even more. "Can you tell me a bit more about your guilt? Where does it come from?"

"I feel so guilty that I didn't love Florence when she was a baby," I gulped, almost choking from the tremendous force of old locked-in sadness that was finally being allowed to come out. "It was such a shocking birth I couldn't feel anything afterwards. I just had to be on autopilot to get through each day. And the days were so long it was like I was drowning."

Julie remained silent, yet completely with me, as I related the tale of the caesarean without enough anaesthetic, and how I was like a zombie afterwards, with no choice but to get on with being a mother. I sobbed and sobbed until there was no more sorrow left.

Then came stillness. Beautiful silence filled my usually noisy mind and allowed my breathing to settle into a balanced rhythm. Finally, peace bloomed within my heart.

"I'm not surprised you couldn't feel any emotion after that appalling birth experience," said Julie quietly. "But I would really like you to know that love is more than just a feeling. Love is an action. It's a giving of care to others without expecting anything in return. Did you get up in the night to feed your baby, even though you had a deep abdominal wound?"

"Yes!" I was a bit surprised by the question. James couldn't get up to help because he was working.

"Did you wash her, change her nappies and make sure she was warm, even when you were exhausted and feeling utterly depressed?"

"Yes, always, and I still always put her needs before mine."

"Don't you think that fulfils the criteria of love?"

That question hit me with a tremendous jolt. I thought about Julie's words very deeply for some time. Suddenly, something clicked in the depths of my consciousness and I realised I had always loved Florence, even though I had mistakenly believed that I hadn't.

Julie was right. Love is more than just a feeling – it's a *doing*. I sighed with deep relief and smiled.

"Now, my next question is, would you want your daughter to only be working and doing household chores? Or would you want her to enjoy some happy times too?" asked Julie.

"I'd definitely want her to have time to have fun," I replied.

"Exactly!" smiled Julie. "So don't you think you should have fun too? And don't you see that you are setting her an excellent example of how life should be? It should be a balance of work that you enjoy… and time to have fun. I bet your lovely mum feels very happy that you have the opportunity to spend time with horses."

"God, yes, you're right!" I laughed. "And yes, my mum loves hearing about my horse riding." I felt suddenly relieved of a huge burden and my mouth broadened into a big smile.

"A very wise hospice nurse once said to me, 'Julie, when you're lying on your deathbed, what will you regret more? Not doing all your household chores or not spending enough time doing what you love?' Food for thought, that, isn't it?" said Julie.

It really was food for thought and it made me realise I needed to stop feeling guilty and that, actually, I had been a very good mother after all. I also felt very glad that I now understood that it is vitally important to demonstrate to children how to have a balanced life as an adult.

Julie invited me to sit down on a chair and take a breather to recover from the enormous emotional release I'd just had. I sat with my eyes closed, just breathing quietly for a while.

Slowly, I began to feel more energised and I opened my eyes. I looked around the indoor arena with awe. I hadn't taken any notice of it at first but it was fantastic. It had been built in the style of an enormous Norwegian log chalet with a seating area down one of the long sides, and it had an adjoining toilet block and kitchen area for when they hosted events. I wished we had something similar at the yard.

After a while, Julie stood up and continued the session. "Now, as you can see, I'm now feeling very calm and I'm just enjoying walking around," she said. "I'm not putting any pressure on the ponies and I'm not asking anything from them but they are choosing to follow me."

The ponies were indeed following Julie even as she walked around and changed direction.

"Look closely," she said and she halted. The ponies, who were all in a line behind her, halted too. "Can you see there is a space between me and the leading pony, and a space between that pony and the next and so on?"

"Yes," I answered.

"That's because I've created an energy bubble round myself and they can feel it. They won't walk into my energy bubble unless I ask them to and they trust me as their leader. So they stop when I stop and walk when I walk because they know that that is what will keep them safe."

Julie started walking again and I noticed even more how the ponies remained the same distance apart and walked at the same speed as her.

"Your turn!"

Julie took me through a guided visualisation to help me create a bubble of energy round myself just like the horses instinctively have.

"Unfortunately, humans have lost touch with their energy auras. I think it's probably because we live so close to each other. We have automatically shrunk our auras in order to be able to sit next to people on a bus and so on. Yet we are all aware of how uncomfortable it is when people stand too close in a queue. So it's that sensation of personal space I'd like you to conjure up." She then invited me to go up to the ponies and take over leadership by being *myself*.

"You don't have to do anything. Just feel good about yourself and feel as if you are here to give them safety. You're not here to force them to do anything or bully them. You are here to give them a break from having to worry about predators. Just be the sort of person who you would feel happy to trust."

I walked up to the group of ponies and stopped at a distance to take a deep breath, relax and think about what sort of person I would choose to follow. I thought about the qualities of a good leader – calm, trustworthy, sensitive, kind, confident.

"Great, the ponies are listening to you. They're licking and chewing, their eyes are on you," said Julie quietly, as she backed away to the edge of the arena. "Now start walking wherever you want to go."

I walked round the arena and the ponies followed me. Not because I'd forced them to or bullied them, just because they chose to. It felt amazing. I stopped. They stopped. I walked, they walked. "Wow!" I said, almost in tears again.

"It's simple, isn't it?" smiled Julie. "And did you notice we didn't have to do any of that unnecessary *chasing the ponies away* like a lot of people believe they have to do for join-up?"

"Oh yes! I hadn't really thought about that. I've never felt comfortable doing any of that stuff. I've seen it done but never really understood why anyone would think that's a good thing to do."

(Join-up is a method usually performed in an arena or round pen. The human behaves the way a horse would towards a new horse entering the herd. This involves aggressively chasing the horse away and then eventually turning their back on the horse, and the horse follows. This is meant to create a bond.)

"Well, as you have just learned, it's completely pointless," said Julie. "In my humble opinion, I think it's more likely to create a barrier in your relationship because the horse will feel unsure of what you are going to do next. Traditional join-up creates stress in the horse and the horse only follows the human through fear not happiness. The way you have just done it is by simply demonstrating you are worth following."

I nodded in agreement.

"We can extend the use of energy in our training sessions with a horse. You told me that you have started to do some lunging with Poppy? Well, let's see how our energy intention can be used instead of traditional methods."

Marjorie collected two ponies and stood by the edge of the arena so that Julie could do a demonstration with one pony.

It was fascinating. She started with the pony on a long lunge line and asked him to walk on. Then she focused her intention, raised her energy by imagining that she was running, and he began to trot. She then breathed quietly and visualised walking and he walked. She then knelt down on one knee and he halted.

"All I'm doing is raising and lowering my energy and the pony is responding to me. He can literally feel my energy. Come and have a go!"

First, Julie guided me through a visualisation of feeling my own energy rise and fall the way it would if I was running or walking. It didn't take long before I was able to encourage the pony to start walking, move into trot, slow to a walk and then halt, simply by altering my own posture, energy and focus. It was a revelation and I much preferred it to the traditional method of shouting out *Trot on!* and flicking the whip at the horse's heels to make it speed up.

"Really focus on his bum and that will drive him forward! Now take a deep breath, drop one hip and think about grazing in a beautiful meadow. Really visualise it. There you go; look, he's slowing down! Now kneel on to one knee... and he's stopped! Excellent, well done!" Julie was a great teacher because she kept it simple.

"I think it's biscuit time!" called Marjorie and we all agreed that it was time for a break. The ponies were given hay nets and a few apples while we humans sat and ate home-made ginger biscuits, followed by goat's cheese sandwiches, which was a funny way round to eat.

Suddenly, there was a snuffling and scratching sound. The door swung open and in came Arnold with a teddy in his mouth.

"Aww, Arnold! Were you missing Mummy? Oh dear! You come and settle down and have some sandwiches." Marjorie, the ever-devoted mummy, greeted him with a cuddle and a plate of sandwiches. "Would you like a tummy scratch?" asked Marjorie, as Arnold rolled on to his side, prodding Marjorie with his snout. "He loves a tummy scratch after lunch, don't you, little man?"

Arnold was clearly in heaven as he rolled around on his back, snorting with pleasure while Marjorie scratched his furry belly. The ponies were too busy eating to be bothered by the presence of Arnold but it was very comical to watch him, especially with his teddy, which he really seemed to love.

The day was filled with amazing training from Julie. It was all so unexpected that I think I was probably in a bit of shock. I had never seen anyone interact with horses in this way before and it was mind-blowing. At one point, Julie had a group of ten ponies cantering around the whole arena. Just with her intention, she managed to take one pony out of the throng, change its direction and have it canter the opposite way to the others and then get it to re-join the herd.

"All I'm doing is focusing my full attention on this one pony and ignoring everything else. I'm bringing her out and that's helping her to feel confident. It's lifting her self-esteem. Now I'm putting her back so that the lesson is complete," called Julie from the middle of the arena. "Everything we do with horses must have a benefit for them. We are doing it *for* them, not *to* them. We are supporting them as good leaders."

Julie then helped me to learn how to help Poppy feel calm when being tied up for grooming. She taught me how to step out of the way and allow Poppy to have a *conversation* with the rope and learn how to work out for herself what she needed to do to release the pressure by walking towards the rope instead of pulling away.

It was an amazing lesson because, unknown to me, the pony

I was working with had literally arrived wild from the hills the day before. He was not used to humans, yet there I was merrily working with him and it didn't take long before he happily stood still and enjoyed being brushed. I was amazed when they told me he'd never been handled.

"We have taken away the horse's ability to think by being overly dominant and bossy. This makes an unsafe horse. By reminding them how to work out problems in their own mind, we allow them to feel confident so that if they are faced with a spooky situation they will think instead of reacting with fear," said Julie.

The day became evening almost without noticing. Isn't it funny how that always happens on the best days? We took the ponies back to the field and we all lay down on our backs among the dandelions and looked up at the endless sky, which was just beginning to turn pink.

Wow, what a day! I thought to myself, breathing in the sweet smell of the grass. I felt so different from how I'd been feeling ever since becoming a mum. I felt alive, awake and more capable of actually *being* a mum.

Although I'd improved thanks to Lucy, I was still quite negative about my ability in that department and I often compared myself to other, more natural mothers. The session with the ponies made me realise that being a good mum was about being a good leader. I just needed to relax, be calm and be fun. I felt so eager to learn more about the nature of the horse as a being in its own right, not just a fun thing to ride around on. How had I never noticed the energy element of horses? How had I not seen how they interact with each other in total silence yet with such ability to move others around without force and without even touching? And how could I relate that to all areas of my life? What sort of energy do I give off to other people? My mind was exploding with new thoughts and so many millions of questions.

"Who's hungry?" asked Marjorie, breaking the silence. "I'm famished! Let's go and eat."

Dinner was excellent once again, as Marjorie had made the best vegetable flan the world has ever known. We were joined, of course, by Arnold, who jumped up and sat on a chair at the kitchen table.

"Oh dear, Arnold, we have guests – must you really sit here?" asked Marjorie, looking a little bit flustered.

"I don't mind – it's quite funny!" I laughed.

"Oh, jolly good. He is such a dear little fellow, isn't he? Now do eat nicely, Arnold. Try not to make too much of a mess." Marjorie tied a pretty floral bib round his neck and gave him a massive slice of flan and a ladle of home-made baked beans with a sprinkling of parmesan, which he hoovered up in about three seconds.

I suddenly realised that I still hadn't learned anything about the bitless bridle, which was actually the reason why I'd gone there in the first place. I mentioned it, as I was anxious to learn all about it.

"Ah yes, don't worry about that. All will be revealed tomorrow. We have a very interesting day planned for you!" said Marjorie.

After dinner, I had a wonderful hot bath with strawberry-scented bubbles, in a peculiar-shaped bathtub that was in a sort of shed next to the cottage. It was so bizarre because from the outside, the building appeared very shabby, the sort where you'd store old bits of machinery. But inside, it was beautifully decorated and had underfloor heating and plush towels all folded neatly in a pretty wicker basket. The soothing water calmed my busy mind and I could feel my subconscious absorbing the lessons of the day.

Chapter 24

It was my last day in Wales. I was awoken by a strange scratching sound, followed by a loud crash as the curtains, separating the conservatory from the living room, fell down. I leaped out of bed in shock. Furious squealing sounds emanated from a large lump underneath the curtains and I breathed a sigh of relief as I realised it was Arnold and not a murderer.

"Arnold, you big idiot!" I laughed, as I rescued him from suffocation under the swathes of material. "I don't think your mother is going to be impressed with this!"

"What's happened? What's happened?" yelled Marjorie, flying into the living room, wringing her hands. "Oh dear! Are you OK?"

"Yes! It's just Arnold!" I grinned.

"Arnold! What are you doing? Oh dear, are you hurt?" Marjorie checked Arnold all over and luckily, he was fine. "Come along and have breakfast and we'll sort the curtains out later."

I noticed that Marjorie looked like she was wearing the curtains. In fact, on closer inspection (when she had her back to me, of course) it was clear that this particular pair of dungarees were indeed made of the same floral material as the curtains and they had at least six pockets.

Breakfast was amazing. Home-made bread (from the oven, not a bread-maker) with home-made goat's cheese and home-made strawberry jam. It sounds like a weird combination but it was delicious beyond description.

"So today is your last day and we shall be teaching you all

about the bitless bridle!" said Marjorie enthusiastically. "You run along and get ready and Julie will probably be here by the time you're back."

I trotted off to the inside bathroom, which was in such a tiny room you had to bend over to move around in it as the ceiling was so low – and I am by no means tall. I hastily dressed and then dashed back to the kitchen to find Julie having a cup of spicy tea.

"Morning!" she greeted "Let's get cracking!"

We went into a large glorified shed that was decked out like a classroom with a desk and some chairs. On the desk were some examples of really extreme bits that Julie had found in various foreign countries. They were nasty and sharp and it was horrible to imagine the pain those horses must have suffered while wearing them.

"Now, before we start talking about the Dr Cook humane bitless bridle, I'd like you to put this in your mouth," said Marjorie, handing me a dessert spoon.

She asked me to put the handle, widthways, into my mouth. It was very peculiar. Julie then launched into a speech about bits but I couldn't really focus on what she was saying because the spoon felt so weird and I couldn't stop salivating. I had to keep swallowing and wiping my chin with the back of my hand, which was really grim.

"...and that's why we personally prefer to use a bitless bridle," said Julie as she concluded her speech and signalled for me to take the spoon out of my mouth. "Any questions?"

"Er... well, actually, I couldn't really follow most of that," I said. "I couldn't think about anything except the spoon, and my mouth just kept filling up with saliva!"

"Exactly! Now you know how hard it is for a horse to listen when it's got a piece of metal in its mouth! Having anything in the mouth triggers the digestive system to get ready for the arrival of some food because the salivary glands are being constantly stimulated. It's much easier for a horse to concentrate without the distraction of the bit."

"I'd never thought about that before," I replied, deep in thought about what I had just experienced. "I just noticed that Poppy hated opening her mouth for it – that's why I thought I would try her bitless. It really makes sense though."

We went outside and Marjorie collected a small black horse to demonstrate the fitting of the Dr Cook bitless bridle. She showed me how to test that it was all in the right place on the horse's face and then demonstrated how it worked. It was so simple yet so effective. Two straps crossed from the side of the face to underneath the face, which exerted a pushing pressure when the reins were pulled. So, if you pulled the right rein you effectively pushed on the left side of the head and the horse would turn to the right and vice versa. The pressure was in a large area so it didn't cause pain, it literally just pushed the head round. Pulling back on both reins put pressure on the whole head and brought the head down for slowing and stopping.

"OK – get your hat on and let's do some riding!" said Julie, and we went into the indoor arena.

The horse was called Flora. She was a lovely black cob, my favourite type of ride, and I felt very safe and familiar once on board. However, like a lot of little cobs, she was in no hurry to go anywhere and it was rather comical to experience such a sluggish horse after having ridden super-speedy Poppy for the past couple of months. I did everything I could to get her going but all she did was amble along for a few steps and then she stopped to give her leg a bit of a scratch.

"She's so slow! I'd forgotten how it feels to ride a horse like this!" I wailed in a slightly pathetic manner.

"Over to you, Julie!" grinned Marjorie.

Marjorie sat down on the mounting block and fished around in one of her many pockets for a biscuit.

"Riding a lazy horse can be a bit irritating, can't it?" Julie smiled.

"Yes, very!" I replied, feeling more than a little frustrated.

"And when we feel that irritation," continued Julie, in her lovely non-judgemental, relaxed manner, "our body generally tenses up and we begin to feel like a big heavy clamp from the horse's point of view. This is basically telling the horse to stop moving." Julie came over and pointed out the tension in my arms and legs.

"Oh blimey!" I said. "I'd never realised!"

"Also, what we tend to do when we feel this irritation is to inadvertently look down at the horse's neck as if we are having a conversation with it. We look at the back of their neck or head and say, 'Come on, get moving!' completely forgetting that horses use body language more than spoken words, and in that moment, our body language is rooting them to the spot."

"Because we're looking down?" I asked, as I slowly awoke to a different way of understanding things.

"Yes, exactly! We are looking down and focusing all our attention there, so that's where the horse stays. And even if you look ahead, but feel irritated, you will find that the tension in your body is in a downward motion that will also keep the horse either standing or moving very slowly as it desperately tries to interpret your mixed messages. We rarely notice how much our horses *try* for us."

"Oh my God! I didn't realise any of this but it's so obvious now!" I was stunned.

"Let's take a deep breath and relax your body," said Julie, and she did a basic visualisation to help me let go of tension.

"So, sitting as quietly as you can, keep your legs relaxed and still. I'd like you to look over to the other end of the school and feel that you need to go there. Really focus on that spot and imagine it's very important to get there! Visualise yourself walking very fast over to the wall!"

I looked over to where Julie had suggested and conjured up a desire to go there. Flora lifted her head and started walking.

"Great! Now without using any leg aids, feel as if you need to get there faster! Quick! Your life depends on it!" called Julie.

I visualised myself walking really fast. Flora picked up the pace.

"Excellent! Now, keeping your hands nice and still, turn your head to look over to your right. Focus on walking towards that cone over there in the corner!" said Julie, gesturing to a cone in the corner of the arena.

Keeping my hands and legs relaxed, I looked over to the cone and really focused on it. Amazingly, without even using the reins or my legs, Flora turned and walked to the cone.

"You see, horses are basically doing tai chi all the time! She's feeling your energy and she's going to where you are sending your energy."

It really was the most fantastic experience. Flora walked where I asked her to walk but I didn't use my voice or my hands or my legs, I just used my intention. For a scatty person such as myself, it was a revelation. I am rarely focused. My mind is usually in several locations all at the same time but Julie taught me how to be aware of how my thoughts were affecting the horse. It was very grounding. For the first time in my life, I felt present. I also became aware that my general sensation of low-level background worry had dissolved.

"OK. Now I want you to come down the centre of the school and halt. Just visualise halting," said Julie.

Incredibly, it worked. Flora halted. "Wow!" I said. "I don't know what else to say except *wow*!"

"It's great, isn't it?" laughed Julie. "If you lived nearby we'd be able to build up to riding with no tack and even jumping with no tack but at least you've got the basics to take home with you."

"Yes! With Poppy it will be the opposite, though. I'll have to imagine her walking very slowly!"

"A good way to do that is by counting *one, two, three, four* very slowly over and over in your mind and eventually you'll notice her feet fall in time. Let me know how you get on!" smiled Julie.

I untacked Flora and gave her a big kiss and then all three of us walked her back to her beautiful meadow. It was the most perfect place for a horse to live with the most indescribably stunning views of mountains in the distance. My eyes drank in the scenery and I stood quietly for a while with no thoughts in my mind, simply being with nature. I watched the alpacas wandering about, grazing, the goats lying in the sun – and there was the peacock treating me to another display of his fabulous feathers.

After a tearful goodbye, it was time to load up the car with Poppy's new bridle, a lovely green rope halter and a few lunge ropes of different lengths. Arnold gave me lots of snuffly kisses and

Marjorie gave me a home-made wicker basket full of wonderful food for my journey home. She really was the best cook ever.

I drove away feeling like a very different person. I felt calm and confident. I didn't even feel remotely flustered when I took a wrong turning and ended up at the end of a very narrow dirt track. Usually, that kind of thing would induce a lot of stress but I just laughed and reversed. I was amazed by my reaction and sang loudly all the way home. What struck me the most was the realisation of being present in the moment. It had felt so comfortable to be focused in that moment when I was riding Flora, I wanted to be able to be similar in everything I did.

Chapter 25

I had a very busy work diary the next few days so I didn't have much of an opportunity to practise anything with Poppy. It was a bit frustrating but such is life. Finally, there was a quiet day so, after a pleasant walk with the dog, I drove to the yard full of enthusiasm. My plan was to try the energy-lunging I'd learned in Wales before the farrier arrived. However, it seemed fate had decided it was the day I should meet Brenda instead.

She was standing by the gate with Jack and Sally, looking rather mournful. Brenda had dreamed of having a pony ever since she was a child. "They take a lot of looking after!" her parents had told her and promptly enrolled her into a ballet class in the hope that she would forget about ponies. Unfortunately, this was the reason why, as an adult, Brenda thought it would be a great idea to buy two untrained Fell ponies straight off the moor...

"I thought I'd train them at the same time as learning to ride," explained Brenda, twiddling her hair apologetically. "I didn't realise it would be so difficult! I thought it would only take a few weeks."

"Are you serious?" I asked, laughing, and then quickly stopped when I realised that Brenda was deadly serious and looked like she was about to cry.

"Well, it's not going to help whingeing about it now. The farrier's on his way and those ponies need their feet trimming – they're in a right state," said the ever-practical Jack, leaning over the gate and chewing on a long stalk of grass. "How on earth are you going to catch the buggers?" she mused.

"It's not going to be easy," said Sally, shaking her head.

Brenda wrung her hands, clearly very stressed. "I don't know how to catch them any more! It's been so long since I did anything with them. They've gone a bit wild!"

"Yes, they are a bit wild." I grimaced.

"A bit wild? That's an understatement! They are dangerous and you should be ashamed of yourself, you stupid woman!" scolded Louise, who had suddenly appeared behind us. Of course she was right but she didn't need to be so nasty to poor Brenda, who was obviously just a bit dim.

"Well, as you are such an experienced horse owner I'm sure that you will know exactly how to catch them!" said Sally with a gleam in her eye.

"Ha!" scoffed Louise. "Of course I do but Brenda needs to take responsibility and work it out for herself." She tossed her perfect hair and flounced away. As ever, Louise was dressed immaculately in speck-less white breeches and a floral silk blouse that made the rest of us look like Compo from *Last of the Summer Wine*.

"Silly cow," muttered Jack.

"Have you not got those ponies yet, Brenda, love? Oh dear. You know I'm very sorry but I will have to call the RSPCA if you don't get their feet sorted out this time. I don't like to make a fuss, as you know, Brenda, love." The mysterious yard manager had finally made an appearance.

I stood back to get a good look at the very softly spoken man. He was around the age of sixty. Thick, wiry grey hair framed a round face with watery blue eyes and red cheeks and he was very tall and lanky. He seemed about as effective as a wet flannel.

"I've been asking you for months to deal with their feet and you've not bothered to even reply. I'm very disappointed, Brenda, love, really I am!" he continued, all the while buttoning and unbuttoning his cardigan.

"I'm so sorry, Bob!" replied Brenda. "I've just been so busy with work and kids."

"I'm sorry to have to be cross, Brenda, but it's gone on a bit too long," said Bob, shuffling his feet and still messing with his cardigan.

Jack rolled her eyes and I bit my hand to stop myself from laughing. I had never heard such a feeble telling-off in all my life. No wonder those ponies had been allowed to cause such chaos for so long.

"The farrier's here!" announced a very brisk voice that made us all jump.

"Oh! Right. Well, Brenda, dear, you'd better get those ponies," said the yard manager and then he oozed away.

"Hello, I'm Morag! You must be Grace?" Morag, who had a wonderful crisp Scottish accent, shook my hand vigorously. "Brenda, you need to bring your ponies in now."

Morag was a short and stocky woman in her early fifties. She was also ex-army and a keen bagpipe player. Her voice had a thunderous, commanding tone that had the effect of making everyone stand up very straight. It was most amusing to observe.

"I don't really know how to catch them, Morag," quivered Brenda.

"Oh, Brenda! Really, this is ridiculous! Right. We need a sensible plan – where is Danny? Oh, there he is. Danny! Come here immediately, please!" Morag's foghorn voice bellowed over to the most drop-dead gorgeous man who was walking towards us from the stable block.

"Oh my God! Who is *he*?" I hissed at Sally.

"That's Danny! He owns Boudicca, the big bay horse," whispered Sally.

"Wow! He rides here? He's gorgeous!" I whispered back.

"He's gay!" She smirked.

"Oh, *no way!*" I couldn't believe it. He was so *masculine*, for want of a better word. Tall, dark and ruggedly handsome with fabulously broad shoulders and a rough beard, he was textbook gorgeous.

"Yes, good job really. Haha!" laughed Sally.

"Ladies, really! We have a job to do!" said Morag, giving us a withering look.

I didn't like the sound of the word *we*. Why did *we* have to be involved in this situation? I had arrived at the yard, eager to start practising all I had learned in Wales before the farrier arrived. It would be my first experience having Poppy shod and I was anxious to do some connection work, hopefully to avoid her kicking his head in. The owner had warned me that Poppy was not a fan of having her feet done and had only ever been cold-shod – whatever that was – so I was extremely irritated to be pulled into someone else's drama on this day of all days.

"Hello, girls!" greeted the delicious Danny with a flashing smile.

"Hello!" I replied. Fortunately, I managed to stop myself from saying, *I'm gutted you prefer men but actually it's a good job because I'm married* – which was what I was thinking.

Danny started chatting with Morag about the ponies. His voice was deep and very intoxicating.

"I know what you're thinking!" whispered Sally and laughed like a drain.

Morag shot her a look that immediately stopped that bit of banter.

"Right, everybody! We need to decide who is going to go where and what roles we will all take on," said the super-efficient Morag with her hands on her hips and a businesslike stance.

"OK," we all muttered. None of us dared to say otherwise. Even Jack, who would normally have a lot to say, silently waited for instructions.

"Now, Danny and Jack, you go and get that trailer over there and wheel it up here. I will stand on it and shout instructions."

We all looked over to the barn where there was a large trailer parked by the side of it. Danny and Jack pulled it up to the gate and Morag clambered on.

"Right! Now then—"

"Look, it's obvious what we need to do," interrupted Jack finally. She had a good brain for problem-solving and was clearly irritated by Morag. "We need to collect the other ponies and put them in the school and then herd the two nutters down here, get them cornered and get head collars on them. Then someone needs to get a dart gun and put all of us out of our misery!"

Sally and I guffawed with laughter.

"That's not helpful, is it?" said Morag, glaring at us. She was terribly serious. "OK, Jack, that's a good idea. Apart from the dart gun, of course."

"She might have a point, though," Danny interjected. "They are totally nuts and probably need sedating or no farrier will ever come here again if these two kick the crap out of him."

Danny's words made me feel a bit sick as I wondered what Poppy was going to do to the farrier, and I wished that her owner was here instead of me. However, I kept my anxieties to myself.

"I think that once they are caught they'll settle down," said Morag very hopefully. "It's not as if they've never seen a farrier before."

The three non-feral ponies were easily caught and moved into the school while the two Fells stood watching suspiciously from afar. It was obvious they knew we had plans to capture them and they were having none of it. Honest to God, it was the most ridiculous charade I've ever been involved with in all my life. What started with military precision ended up as a terrible version of *One Man and His Dog* in a Carry-On film style. Morag gave us all places to stand and from her position on the trailer she shouted instructions to each of us, with no need for a megaphone.

"Grace, move forward!"

"Danny, close in on your right!"

"Jack, run to the left! No! The *left*! That's the right!"

"God give me strength!"

"Brenda! What are you doing? Get off your phone!"

Just at the crucial point where we almost had the ponies contained and moving towards the gate, Brenda got a phone call... and she answered it.

"For fuck's sake, Brenda, what are you doing?" shouted Jack, who had lost the will to live.

"Oh, I'm so sorry! It's my mum. She wants to know how it's going!" replied Brenda, looking embarrassed.

"Well, it's not going so great now, is it, you idiot!" Jack retorted as the ponies, spotting the chance of escape, galloped back to the top of the field.

The whole performance began again and the wild-eyed Fells gave us all a good run for our money. This time they bucked and farted and lashed out at us with their back legs. It was really scary and they had us flying in all directions to get out of their way.

"*No! No!* Go the other way, Grace, for goodness' sake, lass!" yelled Morag.

"Danny, watch out for your head!"

"Sally! *Sally!* What are you doing, woman? Get out of the way! You're going to get kicked! Oh my God!"

"Brenda! Why are you just standing there? These are *your* ponies! Oh no, now they've escaped again!"

We were all out of breath and almost collapsing, when Louise turned up with two giant buckets full of food. She stood at the gate shaking the buckets and, of course, the two ponies trotted up to her like butter wouldn't melt in their mouths. They shoved their heads into the buckets and began eating very noisily. Louise then put head collars on them with no problems whatsoever and with a smug expression said, "Well, that's that sorted. Brenda, would you like to take them to the farrier? He's ready for you now."

Morag jumped down from the trailer and took hold of the lead ropes and handed the calm ponies to Brenda. Brenda and the ponies walked towards the stable yard as if it was something they did every day.

"Oh well! Thank you, Louise!" said the very flustered Morag.

"No problem!" said Louise sweetly, tossing her hair again and walking off towards the stables.

Why we hadn't thought of doing that ourselves is beyond me. With hindsight it was such an obvious thing to do. Sally laughed her head off as she had a tremendous capacity to see the funny side in everything, even if it included laughing at herself.

Jack, on the other hand, was not amused. "I can't stand that woman!" she fumed and stormed off to get Buddy.

The rest of us just plopped on to the ground, exhausted, and said things like, "Oh yes! We should have tried that first!"

We all waited with baited breath, expecting to hear all sorts of curses and yells emanating from the indoor stable barn. Nothing. Not a sound emerged.

"Do you think they're all dead?" asked Sally.

"Maybe you should go and take a look?" suggested Morag.

"No way! I'm not going down there! Danny, you go!" said Sally.

"No chance! I'm sick to death of those ponies. But, yeah, actually, you've got a point. Why is it so quiet?"

The silence was eerie and we were just about to go down as a group when out of the barn came the two little menaces. They were walking very nicely. We all stood, open-mouthed with surprise.

"What the hell?" said Danny, stunned. "How did that happen?"

As it turned out, green-haired Alex had arrived, armed with dried chamomile and valerian herbs in a feed that she had prepared for the two ponies. These herbs had completely relaxed them enough to allow the farrier to do his job without any injury.

"Bloody hell!" exclaimed Sally. "I always thought Alex was just a bit mad but that's amazing!"

Alex looked very pleased with herself and rightly so. The ponies, slightly sore-footed, wandered back into the field and then galloped off to the tree at the top, where they stood, giving us all dirty looks. And now it was the dreaded moment where I had to catch Poppy and take her to the farrier and hope to God that she would stand nicely. It seemed like a hopeless proposition but I remembered Julie's wise words.

I stopped at the gate, took some deep breaths and made sure

I was relaxed and not thinking about all the other jobs I had to do at home. Then I walked into the field and totally ignored Poppy and stood very calmly looking at the other horses. I really focused on being present and allowed my breathing to be calm and rhythmical. After a few moments, I wandered slowly over to her and opened my heart to allow some sort of nice feeling to emanate from me instead of the usual mix of fear, stress and anxiety.

"Would you like some new shoes?" I asked Poppy, almost as if I wasn't bothered if she came to me or not.

OK, yes. Why not? she quite possibly replied, as she walked over to me to scratch her head on my shoulder.

I quietly put the head collar on and scratched her head, feeling as if we had all the time in the world. Then I had the bright idea of walking round the field for a few minutes, just to connect and relax together. It was very pleasant, especially after the mad experience I'd just had chasing the two wild ponies. Poppy walked with me towards the stables more relaxed than I'd ever known her to be, and when she was tied at the bar she danced around fifty per cent less than normal, which was a lot better than I had expected.

"She's not my horse! And her owner said she's only ever been cold-shod because she's got sensitive feet. And she can be really nervy so you might want to get your dog out of the way in case she kicks him!" I said, all in an anxious jumble, to the farrier.

I was terrified of what Poppy might do to his dog that was running around dangerously close to her back end.

"Well, let's have a go with some heat and see how she is. She'll be fine – don't worry," he replied, doing nothing at all to remove his dog, who began sniffing Poppy's belly. Luckily, she didn't kill him.

The farrier turned out to be a very lovely guy. He talked to Poppy very gently and gave her a scratch and with no fuss at all she let him shoe her as if she'd known him forever. I couldn't believe it. I almost cried from the relief as it was the total opposite of what her owner said she would be like.

"I've got the gift!" said the farrier, straightening up and stretching his back. "I know how to treat the ladies – that's why they all love me!"

I laughed my head off.

"It's true!" he replied, giving me a cheeky wink.

I didn't really know what to say to that but I didn't care. I was just so relieved. I walked Poppy back to the field, feeling confident and relaxed. I was a bit disappointed that I'd not had a chance to practise the lunging but I felt positive because it had gone so well with the farrier.

I drove off to collect Florence from school, feeling much more mellow than I usually did. "Be in the moment and be a good leader!" I reminded myself.

Instead of feeling irritable and thinking about various jobs I had to do, I greeted Florence with a relaxed, open heart, just like I had with Poppy. I listened with full attention to all her crazy chatter and we had a lovely afternoon together.

The food shopping was much more enjoyable than usual as I involved Florence with decision-making. It was interesting to see her learning how to think and choose the right things. It was like letting the horses learn how to think. Her behaviour was much better for it too.

Chapter 26

Finally, a window of opportunity opened for me to practise using the new bitless bridle I had bought in Wales. The yard was quiet and the only sound in the air was that of a tractor on the neighbouring farm. Peace at last. I was too self-conscious to attempt to try Poppy with a new bridle in front of anyone in case it all went horribly wrong and they all thought I was an idiot. Looking back, I don't know why I was so bothered about other people's opinions but several people at that yard were successful competition types. I was a mere 'happy hacker' so I felt a little inferior when they were around.

The two annoying Fell ponies were busy sleeping in the sunshine so the walk up to the horse field was, pleasantly, without incident. I had a loaded water gun with me, though, just in case. I felt very enthusiastic as I walked into the field to get Poppy and she must have sensed it because she stopped grazing and watched me with her ears forward, looking interested. Poppy stood very still as I walked to her shoulder and I told her about her new bridle.

"Let's go and try it while no one is around!" I said eagerly and she really looked as if she replied with *OK!* because she actually lowered her head for me to put her head collar on, which was a first.

Water gun at the ready, we slipped into the dreaded pony field and I closed the gate as quietly as I could. Which, of course, wasn't quiet at all because it was metal and made a very loud clanging sound. Why there wasn't a fence to keep the ponies off the path was beyond comprehension. Unfortunately, the two menaces woke up and decided to behave like idiots once again. They came careering over, snorting and bucking but I was armed and ready.

"Take that, you little gits!" I shouted as I squeezed the trigger and a fountain of water jetted out at them.

I wasn't expecting their reaction. They stopped and actually appeared to enjoy it. So I sprayed them again and they turned round as if to say, *Do this side!* It was very amusing. Poppy seemed amused too because for once she stood quietly and just watched.

"I'm afraid that's your lot!" I said, as the water ran out. And can you believe it, the two ponies just began cropping the grass quietly.

"Well! I think you two just pretend to be wild when it suits you!" I said to them, as Poppy and I walked off.

There was not a soul in the barn as I tied Poppy at the bar for grooming. This was great because it gave me the opportunity to try out what Julie had taught me, about allowing Poppy to learn self-release. As usual, Poppy was dancing around, pulling back on the rope. I took a deep breath and switched the lead rope to the much longer, smooth, tubular rope I'd bought in Wales. A flat lunge rope or ordinary lead rope would not work for this technique as they don't release fast enough.

Usually we tie horses by threading the lead rope through a loop of string that is tied to a metal ring, for safety reasons. If the horse panics, it can snap the string and run without hurting itself. For this method, though, I needed to thread the rope through the metal ring and put some slight pressure on. This can be dangerous and should only be done with the correct equipment and with a thorough knowledge of the technique.

I made a conscious effort to remove my *energy* and my *self* from Poppy and her stress. Julie had taught me to *reward the try*, so I had to be very aware of the exact moment when Poppy thought about how to free herself from tension. As soon as Poppy's face appeared to think, she stopped pulling back and I instantly released the rope.

I gently took up the slack again and Poppy felt the pressure of the rope. Again, she pulled back and I watched keenly to ensure I released the pressure the moment she thought about not pulling. The third time, she didn't pull back, she took a teeny tiny step forward. I instantly released the rope but continued to keep myself out of Poppy's *conversation with the situation*.

I waited a few moments then, once again, I took up the slack and felt the tension in the rope. Poppy took a smooth step forward towards the bar as I simultaneously released the rope and, therefore, the pressure. She'd got it. Poppy had used her own thought processes to work out what she needed to do to make herself feel comfortable, and in a very short space of time too.

"Wow! Well done! Clever girl!" I said, shedding a few tears of *mother's pride*.

Poppy had a very pleased expression on her face that was so lovely to see and she stood very happily for a change. She still moved about a bit but nothing like the crazy dancing and pulling that she usually did. Grooming was so much easier as I didn't have to keep moving the grooming kit out of the way of her massive feet. I put her saddle on. She still nipped my leg but it was a half-hearted attempt, more like a habit than any real need to express herself. And then we headed for the outdoor school.

We began by walking around together as Elise had suggested

and I made a conscious effort to be more self-aware. I focused on where I wanted to go and what speed I wanted to walk at and Poppy responded very well, so we were in harmony, as it were.

"Right, Pops, it's now or never," I said, as I slipped the reins over her head and removed the head collar. "Welcome to your new bridle! I hope you like it."

I opened up the bridle and pulled it over Poppy's ears. A look of surprise filtered into her eyes as it began to dawn on her that nothing had gone into her mouth. Poppy breathed a deep sigh of relief and happily stood quietly as I faffed about getting all the straps the correct length so the bridle sat properly on her absolutely giant head. The bridle was extra-large and even then it only just fitted her.

I wished I'd videoed her initial response to the bitless bridle. Her loud sigh said it all. Once on board she walked very nicely, in a forward yet relaxed manner. She was alert and listening for instruction. I tried a few turns using the reins just to check that it did work – and it did. Then I tried a halt and that also worked. Then I decided to have a go at using my energy to direct Poppy, instead of relying on hands and legs. However, the gate clanged in the next field, which startled me, and I looked round to see that gorgeous Danny was in the jumping field with his eye-catching bay sports horse, Boudicca.

Danny rode round the field a few times and smiled shyly as he passed. He really was fabulously good-looking in his faded, boot-cut jeans and a tight T-shirt that showed off his wonderfully muscular chest. He was also a very efficient rider and it was a real treat to watch him and Boudicca fly over the jumps with such wonderful balance and timing. Unlike a lot of thoughtless showjumpers, Danny didn't fly out of the saddle and bang back down again on to her back. He merely leaned forward and stayed glued to the saddle. It was so impressive. He had clearly spent a lot of time working on his own core strength in order to jump as smoothly as that.

Danny trotted and walked Boudicca to cool her down and came over to say hello. Unfortunately, just as I opened my mouth to reply, the unmistakable foghorn voice of Morag hit us both at full whack.

"Ahoy there, you people!" she called with a cheery wave. "How about a group ride out in this lovely weather?"

As I mentioned previously, Morag had the type of commanding voice that was almost impossible to disobey. I can only put it down to her years in the tough Scottish army. I wanted to say, *No, thanks! I am really keen to continue with some schooling*, but when I opened my mouth I found myself saying, "OK!"

Damn, why did I say that? I thought to myself, but it was too late.

Danny and I dismounted and led our horses over to the stable yard where Morag was busy instructing a youngish woman, named Noor, how to fasten her girth. I'm sure Noor probably had a fair idea how to fasten a girth as I had seen her before at the Otley show, winning a jumping competition, so she was certainly not a novice rider.

"It's always best to hold the strap upwards instead of at an angle and then it's more comfortable for the horse, you see?" said Morag in her forthright way.

"Er... yes. Thank you, Morag!" answered Noor in a resigned sort of a way.

"Right, everybody! It's a super day to go out and get to know each other better!"

Morag was very enthusiastic, which began to rub off on me. It is always nice to get to

know the people you are sharing a livery yard with and I was grateful to Morag for making the effort to include me. Morag introduced me to Noor, who had a lovely skewbald horse named Jigsaw.

"Now then, do we all have hi-vis? Grace, have you got hi-vis? Noor?"

I went to get my pink hi-vis tabard while Noor went to get her yellow hatband.

"*Tch tch tch*," tutted Morag. "Is that all you have? That won't do at all. Danny, where's your hi-vis?"

Danny smirked – he was used to Morag and didn't seem to mind being chivvied along by her. Morag marched us all to her stable's back room in which there were dozens of high-vis garments of all shapes, sizes and colours. It was like an Aladdin's cave of safety wear.

"Here you are, Danny, you can wear this," came the muffled voice of Morag as she bent over, rooting through a box. Morag stood up and handed him a neon-pink T-shirt.

"Grace, here's a hat cover for you," she announced, handing me a terrible, large plastic, fluorescent yellow thing. It was like a giant, Day-Glo shower cap. Danny laughed but I was too shocked to say anything.

"It's no laughing matter, Danny. We must all be as visible as possible or our insurance is null and void! Here, Grace, let me put it on for you." Morag stretched the ghastly cap over my riding hat and I was so stunned all I could do was mutter, "Thank you!" through gritted teeth.

"Here's an orange hatband for you, Danny. Oh, and Noor, you can wear this green waistcoat." Noor's face was a picture of horror but she obediently put the green waistcoat on as she daren't do otherwise.

"Now let's get the horses properly attired." Morag marched towards the horses, carrying an assortment of brightly coloured items. In no time at all, Morag had all four horses covered in colourful neck straps, tail straps and leg wraps. They all stood stock-still while this was going on as they too daren't argue with Morag.

"Right! I think we're all ready, so let's mount up and away we go! Come along, everyone!" Morag was unstoppable and we all silently obeyed – it was very comical. We rode out of the yard in our multicoloured, fluorescent outfits that I feared would probably make us more dangerous than ever. Surely it would dazzle car drivers and stun them completely?

However, I soon forgot about what a prat I looked when I realised we had suddenly arrived at the entrance to a massive open field. My veins turned to ice – as they say in horror novels. This was my biggest fear right here in front of my face.

"I've never ridden on an open field with Poppy!" I squeaked.

"Well, it's an opportune moment to get the experience now!" replied Morag enthusiastically.

I felt sick. I also felt really, really inferior and embarrassed. Danny, Morag and Noor were such competent riders. All of them did regular showjumping and cross-country competitions so in comparison to them, I felt like a beginner. It was such a horrible, uncomfortable feeling. I gripped tightly on the reins and my legs were like clamps round Poppy's sides. Everything I was doing was the polar opposite of what Julie had taught me but in that moment of colossal fear, all I could think of was, *Help! I am on a super-fast horse that could bolt at any second!* The worst of it was I didn't feel able to speak up because I hardly knew these people.

"We'll just walk," said Danny, who had noticed my ashen face.

"Yes, good idea, Danny!" agreed Morag. "Let's walk round the whole field twice so that Grace and Poppy can get the most out of the experience!"

I was horrified. Instead of taking a direct route straight across the edge of the field, Morag guided us all round the entire perimeter – twice. My heart was in my mouth – I could literally feel it beating in my throat. And I couldn't understand how Danny and Morag, who were both in front of me, were so chilled out about it. Both of their horses were very full on, jogging sideways and snorting the entire time and it was really stressing me out. I was certain that their jogging and snorting would wind Poppy up and make her explode like a rocket into the next county.

However, just as we approached the final edge of the field, it dawned on me that Poppy was not stressed out. She was not remotely affected by Boudicca or Morag's striking grey horse. Poppy was ignoring them and was walking very steadily. She was even ignoring me and my fearful body language. I relaxed my legs and my hands. Poppy sighed, no doubt thinking, *Thank God for that. What on earth is your problem?* and she continued to walk, like a chilled-out cob, across the field behind the two very joggy horses.

Wow! I thought to myself as I realised how wrong my thoughts had been. I was stunned by how relaxed Poppy was, not to mention relieved. She had taken control of the situation and had sensibly realised there was nothing to fear so she just walked. I could only put it down to her own renewed self-confidence following the self-release experience. She had learned how to think for herself. It really was truly remarkable.

We arrived in the village and trotted along some very pretty lanes. I was feeling much happier and more relaxed so I enjoyed having a nosey at all the quaint cottages. Then slowly, I became aware of Noor, who was riding behind me. In all of my anxiety on the field, I had completely forgotten that she was with us. But suddenly I could hear her taking a few sharp breaths. I turned round and saw that she looked terrified.

"Are you OK?" I asked, surprised.

"No! I need to get off!" she wailed.

"Oh no! Are you not feeling well? I'll tell the others to wait." I called out to Danny and Morag to stop.

"I need to get off!" repeated Noor.

"Oh no, Noor, not again! Come on now, you're doing so well!" exclaimed Morag, turning her horse and coming over to stand by Noor.

"What's wrong?" I asked, completely confused.

"Noor is terrified of hacking," said Morag "which is why I thought it would be great if we all rode out together!"

I couldn't believe my ears. Noor, a fearless showjumper who went to so many competitions, was scared of hacking? My feelings of inferiority instantly melted away along with all the paranoid thoughts that had been buzzing around my head the entire ride, such as *I'm such a rubbish rider compared to these people.* Poor Noor. I felt very sympathetic as she attempted to slither off her horse. Morag went alongside her and blocked her from getting off.

"Now come on, Noor! Remember you asked me not to let you get off? So I'm not going to let you!"

"But I have to get off! I feel sick!" replied poor Noor, her face growing paler by the second.

"No, you don't!" I said firmly, suddenly remembering the duck-pond ride where Mel had been very nervous. "You're going to stay on and we are all going to sing as we walk slowly along."

"Sing?" exclaimed Noor, looking at me as if I'd gone mad.

"Yes, sing! All of us!" I repeated. "OK, let's get going."

"The wheels on the bus go round and round!" I sang loudly. "Come on, everybody!"

"Round and round! Round and round!" sang Morag and Danny, grinning.

"Come on, Noor! You too!" I insisted.

Noor joined in and we all began to walk very steadily down the lane, all of us singing 'The Wheels on the Bus'. Very soon, Noor forgot her fears and sang louder. We got some funny looks from passers-by, what with the excessive, multicoloured hi-vis clothing and singing a children's song, but it worked. Noor stayed on all the way home.

"We made it! Well done, everybody!" laughed Morag, as we clattered into the yard.

"Thanks for helping me, everyone," said Noor very humbly. "I wouldn't have managed without you all."

"And thank you for helping me with my fear of riding on the field. I was absolutely terrified!" I said.

"You didn't show it," said Danny. "You were fine – you only looked a little bit worried!" Which was very nice of him to say, considering I was on the verge of vomiting.

I walked back up to the field with Poppy, my head full of the events of the morning. Firstly, Poppy had learned some self-release, which had been a pivotal moment. Secondly, I'd faced my fear of open fields and Poppy had been amazingly relaxed, like a totally different horse. Thirdly, I'd ridden with people who I thought were so much more competent than me, who had turned out to have fears too. And last but not least, the bitless bridle had been absolutely fine. All in all, it had been a very successful morning and I felt super-charged with positive energy.

When I arrived home, I walked the dog, dashed to school, collected Florence and did a supermarket-shop before loading the washing machine, cooking dinner and sitting down with a cup of tea before James got home.

"I don't mean to be funny," said James after dinner, "but I've noticed the house is a bit of a mess and you haven't washed any of my clothes yet this week."

"Oh, really?" I replied.

"Yes," continued James. "I know you're enjoying your riding but I don't want it to get in the way of other important things. Remember, I'm working a lot more than you."

"Actually, James, maybe you could do a bit of parenting and then see how draining that is? And then do some massage work followed by fifty tons of housework? Maybe then you might shut your old-fashioned mouth and start doing your own washing? I'm going out. Bye."

I walked out of the house before James had time to process what I had said. I had no idea where I was going but it suddenly dawned on me I was wearing my pyjamas and dressing gown. I couldn't go back home, though, so I sat on a wall at the end of our street, praying nobody would see me.

"Grace!" James appeared, puffing and panting from running after me. "I'm sorry. I'll do my own washing. Please don't leave me!"

"I'm not leaving you. I'm just sick of doing everything and sick of feeling guilty every time I spend time with Poppy. You have never spent more than two hours looking after Florence on your own! Are you even aware of that?"

"No? Yes! Really? I'm sorry. Can we go home and talk about this?" he pleaded.

I was like a volcano that had blown its top. All my pent-up stress poured out and I'm very glad to say that James didn't interrupt. He sat and listened and from that day on he did his own washing and even began loading the dishwasher after dinner every night.

Chapter 27

My time loaning Poppy should have been coming to an end. Originally, her owner had vaguely mentioned finding her a permanent situation somewhere else because Poppy was only signed up for temporary livery at the yard. However, she decided that she was very pleased with how I had been getting on with Poppy so she changed her mind about moving her or finding someone else.

As I had just bought Poppy a new bridle, this was welcome news but at the same time, I still felt out of my depth. I was acutely aware that there wasn't as much of a bond between us as there had been with Monty or Lucy and it really bothered me. I was ruminating over these facts during my lesson, instead of focusing on riding, and before I knew it, Poppy had begun to wander aimlessly about.

"Would you mind explaining why you are drifting across the school about to crash into me?" asked Elise, snapping me out of my thoughts and bringing me back to the present moment.

As usual, Elise was dressed in her smart tweeds and breeches along with a silk headscarf so she looked a lot like the Queen.

"Oh heck! Sorry, I wasn't paying attention!" I exclaimed as Poppy walked straight over to Elise and stopped, which was her way of saying, *I'm listening to her not you.*

"May I ask what you were paying attention to instead?" asked Elise, bemused.

"I was just thinking about Monty," I sighed. "I had such a great bond with him instantly and I just don't really feel that sort of magical connection with Poppy."

"Good heavens, Grace, this isn't a romantic film!" exclaimed Elise briskly. "It can take years to form a bond sometimes, especially with a mare!"

"Really?" I replied, surprised.

"Yes! Even more so if she's had a history of being bullied, which I suspect she has," Elise continued, with her hands on her hips. "Nobody has patience these days. People seem to expect an instant rapport with their horses and to be feeling this, that and the other. Utter nonsense! You have to earn the relationship by demonstrating that you are worth listening to, especially with a mare and definitely with a stallion."

"That makes sense," I conceded. "Am I being an idiot doing all of this with a horse that I don't own? Having lessons and buying a bridle?"

"Not at all!" replied Elise sharply. "There are so many positives. You have full use of a young, athletic horse. You could do a bit of jumping and dressage and learn things that we couldn't do with Monty. You'll become a much better rider so when the time comes that you're able to buy your own horse, you'll have more options. Now stop being ridiculous and let's get on with the lesson!"

I loved Elise. She always helped to bring me back to earth feeling more knowledgeable and better about things. I had been so stuck in my expectations of how I believed it should be, that I hadn't been able to allow it to be what it was.

"Now look, isn't she walking nicely now? This is how you will get that bond you're wanting," continued Elise. "And if you want to work on getting to know her, spend more time grooming, massaging and just walking with her. There's a lot to be said for in-hand work."

The lesson was great. Elise was initially very sceptical about the bitless bridle and had asked to begin the session in the old bridle. We did walking, changes of direction and halting. Then Elise asked me to dismount and put the bitless bridle on. Once again, Poppy let out a loud sigh and instantly relaxed.

"Wow! Now that is very interesting indeed!" said Elise with great surprise. "I have to admit I wasn't expecting such a noticeable reaction."

Elise continued the lesson and was very impressed with how Poppy went in her new bridle, to the point where she asked if she could try it on her own, giant horse. I was amazed and pleased because Elise had always been very traditional.

"Right, let's work on that bond with a few poles. Off you get and run the stirrups up!" called Elise.

Excited, I immediately jumped off.

"Dismount correctly, please, in my lessons! We'll have no bad habits! We are not in the middle of a musical chairs game."

Elise was a stickler for doing things safely and correctly, which of course is only sensible. But I was so interested to find out what we were about to do next that I just hurled myself off. Elise marched over to a pile of poles and began arranging them in various patterns around the school.

"OK! Now, the aim of this is to walk over the middle of the poles together, with you walking level with her shoulder. Look at it as an analogy for life – you're facing obstacles and going over them *together*. This will increase her respect for you not just as a leader but as a partner too. She will grow to trust you and then she will be happy to do more for you when you're in the saddle. Also, it's a good way of strengthening her core muscles and helping her control her feet. She's still a bit clumsy."

This was true. Poppy was a bit clumsy and occasionally seemed to trip up over her own feet.

Together, Poppy and I walked round the school, going over the poles. At first, Poppy clonked her feet on most of them but very quickly she learned to pick her feet up and realised how to pace herself to go over several poles all in a line without hitting any.

"You need to look ahead as soon as you've gone over a pole! Give her a longer length of rein. She needs to be able to lower her head or you'll hurt her back," called Elise, from where she was standing in the middle of the school.

She then explained how it was important for Poppy to lift her back and core as she walked over the poles and this required a low head carriage. If her head was held high, that would cause her back to hollow, which would put stress on her lumbar vertebrae.

"You must remember she's still growing so it's vital to strengthen her body correctly. You're not together, you're drifting again! Get focused!"

I pulled my mind back to where I was and thought about all I'd learned in Wales. I really concentrated my energy on where I wanted Poppy to go and put my heart into it.

"Well done! Much better! Remember, if it's sloppy when you're walking, it'll be impossible to do it ridden," said Elise as she walked around changing the poles, raising the heights of some with a few handy bricks.

We went round the course again and it was really fun and I could tell that Poppy was enjoying it too, especially as I was more grounded and focused.

"Right, that's enough for today! Didn't you both do well? Keep practising and stop worrying about bonding – it will happen eventually so long as you keep up with in-hand work," Elise said cheerily.

Elise headed off to the car park while I led Poppy back to her stable, feeling happier, and gave her a hay net while we waited for the horse dentist to arrive. According to her owner, Poppy disliked dentists so I was a bit apprehensive but I was hopeful that the great time we'd just had would transfer to her dental experience. Green-haired Alex (as everyone called her) had kindly made me a chamomile and valerian feed to help relax Poppy, which she happily ate.

"Goodness me, Brenda, they've not seen the dentist in nearly two years so you really must go and get them!" came the unmistakable, commanding voice of Morag from outside.

"Looking forward to this! *Not.*" Jack smirked as she walked in with Buddy. "I'm not running after those buggers again – I'm too old for that rubbish!" Buddy waited at the bar while Jack came over to chat.

"How is it that he will stand wherever you put him and you don't even have to tie him?" I asked, feeling slightly envious of how easy it was to do things with Buddy.

"I don't know! He's always been like that. He's lazy!" laughed Jack. Buddy was literally standing quietly, not tied to anything and he wasn't wandering off. It fascinated me.

"We need a bucket of grass-nuts quickly, please!" called Morag as she marched into the barn, huffing and puffing. "Honestly, that woman will be the death of us all. Why is she never prepared for these events?"

"I've got loads," said Jack generously and she went to her stable to get some. Buddy still didn't move.

"I don't really feel confident to go and get them myself!" said Brenda, coming into the barn, looking worried.

"Brenda! If you shake the bucket at them they will be fine," said Morag, clearly exasperated. "Alex, did you make the magic food again?"

Alex was just walking in with giant Jenny. "Yes, it's in their stables!"

"Excellent! Right, come on, Jack, we'll help Brenda catch the two monkeys," said forthright Morag.

Jack raised her eyebrows and sighed but resigned herself to her fate and walked off with Morag and Brenda while Buddy still stood quietly at the bar.

"How is that possible?" I exclaimed.

"He's Buddha!" laughed Alex.

My mouth dropped open as the most enormous man I'd ever seen suddenly walked into the barn.

"Hello! Hello!" he greeted in a very cheery way. "Who's first? Oh, you can be first! I love chestnuts!" he said striding over to Poppy. "What's your name, little horsey?"

The dentist had arrived and he was a giant of a man. He must have been at least six foot five, very broad and had an aura of Baloo from the *Jungle Book*.

"Hello!" I said. "This is Poppy. She's new to me and apparently she's not keen on dentists so I'm a bit worried about how she might behave."

"No need to worry!" said the dentist, letting himself into Poppy's stable.

"Now then, aren't you a little cutie?" he exclaimed, grabbing her nose with his giant hand and wobbling it around. He was so massive that Poppy looked like a pony next to him.

"What a lovely shmutsky face you've got!" he said, smothering her face with kisses.

Amazingly, Poppy clearly liked it as she blew on him softly.

"Ahhh, friends already! Let's have a raspberry!" The dentist blew several raspberries on Poppy's cheeks and if she could have laughed she would have done. I'd never seen anything like it. He was like a children's entertainer and Poppy was like a little kid, loving the attention.

"Right, let's have a look at your head and neck first." Dave, the dentist, checked her lymph nodes for any swellings and then checked her bite. "Lovely, lovely! Now we'll have some more kisses!" He gave Poppy a few more kisses and then effortlessly put the weird contraption into her mouth that equine dentists use to keep horses' mouths open. In case you've not seen one before, they look like something you'd expect to see in a medieval torture museum. It's a leather head collar with a great big metal thing that goes in the horse's mouth with a mechanism that allows it to stay open so the dentist can work easily.

Poppy was so relaxed and unconcerned, it was incredible. I was fully expecting her to react very badly to having that device in her mouth but she didn't seem bothered at all. It was clearly down to the energy Dave was emitting. He was confident, calm and jolly, which are attractive qualities that rub off and make you feel similar.

"Ahh she's only a bibbly baby!" said Dave, peering into her mouth with the light of a headtorch.

"Is she really? My riding instructor said that too but I was told she was ten."

"Ten?" laughed Dave, looking round at me and blinding me with his torch. "Not this horse! Have a look. Now these corner incisors are just in full wear and all the lowers have open *infundibula*. So I would definitely say this horse has only just turned five very recently. Happy birthday to you, Popple Wopple!"

Of course, none of that made any sense to me so Dave kindly showed me what to look at. "When I do Buddy, you'll see what an older set of teeth looks like," he said.

"So it's official. Poppy is a baby! Oh my God, what a nightmare!" I felt very stressed.

"It's not a nightmare at all! I think it's great!" said Dave enthusiastically, filing her teeth down with a giant rasp that made an awful sound. "It means you've got lots and lots of years to have lovely shmutsky kisses!" He gave Poppy more kisses. He was so lovely with her and she looked so happy it made me feel quite emotional – as usual.

"Shmutsky kisses!" I laughed. He was such a crazy guy.

I was half expecting Dave to give her a balloon animal and a candyfloss when he'd finished. But instead he opened a large Tupperware container and gave her a few chunks of watermelon.

"They love watermelon and it's a nice treat after a filing," said Dave, washing all his equipment off in a bucket of water and disinfectant.

I'd never seen a horse eat watermelon but he was right, Poppy absolutely loved it.

"Right, who's next? Jack's not back so we'll do Jenny instead. Come and have a look at her elderly teeth!" Dave marched over to

Jenny's stable and got her in a headlock, smothered her face with kisses and then blew raspberries on her nose. Jenny loved it.

It was very interesting to see the differences in an older horse's teeth and Dave, although totally crazy, was good at explaining what it all meant. He was such a giant of a man that even Jenny, who was enormous, looked small next to him. Apparently, Dave had miniature Shetlands as garden pets. I couldn't imagine how he managed to do their teeth. He must have had to stand them on a table or something.

A barrage of crashing and banging accompanied by several swear words heralded the arrival of the two annoying Fell ponies.

"Ah! Trouble's arrived!" laughed the dentist. "Brenda, pop them in their stables while I finish the well-behaved horses!"

Brenda, Morag and Jack managed between them to get the two menaces into their stables.

"Bloody hell," muttered Jack, wiping the sweat off her brow as she walked over to Buddy, who was happily eating his hay net completely unconcerned about anything going on around him. "Honestly, those ponies are a couple of ba—"

"*The loooong aaand winding road da daaa da daaa!*" sang Veronica loudly, as she walked in. She was wearing a very expensive-looking traditional Japanese kimono and wellies. I couldn't stop myself from laughing.

"Ahh, the darling dentist is hither!" she said and waltzed off to her stable to get a head collar. "I shan't be long!" she called out as she wandered off to get her poor unfortunate horse.

"She is so mad!" I laughed.

"Yes!" replied everyone in unison.

"She's certifiable," said Morag, shaking her head.

I suppose we were all so occupied watching the dentist that

we didn't hear the scuffle, the crash and the shriek from Veronica until she came back into the stable barn crying. She hurled herself on to a pile of hay, sobbing dramatically.

"Here we go again!" sighed Jack, as if she'd seen it all before. "Take me away before I kill someone!"

"Oh, for goodness' sake, Veronica, pull yourself together, woman!" snapped Morag. "What are you crying about this time?"

"The little black pony has run away!" Veronica gulped, dabbing the tears from her splodgy eyes with a lace handkerchief. "I opened the wrong stable and he bolted!"

Veronica kept her hay in the empty stable next to the Fells, which were the only three outdoor stables.

"Oh no!" wailed Brenda as she dashed out into the yard.

"Well, he won't get far. He'll only be back at the gate, I'm sure. Veronica, do stop crying!" said Morag as she strode out after Brenda.

It wasn't long before Brenda and Morag ran back into the barn, their faces lined and drawn with horror.

"Somebody left the main gate open! Bobby has escaped!" shouted Morag. Her usually alto voice was raised an octave higher.

There was a momentary pause in which everyone, myself included, froze. We were all suspended in a shocked silence. Then suddenly, the space filled with a tidal wave of noise as everyone went into panic mode.

"Oh my God! Which idiot left the bloody gate open?" shouted Jack.

"I don't think shouting is the appropriate response, Jack!" replied the flustered Morag at full volume.

"Well, you're shouting!" retorted Jack.

"Oh my God!" wailed Brenda, shaking her hands. "What shall we do? What shall we do?"

"He's called Bobby?" I mused. "I didn't know they had names!" I had only ever heard them being called words I probably shouldn't write here.

"The other one's called Simon!" Alex called out from inside Jenny's stable.

"Can we stop the discussion on their names? For God's sake, everyone, we need to find Bobby before he kills someone!"

That statement made everyone shut up as we realised that it wasn't just an ordinary escapee pony, it was the worst of the two naughty and bored Fells.

"What's going on?" asked Gorgeous Danny, who had just sauntered in, looking delicious as ever in casual jeans and a checked shirt that made him look even more rugged than usual.

"Bobby has escaped! Someone left the main gate open!" yelled Brenda, her face bright red and her eyes almost popping out.

"No prizes for guessing who that was," smirked Jack, glancing over to Veronica, who was still lying down sobbing very dramatically.

"Oh, for goodness' sake, Veronica, was it you?" demanded Morag.

"Yes! It was I! Oh dear, I am so foolish!" came the muffled response of Veronica in between sobs.

"Right, everyone, get your horses and follow me!" The usually quiet Danny took charge of the situation. He fancied himself as a bit of a cowboy after having recently been on a ranch holiday in America.

"Wouldn't it be easier to catch him on foot?" I asked.

"No, he could be anywhere! We'll never catch him!" shouted Danny as he dashed off to get his horse tacked up.

"But he might just be on the grass verge by the road!" I called after him.

"I'll drive out and see if I can find him. Come on, Brenda, bring his head collar. Grace, you can ride Buddy – his tack's in there," Jack gestured to her stable and ran off to her van.

Poppy seemed quite happy to stay in her stable with a load of hay so I left her to it and hurriedly tacked up Buddy. I had ridden him a couple of times so I felt very confident as we zoomed out of the yard like the Charge of The Light Brigade. Buddy may have been very laid-back but when asked to run he generally went hell for leather, as the saying goes.

"Which way shall we go?" I shouted as we approached the end of the long driveway.

"Dunno!" shouted Danny. "I'd not thought of that!" and he suddenly pulled up. Buddy almost crashed into his horse but managed to stop just in time. We looked around but Bobby was nowhere to be seen.

"Oh God! Which way?" wondered Danny. "Which way did Jack go?"

"No idea!" I replied.

Morag, Alex, Sally and Ije were close behind and we all began arguing as to where we thought Bobby may have gone.

"Whoa, everyone!" shouted Alex and, amazingly, everyone shut up. "Did anyone check the garden?"

"What garden?" I asked.

"The yard-owner's garden!" she replied.

"No! Why?" asked Morag, looking perplexed.

"I know I'm not one for logic but logically speaking, why would a horse run away from its territory? Surely, he's more likely to have hopped over the fence and is probably just destroying the veg patch," Alex suggested.

"Oh, for goodness' sake!" Morag almost exploded with exasperation. "Come on, everyone, let's go and look!"

We all turned round and galloped up the track back towards the yard. It was excellent fun and Buddy was perfect for that sort of caper. It was so nice just to ride without having a mind full of fears. We skidded to a halt near the farmhouse, which was old and beautiful, if slightly mouldering, and as if on cue, Bob the yard manager opened his door and stepped outside.

"Oh, hello, everyone!" he said, looking very surprised to see us all so close to his house. "Is something wrong?"

"Is Bobby in your garden?" yelled Morag at full volume.

"Er... no... not that I know of. Why?" Bob looked very taken aback.

"Because Looney Tunes left the gate open and he's gone!" laughed Danny.

"Danny, it's no laughing matter!" scolded Morag.

"It's the best excitement we've had in a long time, though!" Danny replied, still chuckling.

"Oh dear," said Bob, scratching his cheek. "Oh dear, oh dear! Now that is a problem. Shall I have a look in the garden?" he asked in his painfully slow way, cocking his head to one side.

"Yes!" we all replied in chorus.

Danny laughed his head off while Bob walked back into his house, carefully closing the door and locking it. He returned a few excruciatingly long minutes later. We could hear him fumbling with the lock and then stopping to answer his telephone.

"No, I'm very sorry. I think you've got the wrong number!" we heard him say. "No, there's nobody here by that name."

"Oh my God!" laughed Sally. "Just hang up, man!"

"Yes, it's definitely the wrong number. I'm terribly sorry," continued Bob. "Ha ha! Yes. Thank you, goodbye!"

"Oh, for pity's sake!" said Morag, getting crosser and crosser.

The door slowly opened and Bob stepped outside, shaking his head. "No, he's not there!"

Danny stood up in his stirrups and surveyed the surrounding fields, double-checking that the errant pony wasn't just having fun nearby. But no luck. He was nowhere to be seen.

"Jack's calling!" shouted Alex excitedly, answering her phone. We all waited with baited breath.

"Oh God, he's by the lake!" said Alex as she hung up.

"How on earth did he get there? And why would he go there?" asked Sally, dumbfounded.

"Come on!" said Danny and off we went back down the track again at top speed. It was tremendous fun.

The lake was at a park not far from the yard but we had to ride down a dual carriageway to get there, which was a bit hectic to say the least. I was very glad that I was on safe, sensible Buddy, who didn't care where he went so long as he was going somewhere.

"He's near the café!" shouted Alex as we neared the park entrance.

"He would be!" exclaimed Morag. "No doubt terrorising all the mums and kids. Oh my goodness, I don't know who I'm more annoyed with – Veronica for being such an idiot as to leave the gate open, or Brenda for buying ponies with no knowledge!" Morag was fuming.

Danny was laughing his head off. "Oh, come on, this is hilarious!" he laughed. But it only made Morag more annoyed.

"There's Jack!" I called out as I spotted her stalking the sandy banks by the edge of the lake, head collar and lead rope in her hand.

"Jack!" shouted Alex.

Jack looked round and rolled her eyes as Brenda came running out of the café with a handful of carrots.

"I got these!" she gasped. "Hopefully, they'll entice him!"

"Good idea!" said Alex.

"Now what the hell do we do?" I asked, watching Bobby trotting up and down by the water's edge, snorting at the swans, which were hissing at him.

"We need to corner him somehow," said Jack. "Two of you need to ride down there and drive him up this way – but be careful. He's such a clever bugger, he'll know what we're doing."

Danny and I rode as casually as possible on the grass above the sandy lakeside, as if we weren't bothered at all about Bobby. He watched us like a hawk and neighed loudly but still trotted back and forth by the swans, tossing his head.

"Wouldn't you think that he would come to us because he knows us?" I wondered out loud.

"Yeah! He's completely weird!" laughed Danny. "God this is fun! I've been so bored lately but this is brilliant!"

I noticed we had a rather large audience gathering to watch the action. Loads of small kids were saying funny things like, "Ooh, look, Mummy, it's a horse and that's another horse and another horse and lots of horses!"

"I think you should all keep well back in case the naughty pony runs into you!" I called out.

"Well done!" laughed Danny. "You can be the health and safety officer today. Morag would approve!"

"Well, knowing how daft Brenda is, she probably doesn't have any insurance!" I replied.

"Ha, yeah! She probably doesn't!"

"Now what?" I asked as we came to a stop a safe distance behind Bobby.

"Dunno! We'll wait till one of them yells at us, I suppose?" grinned Danny. He was so good-looking it was terribly distracting. I had to work hard to stop myself from saying so as I have a terrible habit of saying what I think sometimes.

"Grace! Danny!" yelled Morag, waving her arms.

"Thaaar she blows!" laughed Danny.

"Ride slowly towards us!" called Morag.

"But he'll just nip sideways into those kids!" I shouted back.

Jack said something to Ije and she manoeuvred her pony so that she could block him. Ije did a lot of cross-country competitions and she was a very good rider, despite having flown head first into a tree last time I'd ridden with her.

"OK, Danny and Grace, drive him this way!" shouted Morag.

By this time several of the staff from the café were standing outside watching, along with most of the park and it felt so stressful I started laughing too. Bobby stood still, watching us. Luckily, he didn't seem concerned. Danny's horse, Boudicca, was prancing sideways as usual and Buddy was a bit joggy too but it didn't worry me because I'd known him for years.

"I don't know how you ride that horse and are so laid-back about it!" I exclaimed to Danny.

"What do you mean?" he asked.

"Well, she's jogging sideways!" I replied.

"So's Buddy!" he laughed.

"Yes, but Buddy is a cob so he won't actually do anything dangerous."

"Neither will Boudicca and nor will Poppy because that's what you're really worried about, isn't it?" Danny replied with superb insight.

"Yes!" I exclaimed "You're right! How did you know?"

"Ha!" laughed Danny. "Stop worrying about what you think she might do and remember what she's been like up to now. She's been fine – don't overthink things."

"I always overthink things!" I laughed.

"You ladies always do!" He smiled but then suddenly his smile changed into a frown and I glanced over to where he was looking. "Cyclists! For God's sake, that's all we need."

A group of cyclists were fast approaching on the lakeside edge just round the bend. They were heading towards Morag, Sally and Alex, who were on the opposite side of Bobby, ready to herd him over to Jack, Brenda and the carrots.

"Bikes coming, Morag!" yelled Danny but it was too late.

The cyclists, unaware of our delicate predicament, speeded up, ringing their bells and shouting, "Get those horses out of the way!"

"Oh my God!" I squeaked. "I can't look!"

Morag's horse, Candy, didn't like cyclists at the best of times so she took great exception at being shouted at by a whole gang of them. She spun and reared and Morag fell backwards into the lake with a very loud splash. The cyclists screeched to a stop, piling into each other and falling all over themselves on to the ground in a big heap. It was like a terrible cartoon.

"Christ!" yelled Danny, dashing to the rescue with me and Buddy in hot pursuit.

Some people from the audience started shouting at the cyclists for being so rude. The cyclists were shouting at us saying, "Horses shouldn't be in the park!" but Alex, who was always so lovely and calm, sorted everyone out by simply explaining the predicament.

Jack was busy dragging Morag out of the lake, which was lucky for the cyclists because she probably would have punched the lot of them. The cyclists apologised and offered to help and the café staff brought a few towels and a cup of tea for poor Morag. Meanwhile, Candy took full advantage of the situation and scrambled up the sandy bank to graze on the grass above.

Candy's grazing seemed to be quite magnetising for Bobby. He sidled up to her and began munching away on the grass too. Something about what I had learned in Wales started niggling in my mind as I watched them.

"Danny!" I hissed as I slid off Buddy. "Get off your horse and let her graze!"

"OK!" Danny got down and we let Buddy and Boudicca graze the very thick and tempting grass.

"Hold Buddy's reins!" I whispered and then walked calmly over to Jack and took the head collar.

Everyone was fussing over Morag so it was very easy to take a deep breath, check my energy, lower it and stand near the grazing horses with my head down and a knee bent as if I was eating too. Very quietly, I started stroking Candy, totally ignoring Bobby. Bobby came up close of his own accord and didn't react while I gave him a stroke on his shoulder. I took another deep breath and slipped his head collar on. The fact he wasn't totally feral and knew our horses obviously helped.

"Phew!" I said, silently thanking Julie's excellent teaching.

"Wow, good thinking!" said Danny, giving me a thumbs up.

Brenda dashed over and took Bobby very gratefully.

"God, what's that awful stench?" I suddenly got a whiff of the most pungent, foul smell.

"It's Morag!" laughed Jack. "Oh my God, Morag, you stink!"

"Yes, thank you, I am aware of that," grimaced poor Morag, who had unfortunately landed in the swampiest part of the lake. Her clothes were smeared with revolting green slime and she stank of rotten fish.

The walk home was very funny and very smelly, thanks to Morag, while Bobby walked along very meekly as if he was the best little pony in the world.

"It's a good job none of us had anything else to do today!" Sally chuckled. "This is the best ride we've been on for ages!"

"Speak for yourself!" said Morag witheringly. "I need to hose myself down before I go home. I can't get in my car like this."

Ije obligingly hosed Morag down once we were back at the yard. She sat in the sun wrapped in a towel to dry off, as luckily it was a warm day. Brenda thanked everyone for helping and then received a stern lecture from Morag about the fact that she needed to do something with her ponies, or sell them, and Brenda promised she would.

"I'll believe that when I see it," said Jack as we led the horses back to the field. "Nobody in their right mind will buy those ponies."

"True, but it was a really funny day!" I said. "Buddy is ace. You're so lucky to have such a laid-back horse."

"Poppy is getting better, though, isn't she? I don't think you need to worry so much any more," Jack replied.

She reminded me of what Danny had said and I realised that they were both right and that I needed to put into practice all that I had learned in Wales. I had discovered that the *energy thing* really did work, after being able to catch Bobby so easily. I thought about that over the course of the day. I realised I used the energy thing without thinking in my work as a massage therapist. I kept my energy low and that helped to relax people. I concluded that it was obviously an automatic ability that we all have but we just aren't aware of. Now that I *was* aware of it, I wanted to use it more often.

Chapter 28

"Today we will be getting to know each other!" announced Elise as she marched briskly into the barn where I was grooming Poppy for our lesson. "Come on, let's get going!"

"Oh!" I jumped as I was in a bit of a daydream. "I've not tacked up yet!"

"Hurry up! We're going for a walk – in hand!" Elise could be very sergeant-majorish when she wanted to be so I hastily got my hat on and put Poppy's bridle on and led her out of her stable.

"Walking is one of the best ways to improve your relationship with your horse," said Elise as she turned and strode out of the barn at top speed. Poppy and I followed. "Can you tell me why? Oh, hang on, this is the awkward field, isn't it?"

We had arrived at the gate of the pony field and, as usual, the two annoying Fells were looking for entertainment.

"Right, we'll have none of their nonsense. I'll go in and sort them out and I'll meet you on the other side," said Elise, opening the gate.

"The other side? That sounds a bit final!" I laughed.

"The other side of the field, you ninny!" replied Elise, rolling her eyes. "Bloody hell, this gate's a bit awkward, isn't it?"

Elise managed to get the gate open and we all walked through. Bobby and Simon (the two Fells) came trotting towards us with a menacing gleam in their eyes. Unfortunately for them, they hadn't reckoned on Elise's strength of character. Although she wasn't much more than five foot four, she had a very big personality and a great deal of self-confidence. She marched straight at the ponies, stared them in the eyes and kept walking.

"You two can bugger right off!" she commanded and amazingly they turned, gave a small flick of their heels in mild protest and trotted away fast.

"Right, that's them sorted!" said Elise with great satisfaction as she met me on the other side of the top gate.

"That was impressive!" I said.

"Not really," replied Elise. "It's about attitude, that's all. So many people have begun to label things with fancy names like 'Natural Horsemanship' and this, that and the other. In my day it was called common sense!"

"Now, where were we?" she continued. "Ah yes, walking. Can you tell me why it's so good for bond-building?"

"Er... umm... no!" I tried to think but couldn't really see why we were going for a walk. It felt a bit funny, like I was walking a giant dog.

"Because you aren't asking anything of her," said Elise. "You are next to her, she can see you, so she can relax. You are not busy worrying about falling off so you can relax too. Simple!"

"Yes, I am feeling relaxed!" I laughed as I realised that walking this way meant I could enjoy where we were and finally see my surroundings. I hadn't taken much notice of this particular pretty lane due to the fact that I was always busy concentrating on what Poppy might do. The lane wound round the surrounding farm, which had fields full of cows and sheep. Normally, Poppy would jog along this part of the lane because of said cows and sheep but today she was more settled and walked nicely.

"She's taking confidence from you," Elise explained. "Remember that in her brain, you are a hunter. She is a prey animal, therefore she is *dinner*. However, because she is a domesticated horse, she automatically looks to you for protection and here you are at her shoulder protecting her."

"Wow! I'd not thought of it in that way. That's fascinating!" I exclaimed.

"Furthermore," Elise continued, "when we sit on their backs, that feels similar to having a predator attack them so it's incredible that they learn to accept it. It's no wonder a lot of horses are jittery under saddle."

"God, yes, wow!" I loved my lessons with Elise I always learned something valuable each time.

"OK. Now can you see that she's feeling a bit nervous here? Her neck's like a giraffe and she's sniffing the air," said Elise.

"Oh yes! I think it's the cows," I replied, feeling a bit uneasy.

"Now all you have to do is let her stop and look at them while you relax and talk to her. She's young – she needs to learn that if mum's OK about cows, then she can be OK too."

We stopped to let Poppy have a good look at the cows, who were craning their necks over the fence to get at the cow parsley and sticky weed. Poppy seemed a bit disgusted by them at first. She probably thought they were very smelly. So I stroked her and went to stroke the cows and that helped Poppy to calm down and start eating the cow parsley too. I lifted her head to stop her.

"It's OK – let her eat! It's a reward for being relaxed," said Elise. "Good girl, Poppy. They're only cows. Now you won't have to worry next time you ride past. So many people don't let their horses stop to look at things. They get their knickers in a twist about always making the horse keep moving and insist the horse must be listening to them all the time. But I think the way to create a safe riding horse is by slowing down. Let them look and learn for themselves what's scary and what's not."

The end of the lane opened out on to a busy road so we turned back and headed for the school. We had twenty minutes of riding under Elise's eagle eye and it was obvious the walk had definitely improved Poppy's frame of mind as she moved very nicely. I felt very chipper as we walked back to the barn after the lesson and decided I would hack out.

The main driveway led to a very busy road and as I was feeling brave we headed that way. Luckily the road was quiet so we crossed it easily and went into the large council estate opposite.

"Let's turn right," I said to Poppy and off we went.

It felt a bit weird because it was a street I'd never been down before. Poppy was very forward but this time she was much more relaxed. It was a stark contrast to the first time I had ridden out alone, which was horrifying to say the least. The walk and the lesson had definitely changed something between us – we were more connected and for the first time I could almost relax.

"That's looking a lot better today!" called out a familiar voice. I turned to see Jim, the traveller, walking along with a bag of shopping.

"Hello!" I grinned. "Thank you! Yes, it's loads better now. We've been doing a lot of connection work!"

"Well done, lass! That's what it takes. Slow and steady and you'll get there."

Poppy stopped to have a nosey in his shopping bag.

"Poppy!" I shouted. "Stop it!"

"It's all right," laughed Jim. "Reckon she can smell the apples. Here you are, darlin'. Sounds like you've earned it." He reached into his bag and gave Poppy an apple that she ate very messily, spitting apple juice all over Jim. Luckily, he found it amusing. Then a group of young kids ran across the road to see us and they all wanted to give Poppy a stroke. It was like being with a film star.

"Oooh, she's beautiful!" they all said and Poppy loved the attention.

"Now, don't you be getting lost again... hahaa!" laughed Jim as he went on his way.

Riding through the council estate was bizarre. It was a very busy place and not in the least bit pretty but it had the most courteous drivers I've ever experienced. They all slowed down and passed wide and seemed genuinely pleased to see a horse. I've never had so many smiles and waves. Why can't all drivers be like that?

Poppy continued walking and then we tried a bit of a trot. Her trot was so weird – she almost exploded into it and thundered along like a carriage horse with a very big action. It wasn't in any way pleasant.

"We'll have to work on this!" I gasped, slowing her back to a walk. "Your trot is faster than most horses' canter!" I wondered if she had a bit of Standard Bred blood her.

Just as we rounded a corner we came across another large chestnut horse that was prancing around on the spot. Poppy whinnied and the horse looked over and whinnied back. I recognised her from the yard but I'd not met her owner.

"Oh, thank God you're here!" called the rider. "I was about to get off! Do you mind if we tag along?"

"Not at all!" I replied, pleased to have some company.

"I'm Sara! Are you Grace?" she asked.

"Yes, hello!"

"This is Garnet. She's only three and she's being really annoying! I knew I shouldn't have come out on my own. Stand still, for God's sake!" Sara sat really well despite Garnet's dancing. I was very impressed.

"Poppy's only five, so this should be interesting!" I said, expecting Poppy to revert to being an idiot but she didn't. She stood very calmly and that helped to calm Garnet.

"Phew, that's better! Which way shall we go?" asked Sara.

"Actually, I haven't really got a clue where I am! I always seem to get lost in here," I admitted, feeling slightly embarrassed.

Luckily Sara knew where we were so we continued down the road. Suddenly, Garnet jumped into the air like a cartoon horse with her legs going in all directions at once. Sara managed to stay on – which was very impressive – and Garnet snorted and tossed her pretty head.

"Garnet! For God's sake, it's only a crisp packet!" exclaimed Sara, who was very exasperated. But there was no way Garnet was going to go past that particular monster.

Amazingly, Poppy didn't react at all so I pushed her on past Garnet, who calmed down instantly and followed us.

"Poppy's so chilled-out! It must be really nice to have such a laid-back horse. I hope Garnet will end up like that," said Sara.

"Well, to be honest, this is new behaviour. Up until quite recently, she was really nervy but riding lessons have definitely made a difference."

I was very surprised at how chilled-out Poppy was. She was so *grown-up*, for want of a better description.

"We'll follow you! I think that will be better for Garnet," said Sara and so I took the lead. We went through a small area of woodland and still Poppy was like a steady school horse. It was astounding. It was like she'd turned into Buddy.

"If we turn right here, that will lead us back to the yard," called Sara.

"OK!" I replied.

We had come to a crossing with traffic lights. It was such a peculiar experience to wait at a red light on a horse. Garnet was tossing her head, pawing at the ground and then began trotting on the spot but miraculously, Poppy was completely unbothered by it. She almost looked down her nose at Garnet as if to say, *Hmmph. I am sooo much more mature than you!*" It was most odd but I was very relieved.

The lights changed to green and over we went, Poppy walking very calmly as if it was something she did every day.

"Garnet! Stop it!" Garnet danced sideways across the road, much to the amusement of the car drivers.

The next road was quieter and eventually we turned on to a very steep country lane that led to the farm at the back of the yard.

"We need to be careful of the naughty boys!" called out Sara as we turned on to the lane.

"The what?" I wasn't sure if I'd heard her correctly over the clattering of hooves.

"There's a school up here for boys who've been kicked out of ordinary schools and sometimes they escape and scare the horses for a laugh!" she shouted.

"Oh great!" A sudden wave of fear washed over me. "What should we do?"

"Don't know! We'll have to play it by ear!" said Sara.

The steep lane was very pretty with woodland to the right and a park on the left, which was popular with dog walkers. Poppy was not particularly thrilled to be marching up a lane in walk and kept trying to go into trot.

"Are you OK to trot?" I called to Sara and then suddenly we noticed a gang of teenage lads looming ahead.

"Oh shit! What to do?" Sara shouted.

The gang of boys started shouting obscenities. Nearby was a very ineffectual teacher who was calling for them to "Come back inside now!" in the most pathetic way. Obviously, the boys completely ignored him and walked out into the middle of the road and began chucking stones at us.

"Fuck!" squealed Sara. "Little bastards!"

I saw red. My temper flared up and I let Poppy go into her crazy fast trot. I was so enraged by the boys that I aimed Poppy right for them. Their cool demeanour fizzled away as it dawned on them that I wasn't going to stop. Their faces were a picture of horror as they leaped out of the way, just in time, I might add, because we almost crashed into them.

"You fucking nutter!" one of them cried out. "You could have killed us!"

"That was the idea, you little shits!" I shouted, completely furious.

Garnet quite literally rose to the occasion, rearing and waving her front legs crazily. The boys shrieked in terror and ran off to the safety of their school. How Sara stayed on was miraculous to say the least. She must have been glued to the saddle as she expertly clung on and managed to get Garnet back on all four legs.

We continued at full speed, pounding past the school, zooming round a bend until it felt safe to slow down. I was shaking from the adrenalin.

"Hahaa! Oh my God, that was so scary. They won't do that again!" exclaimed Sara.

"I feel sick!" I replied.

"Wasn't Poppy amazing? She was like a police horse!" laughed Sara.

I had to agree, Poppy had been incredible. She had ploughed on undeterred, despite the idiot boys throwing stones. She was like a warhorse. I was so proud of her and surprised at myself for being so determined under such awful circumstances. It was a very clear demonstration to me about how focusing my energy triggered Poppy to respond in kind.

"You were amazing to stay on when Garnet reared!" I said, full of admiration.

"I haven't a clue how I managed that but at least it scared them off!" said Sara very modestly.

The rest of the journey back to the yard was, luckily, uneventful and the stable barn was quiet when we arrived.

"Well, thanks for that!" said Sara. "What a ride!"

"I think I'm in shock!" I laughed.

My legs felt like jelly and my hands were still a bit shaky. I managed to untack and brush Poppy and then I walked her back to the field. I was quite overcome with emotion. Poppy had gone against her natural flight mechanism and had thundered into a dangerous situation because I'd asked her to. As Sara had said, she'd been exactly like a police horse. We had become one unit and she obviously really trusted me.

However, I felt guilty because it could have been a different story. She could have got injured but in the moment, there seemed no other option. I also felt very sorry for those poor boys. They had made me angry because they were behaving like idiots. But really, what hope did they have to be any better than that? They obviously had never received any love in their sad lives.

I gave Poppy a very big kiss as I turned her into the field and she looked me in the eye and made a little wiffly noise. It felt lovely. There was definitely a connection beginning to blossom. I felt different too but in a way that's difficult to describe. I can only say that I felt taller, more purposeful and strong. Very strong. I hadn't felt that way for a long time and it felt wonderful. It was as if another layer of damage had been erased from my subconscious and the bits of me that had been missing were coming back.

Chapter 29

I looked at Poppy and she looked at me. Well, half looked at me because she was grazing at the time so she had one eye on the grass. Something felt different in a very nice way and I stood for a while, savouring the moment. I was relaxed, grounded and calm. All the attributes I felt were vital to be a good leader.

"Elise is coming soon so let's go and get ready," I said, pulling a bit of grass out of her raggedy mane. Poppy stood, chewing, but she wasn't stressed when I put the head collar on. She didn't attempt to bugger off like she usually did and she walked very happily down the track towards the barn.

Such a small thing but in reality, it was such a big achievement. It showed me how far I had come on my journey of understanding what horses need in order to be relaxed and amenable. All she had ever needed was exactly what I had needed for myself – calm self-confidence.

There had been no one at the yard when I arrived, however the scene in the barn when I returned was surprising to say the least.

"Mum, you are absolutely mad!" fumed a very cross-looking young woman as she marched down the row of stables.

"Oh, stop fussing!" replied her mother, wheeling herself along with a determined look in her eyes.

They were accompanied by an oldish man with a thick grey beard, wearing a brown knitted cardigan over a blue checked shirt. He looked like a dusty old professor, and he raised his eyebrows at me in a subdued sort of a way.

"Hello!" greeted the woman in the wheelchair. "I'm June!"

June had very sparkly hazel eyes and a mop of curly ginger hair and the biggest smile. She had such a warm friendly aura I couldn't help but smile back and say hello and introduce myself.

"Ooh, what a lovely horse!" said June enthusiastically.

Poppy had a good sniff of June's wheelchair and unfortunately deposited a glob of snot on the armrest.

"Oh yikes! Poppy! I'm so sorry about that. I'll wipe it off." I pulled a tissue out of my pocket and hastily removed the snot while June laughed her head off.

"Well, the stable looks OK," said the angry daughter, who had marched back over to us. "Hi, I'm Susan. This is my mad mother June, who is on a mission to kill herself!" she said by way of an introduction.

"Oh, now come on, Susan! I think that's a bit harsh," said the very harassed-looking man who turned out to be called David.

"She'll end up being in that chair permanently if she goes ahead with this!" Susan sounded extremely stressed. "I'm not getting involved any more. I'm going!" and with that, she marched off.

June chuckled. "Don't mind her! She's just worried about me, I suppose, but I've always wanted a horse and no back problem is going to stop me from fulfilling my dream!"

"Oh. Well, that's a very good attitude!" was all I could think of to say.

"Absolutely! It's all about attitude! I've got something wrong with a disc and a facet joint so I need another operation but I can still walk a bit. Anyway, my numbers came up on the Premium bonds so I thought, *June, what have you always wanted?* And the answer was a horse, of course! So I found one I liked the look of on *Horsemart* and I bought it there and then – and she'll be arriving any minute now. I'm so excited!" June's face was red with excitement while her husband seemed apprehensive but in resigned acceptance.

"Wow, that's certainly taking the plunge! Did you go and see her first?" I asked.

"Ooh no! As soon as I saw her face I knew she was the horse for me!"

I was gobsmacked and wondered how she would manage to cope with a horse. I didn't know what to say so I groomed Poppy while June told me all about her back problems, which had started after having children. She then went on to tell me about her daughter Susan, who had a horse elsewhere; her sons who were both dentists and various other bits of family life. She was very engaging and jolly and didn't seem in the least bit bothered about her back problem or the fact that she'd not really done that much riding. She'd sat on Susan's horse a few times many years ago but, "How hard can it be?" she asked.

"Erm…" I was about to reply when Elise arrived so I had to go for my lesson. It was good timing because I suddenly realised why Susan had been so extremely cross.

Yikes! I thought to myself as I led Poppy to the school. *I hope she will be OK!*

"Walk her round! Let's see you both moving," called Elise as she stood in the centre of the school in her tweeds, looking very commanding as usual.

All thoughts of June left my mind.

"Lovely. OK, mount up!"

I duly got on board and walked Poppy round the school while Elise watched and made helpful comments.

"Now then, let's continue to build on the formation of trust," said Elise as she walked over and attached a lunge line to Poppy's bridle. "Take your feet out of the stirrups and cross them over in front of you."

I felt a bit worried and glanced at the ground, which was a long way down.

"Don't look down there or that's where you'll end up!" exclaimed Elise. "Goodness me, Grace, look ahead!" She was right of course.

We began by just walking round in a large circle a few times while I relaxed and sat deeper in the saddle.

"Lovely! OK, now close your eyes!"

"What?" I was horrified.

"Come along, close your eyes! Don't worry, we're only walking and I've got hold of her."

I closed my eyes with huge apprehension and then opened one eye.

"Grace!" said Elise sharply.

"It's scary!" I squeaked, opening both eyes.

"Nonsense! Now take a deep breath and relax. You look like you're about to have root-canal work!" laughed Elise heartily.

I took a deep breath and allowed myself to relax a bit more.

"Good. Now shut your eyes!"

"Oh God!" I wailed.

"Come on!" commanded Elise.

"OK! Yikes!" I closed my eyes. It felt so disturbing. "This is awful!"

"No, it isn't. Don't be silly! Just concentrate on your seat," Elise said firmly.

I focused on my seat and my balance.

"That's better! Now really be aware of what you're feeling. Be aware of how Poppy is moving and allow yourself to move with her."

It was a very peculiar experience to give up control to Elise and become more aware of how it actually felt to ride Poppy rather than be completely focused on everything I was seeing. Poppy took such big, smooth strides and I could feel that she was also very relaxed, even though she was walking quite fast.

"Now let go of the reins!" said Elise.

"Are you mad?" I exclaimed, opening my eyes wide with horror.

"Close those eyes!" commanded Elise.

I closed my eyes again.

"You know I wouldn't ask you to do this if I thought you weren't ready."

I thought about that and agreed. Elise was an excellent teacher and always knew how far to take someone without going too far.

"OK. Now let go of the reins."

"Aarghh!" I squirmed inwardly but I let go of the reins.

"Excellent! Put your hands on your thighs. Now remember to breathe and let your legs hang long. Move with her!"

Although it was terrifying initially it soon felt quite magical. I became completely relaxed and at one with Poppy and it was so liberating. Elise began to move us round the school doing small circles and large circles and then we went over low poles, all with my eyes shut and no reins.

After a while, a very bizarre thing began to happen. Memories of early motherhood began appearing in my consciousness. All the strict routines I had followed in order to cope with Florence and the upheaval a new baby brings flooded into my mind like a cinefilm unravelling crazily on a screen. Snatches of images came and went and I watched them flit past.

I had needed to be completely in control back then, yet here I was now, totally out of control. But it was OK to be out of control. It felt like fireworks were going off in my brain as the old made way for the new. To trust a large animal as much as I was in that moment, changed me on a fundamental level. It was a very exhilarating and powerful exercise and I began to feel more connected with my true self. It was as if by letting go I was allowing life to happen in a more energetic and fulfilling way.

The images dissolved and I became aware that Poppy had come to a stop so I opened my eyes. I felt very still. It was wonderful.

"Excellent! Well done you!" said Elise with a big smile on her face. "Obviously, don't practise that on your own!" She laughed.

"Ha! No way!" I agreed. "That was amazing! I feel like a different person now. It was like a whole load of rubbish just got cleared out of my mind!"

"Yes! It's very good for mental health, isn't it? I found it helped me when I first did this exercise about a hundred years ago. Obviously, nobody spoke about such things in those days but we all knew that horses kept us sane. Now, all these small steps are what will help to bring you both together."

Elise showed me a few more pole exercises for homework and then went on her way. I led Poppy back to the barn, feeling absolutely fantastic. I was walking on air. I literally felt as if all the last dregs of postnatal depression and the awful memories of early motherhood had been released into the atmosphere and my mind had been reset. In fact, all of me had been reset. I was so amazed by the healing power of just being with a horse.

Sadly, there was no time for me to ponder more deeply on the experience I'd just had because in my absence, June's new horse had arrived. So had Sally, Jack and Green-haired Alex, which was fortunate because at least they knew what to do with a horse and had led her into the stable. David had no idea whatsoever and June wasn't much better. Her excitement had turned to nerves when the reality of buying a horse was suddenly right there in front of her. June's previously glowing face had turned rather pale, to say the least.

"Oh dear. I'm not really sure of what to do first," June mumbled.

"Don't you worry, luv, we'll all help you!" smiled Jack, who had warmed to June's open and friendly nature. "When I bought my first horse I didn't have a clue either. At least you've already sorted out your stable. I had to keep my horse in the garden for the first week!"

"You never?" laughed Sally.

"Yes, she did," I nodded, remembering the sorry tale of Jack's crazy impulse-buy.

"But you seem so sensible!" exclaimed Sally in total shock.

"Ha!" laughed Jack. "Every now and then I get an idea in my head and I just do things without thinking! I didn't even know how to ride."

"No way!" said Alex, who also couldn't believe that Jack could be so crazy. "What happened?"

"Well, I'd always wanted a horse and I woke up one day and thought *Bugger it, I'm buying one.* So I went to the auction and just bought one. Then I realised I didn't have anywhere to keep her so I put her in the garden until I found somewhere!" Jack laughed her head off as she remembered how mad she'd been.

"I didn't even know how to groom her! The livery-yard owner had to teach me!" continued Jack as everyone listened, open-mouthed in shock.

"So how did you ride her?" asked Sally, completely dumbfounded.

"Some of the girls at the yard gave me lessons."

"Wow! What happened to that horse?" asked Alex.

"Well, she turned out to be in foal," said Jack.

"Oh my God! A bogof!" gasped Sally.

"A what?" asked June.

"Buy one get one free!"

"Oh!" laughed June.

"She had a beautiful foal but I didn't have a clue how to train her so I sold her," said Jack sadly.

"Ahh, that's a shame. What happened to the mum?" asked Sally.

"She wasn't well and had to be put to sleep. So then I bought Buddy."

"What a story!" said Alex.

"I'm glad I'm not the only daft woman!" said June, looking a bit more cheerful. "My daughter thinks this will be the death of me."

"Rubbish!" said Jack. "We'll help you to prove her wrong. My mam said the same to me and so far, I'm still alive!"

"Let's give her a brush and some hay," said Alex, grabbing a hay net and tying it up for June's new horse, Beatrix. She really was a truly stunning horse with a beautiful dapple-grey coat and an almost silvery-looking mane and tail. I could see why June had fallen instantly in love with her. Luckily, Beatrix had arrived with a full wardrobe of tack, rugs and grooming tools so we all enjoyed teaching June how to groom. She managed to get out of her wheelchair, with the help of David, and had a great time brushing Beatrix's beautiful hair.

I was so impressed by David's kind and calm manner. He clearly adored June and even though what she was about to do was exceedingly dangerous, he supported her dream to do it. June's neurosurgeon was, of course, totally horrified and completely against the idea but June didn't give a hoot. This was her life. She was sixty-five and she was going to live her dream.

"All my kids are adults and I've spent my whole life looking after them. I even had to look after my parents and David's too. I love you, David, but it's my time now!" said June.

"I love you too!" smiled David and it brought tears to all our eyes.

"Wow, what a great guy!" I gulped.

"Oof, I wouldn't go that far. He does some terrible farts in bed!" June winked and we all laughed, except David, who blushed.

"What would you like to do now?" asked Jack.

"Well, I'd like to ride!" exclaimed June as if that was a really stupid question.

"Do you think that's wise?" asked David tentatively. "She's only just arrived!"

"She's not come far though," replied June. "What do you all think?"

"Bugger what we think!" said Alex. "You live your dream!"

"How about we go in the school and one of us ride her first to see how she goes?" I suggested, feeling cautious.

"Ooh, yes, good idea!" said June enthusiastically.

David breathed a sigh of relief and off we all went to the school. Poppy was happy eating hay in her stable so I left her to it.

Beatrix had an amazing western saddle that looked very comfortable and we were all dying to try it but June asked Jack to ride her as she felt they were kindred spirits.

"You mean we're both mad?" laughed Jack.

Jack was always very cautious of new horses so she asked us to walk next to her just in case Beatrix turned into a rodeo horse.

"Maybe just walk with her in-hand first like Elise taught me?" I suggested.

"Good plan!" agreed Jack and she led Beatrix round the school a few times.

To say she'd just arrived at a totally unfamiliar place with people she didn't know, Beatrix behaved as if she'd known us all her life. She was very happy to walk with Jack and stood very calmly at the mounting block.

"Will you ride her? I'm feeling a bit of a wuss!" said Jack to Alex.

Alex laughed. She didn't need asking twice. "Of course! I'm dying to try that saddle!" and on she got.

"Is the girth OK?" asked Sally as Alex faffed with the stirrups to get them the right length.

"Yeah, it'll be right! I'll just be walking," replied Alex and off they went down the long side of the school.

"Ooh, this saddle's so comfy!" she shouted back to us.

Beatrix walked very nicely, much to everyone's relief – especially June and David. June looked ecstatic as Alex and Beatrix did a couple of circuits in walk.

"Would you mind trotting? I'd love to see her doing that!" asked June.

"Yes, no problem!" grinned Alex, who was clearly enjoying herself. She asked Beatrix for a trot and Beatrix set off very smoothly. "This is great!" called Alex as they sailed past and headed for the top corner of the school. "Oh shit!" yelled Alex suddenly.

"What is it?" I called back.

"Aaargh!" Alex gave a strangled cry as she and the saddle slipped sideways.

"Oh, for God's sake!" said Sally, shaking her head. "She should have tightened the girth."

Beatrix continued trotting and Alex continued sliding round until she was literally hanging upside down. How she stayed on was beyond comprehension. Thankfully, Beatrix stopped and stood stock-still, her eyes wide with surprise.

"Ahh, bollocks!" was the last thing Alex said before letting go and falling to the ground with a loud thud.

Beatrix looked round with a concerned expression on her face and waited to be rescued by Jack, who dashed over. The rest of us were all too busy dying with laughter at such a sight to be of any help.

"Well, I think it's safe to say that Beatrix is a very good horse!" grimaced Alex as she waddled over, holding on to her bottom. "God, my bum hurts! That'll teach me to not be so slack about girths in future. I won't be able to sit down for a week."

"There must be a herbal remedy for that," said Jack, smirking.

As ever, the sarcasm was lost on Alex.

"Ooh, yes, you're right! A bit of chamomile will help." Alex waddled off to her tack room where she kept her herbal supplies.

"What a smashing horse!" smiled June, giving Beatrix a pat.

"She's amazingly calm," agreed Sally. "You've been really

lucky. She could have been a nutter!"

"Any other horse would have freaked out about that happening!" I said, in awe of such a fantastic horse.

"Yes," nodded June. "She's my dream horse! I'd like to go for a ride out on her now."

"Is that wise?" asked David anxiously. "Shouldn't you ride her in here first?"

"No. I want to go on my first hack. Beatrix is as good as gold, aren't you, lovey?" said June with absolute certainty. "When I was a little girl," she continued, "all I ever wanted was a pony. I would spend hours imagining I was riding through the woods. But we couldn't even afford riding lessons so a pony was absolutely out of the question. Well, today my pony has arrived and there might not be a tomorrow so I'd like to go riding now!" said June in a very impassioned manner.

David sighed deeply and realised that there was nothing he could do to change her mind. Alex had returned at this point with her bottom looking a bit bulgy.

"Crikey! Your bum's swollen up, Alex! Do you need to get it checked out?" exclaimed Sally.

"What?" Alex replied, twisting round to look at her bottom. "Oh... ha!" she laughed. "That's just a load of chamomile that I've stuffed in my knickers to soothe the pain!"

"Is it helping?" I asked.

"Yes, it's great!" said Alex enthusiastically.

"Don't encourage her!" said the ever-sceptical Jack. "What shall we do about this ride?"

After much deliberation and discussion, we all decided to support June's wish to ride out but just to do a very short ride round the farm next to the livery yard.

Getting June into the saddle was no mean feat and poor David looked like he was about to have a heart attack from the stress. However, Jack's logical mind was able to figure out a way of directing us to help June on to the mounting block and on to the horse.

First, we got her to sit facing sideways on the saddle and then we lifted her right leg and swivelled her round until she was sitting properly.

"Ooh, ow!" June cried out at one point.

"What's happened?" shouted David in terror.

"It's OK! It just twinged," gasped June, grabbing hold of her back.

"Should we stop?" I asked, suddenly feeling sick with worry. I didn't want to be involved with completely destroying June's back.

"No, no, it's OK now. It just needs to get used to it. Give me a moment!" June took some deep breaths and refused to give in – she was much too determined for that.

Luckily, Beatrix was a narrow horse so when she was actually sitting correctly it was comfortable for June's back, thank goodness. Amazingly, Beatrix stood very calmly throughout the whole performance. June was so excited, her grin was literally ear to ear. It was a really special thing to observe someone suddenly living their childhood dream.

Off we went with Jack leading, followed by Sally, June, then Alex and I were at the back. We felt it would be safest to keep June in the middle.

"How are you feeling, June?" I called out anxiously.

"Ooh, this is wonderful!" said June.

She was sitting surprisingly well, considering her almost total lack of experience, and I was absolutely amazed at how chilled out Beatrix was considering she'd just arrived and she didn't know any of our horses.

"You've got a very good seat!" I said. "And you're holding the reins really well too!"

"Thank you!" replied June. "I always used to watch our Susan when she had her lessons so I learned a lot from that. Couldn't afford for me to have lessons at the same time, mind you. Oh, and of course you can learn a lot from the internet! I often watch YouTube videos of horse-riding lessons and I imagine myself doing it."

I was very impressed.

"Did you ride Susan's horse much?" asked Alex.

"No, only a few times because he was too wide for me. He's a big lad!" laughed June.

We clattered down the farm track, which was nice and quiet, and June enjoyed having a good look at all the fields.

"It's time to turn back!" called Jack from the front, indicating that we were almost at the main road.

"Aww, do we have to? I want to do a proper ride!" said June sadly. "I might be dead tomorrow!"

Jack turned round. "I bloody hope not!" she said.

"She is sitting very well," said Alex. "So maybe we could go into the village?"

"I suppose so," said Jack. "The road's fairly quiet today."

"Fantastic!" said June cheerily. "Let's go!"

We crossed the road with no dramas and soon arrived in the pretty village, with its lovely old stone houses.

"It's a great vantage point for looking into gardens, isn't it?" laughed June, who was thoroughly enjoying herself.

"Yes, and people's bedrooms if you're on Poppy," I replied.

June looked round. "Oh heck, she is tall, isn't she?" she laughed. "Hope nobody's getting undressed with their curtains open!"

"Oh, I hope they are, especially if it's a fit man!" said Sally, laughing her head off and standing up in her stirrups to get a better view. "Can we swap horses, Grace? You've got a better view than me!"

"Sally, you're so naughty!" laughed Alex.

"Well, we only live once so why not?" said June.

"Absolutely!" agreed Sally.

"God, you people," muttered Jack from the front. "You're embarrassing!"

Finally, we arrived at an old railway track that wound through the woods next to the village. It was such a magical place to ride – if you were on a small horse. I spent a lot of time bending over to avoid knocking my head into low branches.

"Ooof, bloody hell! It's not easy bending forward in a body protector," I complained. I was used to doing this ride on Lucy and I never once had to tilt my head out of the way. This was ridiculous. Poppy didn't care, though, and just marched on through the branches, which sometimes swung back and hit me in the face.

"This is the opposite of fun!" laughed Alex, who also had to bend forward on her big horse.

But eventually the trees weren't so low and the track widened a lot so we could sit normally and enjoy where we were. Jenny,

Alex's horse, decided to walk alongside Beatrix. It was amazing to see two horses who didn't even know each other walking happily together.

"This is glorious!" sighed June. "It's a dream come true!"

"Yes, it's beautif—"

"Aaargh!" June let out a strangled cry as Beatrix went up on her back legs, snorting.

Alex reached out and grabbed June with lightning-fast reactions, stopping her from falling off backwards. Beatrix came back down almost as soon as she'd gone up and danced about on the spot for a few moments.

"Oh! Oh! Oh!" cried June, her eyes wide with terror.

Alex leaned over and grabbed the reins and amazingly June stayed on and Beatrix stopped dancing.

"What the heck was that about?" I exclaimed.

"It was a rabbit!" said Jack, pointing to a little fluffy bottom poking out of the undergrowth.

"Oh blumin' heck! I saw my life flash before my eyes!" gasped June.

The rabbit reversed and hopped across the path again and up went Beatrix once more.

"Oh! Help!" shrieked June.

Alex grabbed her again and Beatrix came straight down and snorted and danced. She settled almost instantly so it wasn't terrible but it certainly was very worrying for June, who was very shaken up. Luckily, the western saddle had such a big pommel that June had something to grab hold of, which helped her to stay on.

The rabbit hobbled along, limping, and Beatrix snorted but realised it was OK so she didn't go up again.

"Oh dear!" said June, terrified. "This wasn't part of my childhood dream!"

"Thank God you stayed on!" said Alex.

"Well, that was thanks to you!" replied June. "You must have been psychic!"

"I had a funny feeling something was about to happen," said Alex, who was very intuitive. "That's why I rode alongside you."

"Oh look! It's not well," said Sally, watching the rabbit hop into a tree and bash its head.

"It's got something wrong with its leg," said Jack.

"Oh, the poor thing!" said Alex, leaping off her horse.

The rabbit hobbled into a bush.

"What are you doing?" asked Jack, horrified.

"Rescuing it!" Alex replied, rushing over to where the rabbit was last seen.

"But it's gone now!" said Jack, shaking her head as Alex got down on her hands and knees and crawled into the bush.

"Little bunny! Where are you?" she called in a singsong voice.

"God give me strength," sighed Jack.

Sally sniggered. She loved it when Alex annoyed Jack. June looked on, fascinated, and luckily Beatrix stood quietly. Sally had manoeuvred Malcy so she was ready to help if necessary.

"There you are!" said Alex, crawling further into the bush. "Gotcha!" She crawled out backwards, bringing half of the bush with her.

"Oh no! You've got a little stone in your little fluffy footy! I'll take it out." Alex pulled the stone out from in between the rabbit's toes.

"Ooh, you bugger!" yelled Alex as it bit her finger. She

dropped the rabbit. It didn't move for a few moments and then we could see it was blind.

"It's got myxy!" exclaimed Sally.

"You're going to have to kill it," said Jack.

"What?" yelled Alex. "That's awful!"

"You can't leave the poor thing like that!" Jack replied.

"I can't kill it!" said Alex, horrified at the thought of it. "I'm a vegetarian!"

"So? You can't leave it to suffer!" Jack slid off her horse. "Come here, I'll do it."

"No! The poor thing!" said Alex, scooping up the rabbit and stroking it. "You can't kill it!"

"Oh, but you must!" said Sally. "Imagine what sort of awful life it's got and it will end up being ripped to bits by a fox. That would be so much worse."

Alex considered that and relented. "You're right. Oh, this is awful!" she said tearfully.

Jack quietly took the rabbit and expertly dispatched it in a millisecond. The rabbit made no sound so it was obviously painless but poor Alex cried because she had such a big heart.

"We must bury him," she announced solemnly.

"Are you serious?" asked Jack in disbelief.

"Yes! The poor little soul deserves respect," Alex replied and pulled out a spoon from her saddlebag, which she used to dig a hole.

"Why have you got a spoon with you?" I asked, surprised (but actually not really that surprised. Alex was so potty).

"Because sometimes I like to get ice cream from the farm shop when I'm riding," replied Alex matter-of-factly.

"Right!" I couldn't imagine riding Poppy and eating ice cream at the same time. It would lead to disaster.

Alex dug a deep hole and gently placed the rabbit in, then she covered it over and began saying a beautiful pagan-like prayer.

"Is this really happening?" sighed Jack.

"Yes, it is indeed!" chuckled Sally.

"I once buried a goldfish," I said.

"Why does that not surprise me?" asked Jack, rolling her eyes.

"This is the best day I've had in ages!" exclaimed June. "I love you lot. You're so mad!"

"Ha!" replied Jack. "This is nothing. You've yet to see Flash Dance here doing her crazy routines."

Alex gave us a look and we all shut up. She finished her prayer and smiled. "That's better!" she sighed. Then she found a handy tree trunk lying nearby that she used as a mounting block and got back on giant Jenny, her lovely horse.

"Right! Let's get home before something else happens," said Jack, urging Buddy to walk on.

"Aargh!" yelled June as Beatrix went up in the air again for no apparent reason. June grabbed hold of the pommel and Alex once again thrust her hand out to stop her sliding backwards. "I've got to get off!" said June, terrified.

Sally leaped off Malcy and helped June to get off in the same way we helped her to get on.

"What shall we do?" I asked, knowing that June couldn't possibly walk home.

"How about you ride Malcy, while I lead Beatrix? I think she's probably just feeling a bit overwhelmed and needs to settle before being ridden," said Sally to June.

"That's very kind but I don't think I could – he's so wide!" replied June nervously.

Malcy was very wide because he was a cob. Unfortunately, so was Buddy and Jenny was even wider. That left only one solution.

"You could ride Poppy?" I offered. "She's quite slender! Or we could phone David to come and get you?"

June looked at Poppy. "I don't want to phone David because that would feel like I'd failed. I will ride Poppy," she said resolutely. "She's so tall, though! I'm not sure I'll be able to get on."

"That isn't an option," said Jack determinedly. "Come on, ladies!"

Thankfully, the fallen tree trunk was big enough and between the four of us we managed to get June on to Poppy. It was nothing short of a miracle that Poppy stood very quietly and seemed to understand June's problem. She was so calm it was astonishing. I was secretly terrified that Poppy would start prancing around like she used to do and kill June. But no, she behaved impeccably the whole journey home. She was so sensible and quiet that June was able to relax and thoroughly enjoy riding her. She was under the impression that Poppy was always like that so I said nothing and just agreed. I didn't want to worry her.

"Yes, she's great!" I lied. But I suppose it wasn't really a lie because she was so much better than she used to be. Beatrix was OK to lead too, thank goodness.

David was relieved to see us return all in one piece but was very surprised to see June on Poppy. He came rushing over. "What happened?" he asked and June filled him in on the sorry tale. "She'll have to go back!" said David, understandably upset.

"Absolutely not!" said June, horrified. "I will not give up at the first hurdle! I'll get someone in to help me. Beatrix is my forever horse and she was probably just a bit upset about coming somewhere new, that's all."

David realised there was no point arguing with June when she'd made her mind up so he said nothing more. We helped June to get down from Poppy and, luckily, she could still walk.

"My back's not too bad!" she grinned. "I can't thank you ladies enough. I've had the best day of my life!"

"It was a great pleasure!" smiled Jack, who always loved helping people.

Alex helped June to untack Beatrix and led her into her stable for the night to settle. She put Jenny into her stable too so that Beatrix would have company in the barn.

"You've got to hand it to June," said Jack as we led our horses back to their field. "She's bloody brave, isn't she? I would have pooed my pants if that had happened to me, especially if I had a back as bad as hers!"

"Me too!" I agreed. "She's an inspiration."

"And wasn't Poppy amazing too? You should be proud of yourself," Jack continued. "You've turned that mad horse into something much better. It was obviously meant to be!"

I smiled and gave Poppy a kiss. She was indeed becoming a very special horse, thanks to Elise and the wonderful women from Wales. However, what pleased me even more was that I finally realised it was my perseverance and love that had improved Poppy's behaviour. For the first time ever I valued myself enough to be able to congratulate myself for a success... and that felt excellent. It was a turning point from feeling *less than* to seeing that I had the ability to improve situations in my life – and that was a very empowering thing.

Chapter 30

A week and a half later, I was just about to get in the car to go to the yard when my phone started ringing. It was Bernie, Poppy's owner.

"Hiya, luv!" she greeted. "How's everything going?"

"Really good!" I replied. "How's things with you?"

"Really well, thanks, luv! Listen, would you mind if our Donna came up to see Poppy? She's been missing her and fancies a quick ride."

"Oh… er… no, of course not!" I was a bit taken aback.

"Oh, great! We're nearby so we'll pop in when we've finished here if that's OK? Won't be too long."

"Right! OK, yes, sure," I stuttered.

"Great. See you soon!" Bernie hung up.

"Oh no!" I said out loud to the dog. The dog looked at me and then went back to sleep. I felt nausea rising, my heart began palpitating and my mind went into overdrive.

Oh my God! She's going to want Poppy back!

Not necessarily! replied the very tiny, sensible area of my brain.

Yes she will!

She might not.

Why else would she be coming to see her? Oh my God!

I dragged my boots on and dashed out to the car. Halfway down the street I realised I couldn't remember if I'd locked the door. I reversed back and almost drove into my neighbour's wall.

"For fuck's sake!" I yelled, as I ran down the drive and checked the door. It was locked. "Bloody hell!" I dashed back to the car and sped off to the yard.

I arrived feeling very stressed but luckily, Jack was there so I had someone to talk to.

"It's out of your hands whatever happens," said Jack, who was always very practical and down to earth. "I don't think you need to worry, though. I'm sure she'll probably have one ride and then lose interest again."

"I hope you're right," I said gloomily.

"What's going on? Has somebody died?" asked Sally, who had just arrived.

"Poppy's owner's daughter wants to come up and ride," said Jack. "So Grace is panicking."

"Aww, don't panic! She's a teenager! She won't want the responsibility of having a horse full-time. That's why I'm always here and not my daughter!" laughed Sally. "I never wanted a horse!"

"I hope you're both right. But apparently, she's really missing her. I've put so much effort into Poppy. I don't want to lose her now!" I wailed. I burst into tears and Sally gave me a hug. My heart felt like it was breaking and all the memories of losing Monty came thundering into my mind.

"Oh dear! What's happened?" asked June, rolling in on her wheelchair.

"Poppy's owner is coming up because her daughter is missing her and wants to ride," said Sally.

"Oh, is she not your horse?" asked June.

"No," I gulped sadly. "I wish she was, though!"

"Oh, love! Here, wipe your tears." She handed me a tissue. "I am sorry to see you so down. I think you and Poppy are made for each other. But don't be disheartened because nothing's happened yet so you might find that nothing does happen! And I am sure that the girl won't be wanting any responsibility, so think happy thoughts!" June was very sympathetic and had such a positive aura that it helped me to feel slightly less negative.

A loud crash from outside made us all jump and suddenly we could hear a stream of curses delivered in a very broad Yorkshire accent. "Bluddy 'ell! Who left a soddin' wheelbarrow in the car park right in the bluddy— Oh, hello, ladies. I didn't know anyone else was here!" said the lady, immediately changing her accent and sounding more well-spoken, which was quite bizarre. She was red-faced and flustered.

"You must be June," she continued. "You're the lady who is wanting some help with your new horse, I believe?" The lady looked embarrassed.

"Yes, please!" said June, smiling, and then introducing us all. "This is Philippa. She's our Susan's new riding instructor."

"Right. I'll just nip to the loo and then perhaps you can get Beatrix ready?" said Philippa as she composed herself and marched off towards the toilet.

"Oh dear! I didn't think about how I would manage to bring Beatrix in from the field," said June, biting her lip and looking suddenly very stressed.

"I'll get her. Don't you worry!" said Jack.

"Well, that's very kind but I can't keep relying on all of you," replied June gratefully. "I am a silly old woman. Susan was right, I shouldn't be doing this!"

"Now it's your turn to be told to stop worrying!" said Jack. "It's really not a problem for any of us to bring Beatrix down for you. Come on, ladies, let's go and get her!"

Jack got Beatrix's head collar and Sally and I walked with her up the path towards the field.

"Did anybody bring any fly spray?" I asked, as we reached the dreaded gate into the pony field.

"Oh, for God's sake, are they still here? Brenda was meant to be selling them!" said Jack exasperatedly.

"She changed her mind. She's going to get them trained!" laughed Sally.

"You are joking?" asked Jack.

"Nope!"

"Well, I look forward to seeing that!" smirked Jack. "Here they come, the two nutters. Bloody hell! They're so annoying."

Sally leaped over the gate and pulled out a party blower from her pocket. She took a deep breath and blew hard. The party blower uncurled and let out the most pathetic squeak that rendered us all helpless with laughter.

"Damn, it's broken!" said Sally. "Never mind. I learned a new African tribal dance yesterday at work. It's brilliant! I'll give that a go."

"Oh God, don't – you'll break a hip!" said Jack but it was too late.

Sally had launched and was doing a crazy routine that involved a lot of arm-shaking and shouting. We were transfixed until she managed to trip over her own feet, ending up in a pile of poo that was, luckily, quite dry. Sally swore very loudly. The Fells snorted, backed away, then spun and ran for cover under their favourite tree. Sally came hobbling back, huffing and puffing. "I've pulled a muscle!" she grimaced, rubbing her leg.

"And you've got poo on your face too!" laughed Jack, wiping it off for her.

We continued up the track to the horse field with no further issues and discovered that Beatrix was having a lovely time rolling in some mud. She stood and shook herself off, looking very pleased with herself. Jack walked over to put her head collar on.

"Ouch! You little shitbag!" yelled Jack, rubbing her arm. "She bit me!"

"Wow! I wasn't expecting that!" I said.

"Neither was I. That really hurt!" said Jack, examining the teeth marks on her arm

She tried again, this time more carefully, managed to avoid Beatrix's jaws and got the head collar on. "Come on, you bugger!" said Jack and brought her towards the gate.

The first thing Beatrix did when she got to us was nip both me and Sally at lightning-fast speed.

"Christ! What the hell?" yelped Sally as she leaped out of the way. "She's like a naughty dog!" We all rubbed our arms very crossly.

The weird thing was that Beatrix was very easy to lead. She walked very nicely but she tried to nip us a few more times on the walk back to the barn.

June was very surprised to hear about Beatrix's biteyness but luckily, she stood quietly to be groomed and tacked up and was fine to lead out to the school. We all waited by the rails and watched as Philippa took over and led Beatrix to the mounting block. She was going to ride first to find out how much schooling Beatrix had had.

"Ow! You little sod!" said Philippa as Beatrix nipped her on the thigh. Philippa smacked her on the nose, hard enough for us to hear it.

"Ooh, I don't like that!" said June.

"Well, I don't like being bitten!" replied Philippa. "She has to learn her manners!" Philippa held Beatrix on a tight rein and managed to get on without being bitten again but we could all see that Beatrix was unhappy as her ears were flat back.

"Walk on!" instructed Philippa firmly, giving Beatrix a sharp, unnecessary kick in the ribs. Beatrix began to walk very fast.

"That was a bit harsh," I said to June.

"Hmm, yes. I'm not sure I like this lady," replied June, folding her arms.

Philippa couldn't hear because she was walking away from us up the long side of the school. She walked round the school a few times but Beatrix looked very uncomfortable with the short rein that Philippa had her on.

"We'll try a trot now!" Philippa called out, giving Beatrix another hard kick in the ribs, which only resulted in making her walk faster.

"Trot on!" shouted Philippa, thwacking her with a crop and kicking even harder. "Argh! You little bastard!" she screeched as Beatrix reared up. Philippa tumbled backwards on to the ground. Luckily, it was a soft landing so she wasn't badly hurt. She leaped to her feet and grabbed Beatrix's reins. "Never do that to me again, you nasty bitch!" she yelled as she whacked her round the head.

"Touch my horse again and I'll have you arrested, you horrible woman!" shouted June, leaping out of her wheelchair and marching into the school.

"Do you want this horse training or not?" demanded Philippa quite aggressively. "She needs to learn discipline!"

"Hitting an animal is no way to teach discipline, you ignorant cow!" shrieked June.

Philippa opened her mouth to retort but June was by no means finished.

"Hitting will only make her scared, and a scared horse is NOT a safe horse! I am disgusted by your behaviour and I'll be calling the British Horse Society to complain! You should not be allowed to teach!"

"You won't get anywhere with that horse if you're going to be soft with her!" said Philippa, finding her voice again.

"It is very possible to be firm and kind at the same time, lady. You have got a lot to learn about life. Now get out of here! I don't want to hear another word from you!" June was a powerhouse and that was all it took to silence Philippa, who walked away without uttering another word.

"Wow!" we all said at the same time, rushing into the school.

"That was amazing!" said Sally.

We were all awestruck.

"I can't abide cruelty to animals. I believe there are better ways to train horses!" said June, a bit shaky from the shock of it all.

"Yes, absolutely!" I agreed. "I can recommend my instructor. She's very firm but very kind."

"Well, that sounds more like it," said June, leaning on Beatrix to steady herself and giving her a kiss. "I can't believe our Susan has lessons with such a horrible woman. Ooh, my back! I think I've jarred it."

"I'm not surprised after all that!" said Sally, grabbing hold of June and helping her back to her wheelchair. "I'm so impressed with how you handled that woman."

I was just about to agree when I noticed Poppy's owner approaching along with her daughter. "Oh yikes, they're here!" I said, suddenly feeling sick with anguish again.

"Good luck and don't worry – it'll be fine!" said Jack, patting me on the back.

I left June and the others and went to meet Bernie and her daughter, who were by now opening the field gate and walking towards me. I felt quite ill with apprehension but put a brave face on.

"Hello!" I said, with as much cheer as I could muster.

"Hello!" said Poppy's owner and introduced me to her daughter whose name was Donna. Donna was only seventeen and very tall and stunningly beautiful with waist-length blonde hair and dazzling, sapphire-blue eyes. Her long fingers were perfectly manicured and she was very well dressed as if for a night out, not for a horse ride. We walked up to the field and Bernie asked me how we were getting on. I told her all about my lessons and the hacks out because I wanted her to see I was looking after her well.

"That sounds great! Horses take a lot of time and effort, don't they?" said Bernie.

"Yes! She certainly swallows up all my spare time but there's nothing else I'd rather do," I agreed.

"They're not pets that you can just come and go as you please, are they?" Bernie replied. "It's a lot of hard work, Donna."

We had arrived at the field. Poppy was busy grazing and didn't even bother to look up. Through gritted teeth and with a heavy heart, I handed Donna the head collar and invited her to go and get her.

"I'm hoping this won't go well," whispered Bernie as Donna walked towards Poppy. "She's been talking about Poppy for weeks but I know what she's like. She'll love her for about a fortnight and then she'll be off with her mates, leaving it for me to go and do all the work and I don't have time for horses any more!"

Relief surged through my heart to hear that Bernie was not keen to take Poppy back.

"Let's hope Pops ignores her and this nonsense will be over!" laughed Bernie.

"Pop pops!" Donna called out, walking towards her. Poppy looked up. I felt sick. Then Poppy went back to grazing again. "Hello, Poppy, it's me!" Donna reached out to scratch Poppy's shoulder. Poppy snorted and walked away. I felt very relieved.

"Pop pops!" Donna called out again, walking after her. Poppy started trotting.

"Thank God for that. Good girl, Poppy, keep moving!" chuckled Bernie, and Poppy kept trotting.

Donna looked over to us, shrugged her shoulders and walked back. "I don't think I'll bother. She's not interested," said Donna, slightly sadly, but not too terribly upset. "I thought she'd remember me a bit more!"

"I'm sure she does remember you," I said, feeling a bit sorry for her.

"You can't expect Poppy to come running just because you fancy a ride, Donna! Horses need regular interaction and a steady routine," said Bernie very matter-of-factly.

"Mmmm, s'pose so," mumbled Donna and then her phone pinged so she began texting her friends.

Bernie raised her eyebrows at me.

"Why don't you go back to the car, Donna? And I'll have a quick chat with Grace."

Donna remained glued to her phone as she wandered back to the car.

"Well, that's a relief, I can tell you!" said Bernie when Donna was well out of earshot. "The last thing I want is to look after a horse again."

"I'm relieved too! I've really grown to love Poppy and I was worried this might be the end," I said.

"Oh, don't you worry about that! Donna's not cut out for responsibility. She's too busy with her mates. I'm so glad that we found you. We couldn't have asked for a better person to look after Poppy. I'm hoping that one day Donna will agree to let you buy her. That's if you'd like to? But it's too early to bring that up with her now."

I was stunned. I had not thought about ever owning a horse because of the expense but I knew I didn't want to be parted from Poppy. "I'd love to buy her!" I said, throwing caution to the wind.

"OK, great! Let's give it a few weeks and I'll start to mention it and see how Donna takes it," said Bernie.

I was bursting with excitement as I dashed back into the barn after Bernie drove off and everyone rushed over.

"Well, what happened?" asked Jack, smiling. She could tell instantly it was good news.

"Poppy did her usual and walked off so Donna couldn't catch her and she gave up trying! And Bernie wants me to buy her so she's going to see if Donna will let her be sold in a few weeks!" I was so excited it all came out in a jumble of tears and laughter.

"Oh, brilliant!" said Jack, grinning and handing me a tissue. "You daft lump. I told you not to panic!"

June gave me a hug and I dissolved into floods of tears from the pure relief.

"Horses!" laughed Sally. "Who'd have 'em?!"

"Grace! You need to pull your jeans up or get some new ones. They're halfway down your bum!" exclaimed Jack.

"Oh God, sorry!" I laughed and pulled them up.

"I think you need a smaller pair. They're falling off you!" said Sally.

"Hmm, yes! I suppose they are. I've only just noticed!"

I looked down and pulled my jeans up again. It dawned on me that I had been doing that a lot in recent weeks but I had been too busy to think about it.

"You've lost a lot of weight. How could you not notice?" laughed Jack.

It seemed that all my excess fat had been quietly melting away along with all my misery. I hadn't changed my diet so I could only put it down to the change in my emotional and mental state. That and all the exercise that's involved with horse care too.

I drove away feeling extremely buoyed up about my weight loss. I had been so fed up about my big stomach for so long and had resigned myself to the fact it was here to stay. I decided to nip to the supermarket to get some new jeans before school pick-up. Parking was a bit of a nightmare as all the other hassled mums were desperately trying to get that chore ticked off their lists before school collection too. Finally, I found a space and was just hunting for a trolley when I came across a bit of a commotion.

"What do you mean I cannae park here? Don't you tell me where I can or cannae park, ye impudent little bugger!" yelled a spiky and very familiar voice.

I looked round and my jaw dropped open. Valerie was tying up her four Shetland-drawn, miniature carriage to a bollard by the taxi drop-off and pick-up layby. Obviously, this was a cause for concern for a member of staff who was trying his best to remain polite while asking Valerie to move her ponies.

"Where is the sign saying DO NOT PARK PONIES HERE, eh, laddie?" demanded Valerie aggressively with her hands on her hips.

"Er... ahum... well, there isn't one because we don't usually get horse-drawn carriages in the car park," replied the poor boy, wilting under her powerful glare.

"Well, perhaps more people should take to the roads in horse-drawn vehicles and then there wouldnae be a great big black hole in the environment, would there? I'm doing you a favour by coming here with my ponies and not my car!"

There was no arguing with Valerie. The poor boy couldn't think of anything to say to that and had to admit defeat. "Well, please don't be too long in the shop," he mumbled and then scurried away as fast as he could. He probably had to go and have a lie-down in the staff room to recover.

"Hello!" I grinned at Valerie, desperately trying not to roar with laughter.

"Ah, Grace!" Valerie greeted me like a long-lost relative with a big hug and a kiss. "How are you? It's been so long! How's the new horse? I've heard all about her. She sounds like a beauty!"

I felt very guilty that I'd not been to visit Valerie since starting with Poppy but Valerie didn't seem to mind. In fact, she was very understanding when I told her all about it as we wandered around the supermarket together.

"I don't know how I'm going to get James to agree to buying a horse, though," I sighed.

"Good God, girl! Dinnae tell your husband anything! You

need to be sly!" exclaimed Valerie. "Now what you need to do is get him up to the yard to help you with something really easy that he cannae get wrong. Remember, it needs to be simple because he's a man."

"OK!" I wondered how that would help.

"Then be really, really grateful and tell him he's absolutely amazing," she continued.

"Right..."

"Do that over a number of days and then say, 'Oh, look, she really loves you,' or something similar that will appeal to his vanity. He needs to believe the horse needs him and that being returned to her owner will be a terrible and cruel thing. Mark my words he'll insist on buying her!" Valerie harrumphed and folded her arms across her heaving bosom. She looked very pleased with herself.

I pondered on her words as I drove home and decided it was worth a try, although I wasn't particularly hopeful. I hadn't taken James or Florence to the yard because it didn't feel as welcoming as Valerie's yard. However, I had nothing to lose and no better ideas had come to mind so I gave it a go when he wandered into the living room to sit down later that night.

"Would you mind helping me carry a sack of feed tomorrow? It's really heavy and I don't want to hurt my back," I asked.

"OK," he replied. "It'll be nice to finally meet Poppy."

"Brilliant! Thanks!" I was very surprised at his response.

The following day we all went to the yard as a family. Sally was in the barn when I brought Poppy in to meet James and Florence.

"Grace has done a great job with Poppy," said Sally to James. "Especially considering how abused she was in her first home."

"Abused?" asked James. "You never mentioned that, Grace."

"Well, she wouldn't, would she? She's too modest! But yes, poor Poppy was clearly treated very badly in her first home. She was so scared of the lunge whip, wasn't she, Grace? And she was so nervy you couldn't catch her for ages, could you? Poor Poppy!"

"Really? That's awful!" exclaimed James, reaching out to stroke Poppy. Poppy sniffed his hand and gave him a little nuzzle on his shoulder.

"Ooh, look at that!" exclaimed Sally. "She doesn't usually like men but she likes you! She must know you're a man she can trust." It was amazing. Sally was doing everything for me. All I had to do was watch and say nothing.

"Florence, why don't you stand on this stool and give her hair a brush?" Sally asked, handing her a brush. Florence smiled and nodded so Sally lifted her on to the stool and helped her brush Poppy's mane. Poppy stood very nicely, thank goodness, thoroughly enjoying the little pamper session – and Florence thought it was wonderful too.

"Grace, I can't believe you never told me what an awful time she'd had!" said James.

"Well, she probably didn't want to worry you," replied Sally. "But look at her now! She's such a lovely horse thanks to all the effort and devotion Grace has put into her. God, it would be awful if she ended up somewhere bad again."

"Bad again?" asked James. "Could that happen?"

"Unfortunately, yes," nodded Sally. "If her owner wants to sell her, poor Poppy could end up anywhere!"

"Oh God! That would be awful!" said James, looking quite shocked.

"Poor Poppy!" said Florence, giving Poppy a cuddle.

"Hello!" Bernie called out as she walked into the barn. "Hope you don't mind but our Donna really wants to see Poppy again and have a ride in the arena," she grimaced.

My heart missed a beat from the shock. This was not part of the plan at all. Donna was dressed in jodhpurs and I could see she was very serious about wanting to ride. I felt sick with worry as she walked over to Poppy to try to reconnect with her. Bernie raised her eyebrows and made it clear she didn't want Donna to be doing this but it didn't help me to feel any better.

"Hello, Pops!" said Donna, reaching out to stroke her.

Poppy backed away from her and manoeuvred herself in such a way as to be right behind my husband.

"Oh dear! She knows who she loves!" laughed Bernie as she grabbed hold of Donna's arm and steered her out of the way. "I think Poppy needs a bit of stability, luv. You can't expect her to be happy to see you when you haven't bothered with her for so long."

"Mmm, 'spose so," nodded Donna. "I just fancied a ride."

"Well, Poppy's not fancying it, is she?" Bernie replied. "I think she was enjoying having her hair brushed!"

"Yeah. I think you're right," agreed Donna.

"It's nice to meet the rest of the family," said Bernie, swiftly changing the subject and shaking hands with my husband.

Sally winked at me and wandered off to get Malcy while Bernie and my husband chatted.

"I can't thank your Grace enough for all she's done for Poppy. Honestly, she's been a Godsend!" said Bernie.

"That's great to hear," said James.

"And I bet you love brushing her hair, don't you?" Bernie

smiled at Florence. "She's got a lovely tail, hasn't she?"

Florence nodded and smiled shyly.

"Have you had a ride on her yet?" Bernie asked Florence.

"No!" Florence shook her head.

"Well, why don't you have a little ride now? What do you think, Dad? I bet Pops would like that!"

With some reservation, I tacked Poppy up and led her into the arena. I was a bit nervous because Poppy was so massive and young in comparison to the riding school ponies but Florence wasn't bothered about any of that. She couldn't wait to get on. It was amazing to see how well behaved Poppy was with her. She could tell that Florence was small and needed to be looked after and she did just that. She walked very slowly and carefully and Florence had the time of her life. I was proud of Poppy and proud of myself for having put so much effort into achieving such a wonderful transformation.

"Well done!" Bernie clapped as we came to a halt. "I'm so glad Poppy's got such lovely carers. It's great to see her looking so happy!"

Donna looked on silently and I felt uncomfortable but, luckily, Bernie got a call from her sister so they had to get going. James helped me to untack and lead Poppy back to her field.

"She's a lovely horse," said my husband in the car on the way home. "I can see why you love her. She's definitely helped you to get over your depression, hasn't she?"

"Yes, she has. I don't really have time to think about being depressed any more. That feels like another life ago!" I laughed.

I had become such a different person. The sadness and gloom had gone. I had more energy, better overall health and looked forward to every day. It was a wonderful thing to be free of all that misery and even more wonderful to know that it was all down to spending time with horses. They really are natural healers and excellent teachers. I suppose they are *silent life coaches* if you are open enough to see it that way. I was fortunate that I did see it that way, thanks to Lady Alexa, Elise and the wonderful women in Wales. All of these people had been instrumental in helping me to understand the language of the horse, which ultimately led to the healing of me.

Later that evening my phone rang – it was Bernie. My heart flipped over and a wave of nausea welled up in my stomach.

"Hello?" I answered nervously.

"Hello, luv – you all right?" said Bernie in a very jolly voice. "I've got good news! Our Donna said she can see that Poppy is happier with you and your family than she is with her. So she said she'd like you to buy her if you want to?"

I burst into tears.

"Oh! Are you OK? You don't have to if you don't want to!" Bernie exclaimed with alarm.

"I'd love to buy her! I'm so relieved to hear that Donna would like me to have her!" I sniffed, through great big gulping sobs.

"Haha! Aww, that's great! Shall we meet up next weekend to discuss it?"

After I hung up, I went down the stairs, still crying.

"What's happened?" asked James, running over to me.

"Bernie has asked if we can buy Poppy!" I explained.

"Great! Yes, OK. How much does she want?"

I could not believe that was his reply. *Great! Yes, OK. How much does she want?* were not the words I was expecting to hear. They were the opposite of what I expected to hear.

"I don't know. She said to meet up next weekend and discuss it," I replied in total shock.

"That's a bit silly. Text her now and ask how much she wants. Then we can just give her the cash when we see her instead of wasting time."

Had I died and been transported to a parallel universe? I wondered. Or was I really asleep and this was just a fantastic dream? No, I was definitely awake because the dog did an extremely smelly fart and I doubt I would have included that in such a wondrous dream.

"Are you OK?" I asked my husband.

"Yes, why?" he replied.

"Well, I'm just gobsmacked at how enthusiastic you are about this!"

James sighed deeply. "I have seen such a dramatic improvement in your mood and how you are with Florence. I don't think any therapist could have helped you as much as these horses have. And I don't want Poppy to end up with someone who won't care for her as much as we can so let's just get this sorted. I can't bear to think of her being abused again. Text Bernie now and get the price."

I didn't have to be asked twice. I texted Bernie and she gave us a very reasonable price that pleased my husband.

The following weekend, Jack, Sally, Alex and June were all there to be a part of the most exciting moment of my life. Bernie had a big grin on her face as she gave me Poppy's passport and signed the official form to change ownership while everyone clapped and cheered.

"I'm so glad we found you!" she said, giving me a hug. "It's such a relief to know that Poppy is going to the best family."

It was interesting to see how concerned Poppy looked. She could sense something was happening and seemed worried she was going to be taken away. She stared at me with such intensity it was as if she was saying, *I want to stay with you!* Sally had to calm her down by walking her around while all the paperwork was being signed.

We gave Bernie the money and there it was… my childhood dream had come true. I was a horse owner. But it wasn't just any horse. It was the horse that had rescued me from darkness and brought me back into the light.

About the Author

Grace was born and bred in Leeds, West Yorkshire.

She dreamed of owning a pony ever since she was a little girl but it took until adulthood for the dream to come true. Unfortunately, Grace didn't factor in the amount of poo that was involved with horse ownership. Had she realised that earlier in life she would have found a different hobby!

Grace's day job involves helping terminally ill people to feel more comfortable with their situations. She uses a combined treatment of massage, lymphatic drainage, coaching and healing.

Her big dream is to set up a farm-based therapy centre where rescued farm animals can receive love and care and in turn help to heal the hearts and minds of terminally ill people.

The proceeds of this book will go towards making that dream a reality. So if you have enjoyed reading it please encourage your friends and family to buy it. You can also help by following Grace Olson – Author on Facebook and sharing her website.

https://www.theyardbook.co.uk
https://www.heavenstonehealing.com

About the Illustrator

Ruth Buchanan was born in London but she soon realised that the Yorkshire Dales was a much better place to call home!

Ruth is an award-winning equestrian artist who exhibits at international horse shows as well as in galleries. Her work features in the private collections of notable names in the arts and equestrian spheres in the UK and abroad.

However, the best thing about Ruth is how down-to-earth and approachable she is. Her ability to connect on a deep level with horses is clearly demonstrated in her artwork and it's a lot of fun to be involved in a commission with her. She can see the relationship between horse and human and captures it perfectly on paper.

The watercolour on the cover of this book is Grace and Poppy. It's a moment of their hearts connecting and it has pride of place on Grace's living room wall.

Ruth does a limited number of commissions each year and can be contacted directly via her website.

https://www.ruthbuchanan.co.uk